THE HOLY TRINITY

THE HOLY TRINITY

Understanding God's Life

Stephen R. Holmes

Paternoster:
thinking faith

18 17 16 15 14 13 12   7 6 5 4 3 2 1

This edition first published 2012 by Paternoster
Paternoster is an imprint of Authentic Media Limited
52 Presley Way, Crownhill, Milton Keynes, MK8 0ES
www.authenticmedia.co.uk

British Library Cataloguing in Publication Data

A catalogue record for this book is available from the
British Library

ISBN 978-1-84227-741-6

Biblical quotations are from the NEW REVISED STANDARD VERSION, Anglicized
edition (marked NRSV), or my own translations
(from BHS/NA27)

Cover design by Paul Airy at DesignLeft (www.designleft.co.uk)
Printed and bound by CPI Group (UK) Ltd., Croydon, CR0 4YY

For Elspeth

Quid prodest tibi alta de Trinitate disputare,
si careas humilitate unde displiceas Trinitati?

Thomas à Kempis, *De Imitatione Christi*, 1.3

Contents

Abbreviations

ACCS	*Ancient Christian Commentary on Scripture*
Ad ablab.	Gregory of Nyssa, *Ad ablabium = Quod non sint tres dei* – 'On Not Three Gods'
ANF	*Ante-Nicene Fathers*
AugStud	*Augustinian Studies*
Autol.	Theophilus of Antioch, *Ad Autolycum* – *To Autolycus*
BaC	Zizioulas, *Being as Communion: Studies in Personhood and the Church*
C. Ar.	Athanasius, *Orationes contra Arianos* – *Orations against the Arians*
CCSL	*Corpus Christianorum: Series Latina*
CD	Barth, *Church Dogmatics*
C.E.	Basil of Caesarea/Gregory of Nyssa, *Contra Eunomium* – *Against Eunomius*
Cels.	Origen, *Contra Celsum* – *Against Celsus*
CH	*Church History*
ChrCent	*Christian Century*
Civ.	Augustine, *De civitate Dei* – *The City of God*
CO	*Calvini Opera*
Comm. in Luc.	Ambrose, *Commentary on Luke*
Comm. Is.	Cyril of Alexandria, *Commentary on Isaiah*
Comm. Isa.	Eusebius of Caesarea, *Commentary on Isaiah*
Comm. Jo.	Origen, *Commentary on John*
Comm. Ps.	Theodore of Mopsuestia, *Commentary on the Psalms*
Comm. Rom.	Origen, *Commentary on Romans*
CTJ	*Calvin Theological Journal*
Decr.	Athanasius, *De decretis* – *Defence of the Nicene Definition*

De fid. orth.	John of Damascus, *De fide orthodoxa – On the Orthodox Faith*
De process.	Anselm, *De processione Spiritus Sancti – On the Procession of the Holy Spirit*
De Spir.	Basil of Caesarea, *De Spiritu Sancto – On the Holy Spirit*
De SS. Trin.	Pseudo-Cyril, *On the Most Holy Trinity*
De syn.	Hilary of Poitiers, *De synodis – On the Councils*
De Trin.	Hilary of Poitiers/Novatian/Richard of St Victor, *De Trinitate – On the Trinity*
Dial.	Origen, *Dialogue with Heraclides*
Dial.	Justin Martyr, *Dialogue with Trypho*
Enarrat. Ps.	Augustine, *Enarrations on the Psalms*
Ep.	*Epistula(e)* – letter(s)
Ep. Alex.	Arius, 'Letter to Alexander of Thessalonica'
Epid.	Irenaeus, *Epideixis tou apostolikou kērygmatos – Demonstration of the Apostolic Preaching*
ETL	*Ephemerides theologicae lovanienses*
Exp. Fid.	Eunomius, *Exposition of Faith*
FC	*Fathers of the Church* (trans. series; Washington, DC: CUA Press)
GOTR	*Greek Orthodox Theological Review*
Haer.	Irenaeus, *Adversus haereses – Against Heresies*
Haer.	Hippolytus, *Refutatio omnium haeresium – Refutation of All Heresies*
Hist. eccl.	Eusebius/Philostorgius/Socrates of Constantinople/Theodoret, *Historia ecclesiastica – Ecclesiastical History*
Hom. Isa.	Origen, *Homily on Isaiah*
Hom. Act.	John Chrysostom, *Homily on the Acts of the Apostles*
Hom. Rom.	John Chrysostom, *Homily on Romans*
HTR	*Harvard Theological Review*
In Matt.	Hilary of Poitiers, *Commentary on Matthew*
Inst.	Lactantius, *Divine Institutes*
IJST	*International Journal of Systematic Theology*
JAAR	*Journal of the American Academy of Religion*
JECS	*Journal of Early Christian Studies*
JEH	*Journal of Ecclesiastical History*
JR	*Journal of Religion*
JTS	*Journal of Theological Studies*
LCC	Library of Christian Classics
LCL	Loeb Classical Library

Leg.	Athenagoras, *Legatio pro Christianis*
Lib. Apol.	Eunomius, *Liber Apologeticus*
LXX	The Septuagint
Noet.	Hippolytus, *Contra haeresin Noeti – Against the Heresy of Noetus*
NPNF	*Nicene and Post-Nicene Fathers*
OCP	*Orientalia christiana periodica*
OECT	*Oxford Early Christian Texts*
OED	*Oxford English Dictionary*
Or.	Gregory of Nazianzus, *Theological Orations*
OS	Boethius, *Opuscula Sacra*
PG	*Patrologia graeca*, ed. Migne
PL	*Patrologia latina*, ed. Migne
Prax.	Tertullian, *Adversus Praxean – Against Praxeas*
Princ.	Origen, *De principiis – On First Principles*
ProEccl	*Pro ecclesia*
RelS	*Religious Studies*
SC	*Sources chrétiennes* (Paris: Cerf)
ScG	Aquinas, *Summa contra Gentiles*
Sent.	Peter Lombard, *Sententiae – Sentences*
Serm.	Augustine, *Sermones – Sermons*
SJT	*Scottish Journal of Theology*
ST	*Studia theologica*
ST	Aquinas, *Summa theologiae*
ST	Hodge/Pannenberg/Jenson, *Systematic Theology*
StPatr	*Studia patristica*
SVTQ	*St Vladimir's Theological Quarterly*
Syn.	Athanasius, *De synodis – On the Councils of Ariminum and Seleucia*
ThTo	*Theology Today*
Tim.	Plato, *Timaeus*
TKG	Moltmann, *The Trinity and the Kingdom of God: The Doctrine of God*
Tract. Ev. Jo.	Augustine, *In Evangelium Johannis tractatus – Tractates on the Gospel of John*
Trin.	Augustine, *De Trinitate – The Trinity*
TS	*Theological Studies*
TU	*Texte und Untersuchungen*
VC	*Vigiliae christianae*
WA	*Luther Werke*
WBC	Word Biblical Commentary

WTJ   *Westminster Theological Journal*
ZNW   *Zeitschrift für die Neutestamentliche Wissenschaft*

General Editor's Preface

Many books are written on the history of Christian doctrine, and volumes of systematic theology never cease to roll from the press. The former may or may not include reflections upon the current 'state of the doctrine'; the latter may or may not pay heed to the history of theological reflection upon the subject in hand. Hence this series entitled, *Christian Doctrines in Historical Perspective*, the objectives of which are twofold. First, to trace the biblical roots and defining moments in history of major Christian doctrines, with reference to prominent authors and texts (including recent ecumenical texts as appropriate), concluding with an appraisal of the doctrine in current debate. Secondly, to hold together doctrines which belong together but are sometimes, frequently for good reasons, treated in isolation from one another: for example, the Person and the Work of Christ, Creation and Recreation.

It is hoped that this series will contribute to that biblical-historical grounding of current theological reflection which is necessary if systematic and constructive theology are to be understood as entailing a conversation between the biblical sources, the heritage of doctrinal thought and the current intellectual environment.

Alan P.F. Sell
Milton Keynes, UK

Projected titles:

Stephen Holmes, *The Holy Trinity* (2011)
Andrew McGowan, *The Person and Work of Christ* (2012)
Robert Pope, *The Church and the Sacraments* (2013)
Andrew Kirk, *The Church and the World* (2014)

Introduction

As a sometime hillwalker, I have a prejudice about maps, particularly maps of the British countryside. The Ordnance Survey 1:50 000 scale series, although popular and widely available, is strictly for daytrippers; true walkers use 1:25 000, and rejoice in the extra detail. The printed map I consult most often, however, resides in the glove box of our family car; it is at a scale of 1:253 440 (4 miles to 1 inch), over ten times that of my favoured OS maps. For driving, the detail of a 1:25 000 map is useless; a bigger picture is necessary. If the particular shape of a set of curves in a road is obscured or rendered impressionistically, the ability to take in a breadth of vision more than compensates.

This book is on a big-picture scale, necessarily. Covering in one brief volume two thousand years of debate over what is possibly the central topic of Christian devotion, together with the necessary biblical background, means that at every turn I have obscured details of debates, offered impressionistic sketches of complex positions, and otherwise done violence to scholarly ideals. I do not apologize for this; not only is there value for students in a text which renders a broad vision of the subject, but there is also an argument made in the text that follows that could not have been convincingly made with any less breadth of focus.

In brief, I argue that the explosion of theological work claiming to recapture the doctrine of the Trinity that we have witnessed in recent decades in fact misunderstands and distorts the traditional doctrine so badly that it is unrecognizable. A statement of the doctrine was settled in the fourth century, and was then maintained, with only very minor disagreement or development, by all strands of the church – West and East, Protestant and Catholic – until the modern period. In the twentieth century, there arose a sense that the doctrine had been neglected or lost, and stood in need of recovery. Many brilliant works have been published in the name of that recovery, but I argue here that, methodologically and materially, they are generally thorough-going departures from the older tradition, rather than revivals of it.

Thus stated, the argument is merely historical: I do not, here, attempt to prove that the older tradition was right (by which I mean more ade-quate to the biblical revelation of God). It may be that our recent writers are correct, and the doctrine developed and defended by Athanasius, Basil, Gregory Nazianzen and Augustine, the doctrine which was shared by John of Damascus, Patriarch Photius, and Alcuin of York in the eighth century, the doctrine affirmed with (almost) one voice by Thomas Aquinas, Gregory of Cyprus, and Gregory Palamas around 1300, the doctrine affirmed by Bellarmine, Calvin, and Luther in the sixteenth cen-tury – that this settled doctrine was always wrong. Nothing I have writ-ten excludes that possibility; I do, however, attempt to show just how strongly exegetical the traditional presentations of the doctrine were.

In order to tell this story, the book is rather oddly shaped for a his-tory. I begin with an analysis of the recent Trinitarian revival, tracing its roots in Barth, Rahner, and Zizioulas, and its various flowerings, seeking to show what is generally shared amongst all contributors and strands. I then turn to the biblical material, with one eye on the way the texts have been read, and one on the way they should be read, acknowledging that patristic exegesis worked by rather different rules from our own. The patristic period is treated in disproportionate detail (chapters 3 to 6), simply because this development is so crucial for the doctrine. A brief interlude sums up my reconstruction of the Trinitarian doctrine bequeathed by the church fathers. I move quite quickly from Augustine to the rise of serious anti-Trinitarianism around 1700, simply because, as I read the history, and notwithstand-ing one important argument (the _filioque_ debate, examined in chapter 7) and several idiosyncratic but marginal figures, the story is one of acceptance, re-presentation, and faithful transmission of the patristic doctrine. It would be possible to examine writer after writer, and demonstrate exhaustively the proof of this proposition, but I do not think it is in serious doubt, and the available space is better used on more contested parts of the story, where there is development or change in the doctrine. The nineteenth-century roots of the broad themes of the twentieth-century Trinitarian revival are examined, and the book ends with a brief return to the recent writers, reconsidered in the light of all that has come before.

I hope that the main text of the book will offer an accessible and precise account of my interpretations and arguments, serving the

aims of the series in which the book is placed; I have therefore relegated my engagement with, and occasional intervention in, current
scholarly arguments concerning the interpretation of this or that
thinker or text to the footnotes. This occasionally results in some long-
ish footnotes; the reader who is not interested in how my proposals
relate to those of other scholars is invited to pass over them with the
confidence that he or she will miss nothing of my own argument. The
series of which this volume is a part is intended for upper-level
undergraduates; I have therefore assumed a certain basic familiarity
with technical theological language, and with the shape of certain central historical debates.

The bibliographic references in this book are not intended to be
comprehensive; I have not referenced every text I have read on the
subject, instead using footnotes to either acknowledge the source of
quotations or to point the reader to works I regard as particularly significant or insightful. I have tried in most contexts to reference and
quote English translations where good ones are available; generally,
however, I have worked with original texts, and I have also referenced the best editions of the original. Sometimes English translations are my own; this is always indicated. I have also tried to point
readers towards secondary material in English if at all possible.
Biblical references are often to the New Revised Standard Version
(NRSV), and marked as such; however, there are some places where I
have offered my own translations to make a point clearer. I have tried
not to make reference in the main text to points dependent on the
Greek or Hebrew unless absolutely necessary. All these decisions are
driven by the intentions of the series in which this work is to be
placed.

All that said, particularly with the historical material, I have sometimes found it necessary to work with an untranslated text, to make a
point that demands reference to the original over the translation, or to
refer to scholarly discussions that have not previously been brought
into English-language scholarship, at least as far as I have been able to
determine. Even in the face of requirements of accessibility, it seemed
better to reference this material in case a polyglot reader should wish
to follow it up, rather than leaving it silently in the background.

Some of this text has a fairly complex pre-history. Parts of chapter 1
and chapter 5 are based on my 2008 Tyndale Lecture, and on papers
that covered similar ground later read in seminars in St Andrews and
New College, Edinburgh; I am grateful for the invitations that led to
these presentations, and for the help I received in conversations that

followed. The general thesis of the book has previously been essayed in the Trinity and Christology seminar of the Society for the Study of Theology; the material on Calvin owes something to a paper given at a day conference in Aberdeen celebrating the 500th anniversary of his birth; the material on Coleridge has been presented in several places. Some of chapter 1 was presented at a Rutherford House Dogmatics Conference. I have been helped along the way by conversations with John Webster, Bruce McCormack, Oliver Crisp, Karen Kilby, Paul Fiddes, Sara Parvis, Robert Jenson, Christoph Schwöbel, and with colleagues and students (present and former) here in St Andrews, particularly Richard Bauckham, Grant Macaskill, Alan Torrance, Mark Elliott, Trevor Hart, Ivor Davidson, Jake Andrews, Shawn Bawulski, Jason Sexton, Loe Joo Tan, David Sonju, Shirley Martin, and R.J. Matava. The length of this list is eloquent testimony to the fact that St Mary's remains a wonderfully invigorating place to be about the work of theology. The deep roots of the book lie in many conversations with my former teacher and colleague, the late Colin Gunton. Colin would not have agreed with very much of what I have written, I fear, but he would have been delighted that I, or anyone, cared enough about the subject to write on it, and eager to engage on every one of the various points. It remains a great sadness that such engagement cannot now happen.

Dr Mike Parsons, of Paternoster, has been extraordinarily generous with deadlines to allow me to finish the book I wanted to write; Mollie Barker's editorial work was a model of care and professionalism; to both I am grateful.

The dedication to our third daughter, Elspeth, is an indication of the gratitude which I continue to owe to my family, and particularly to my wife, Heather. Judith, Philippa, and Elspeth continue to fill us with joy, and to challenge our wisdom; our wider family is a wonderful support to us, as is our local church family in St Andrews Baptist Church. Our family life depends on relations and on the vibrancy of the local church; my own ability to write depends so much on Heather's willingness to set me free, to shoulder burdens, and to believe that what I am doing is of some worth.

When I look at the completed text I reflect that I did not set out to tell quite such a catastrophic story of loss, or to be quite so critical of many excellent recent works on the Trinity that formed a crucial part of my own theological formation. The story I have told seems to me to be what the evidence demanded, however; if it is not happy, I hope it is at least clear and honest. The temptation to apologize or defend further is always present in writing a preface; it seems best, however, to conclude simply with Chaucer:

> Go, litel book, go, litel myn tragédie;
> Ther God thy maker yet, ere that he dye,
> So sende might to maken some comédie![1]

Stephen R. Holmes
St Mary's College, St Andrews
The Feast of the Holy Trinity, 2011

---

[1] *Troilus and Criseyde*, Book 5, Roughly, 'Go, little book, to tell your sad story. Pray God that your author might one day be allowed to write a happier tale!'

1.

'The History that God is': Studying the Doctrine of the Trinity in the Twenty-First Century

The Trinitarian Revival

It is now common to note that there has been a surprising revival of interest in the doctrine of the Trinity since the second half of the twentieth century. Christoph Schwöbel comments that 'at the beginning of this period it still seemed necessary to lament the neglect of trinitarian reflection in modern theology and to offer apologies for engaging with such allegedly remote and speculative issues', but goes on to say, 'both, lamentation and apologies, would seem out of place in today's theological situation.'[1] Recent writers have found in the Trinity not just the essence of Christian faith, but a seemingly endlessly generative doctrine for ethical and social ideas. Right belief about the Trinity will determine our understanding of the church, of the proper shape of human society, and of many other pastoral and political questions. As Miroslav Volf put it in the title of a paper, 'The Trinity is Our Social Program'.[2]

Although this book takes its place in a series surveying the history of doctrine, the current interest in Trinitarian theology, and its claim to be recovering historic positions, is such that some awareness of the present intellectual context will be helpful in approaching the history

---

[1] Christoph Schwöbel, 'Introduction: The Renaissance of Trinitarian Theology: Reasons, Problems and Tasks', in *Trinitarian Theology Today* (ed. Christoph Schwöbel; Edinburgh: T&T Clark, 1995), pp. 1–30, p. 1.

[2] Miroslav Volf, '"The Trinity is Our Social Program": The Doctrine of the Trinity and the Shape of Social Engagement', *Modern Theology* 14 (1998): pp. 403–23.

of the doctrine. This chapter, therefore, offers a survey of the renewal of interest in Trinitarianism in the twentieth century, from its roots in Karl Barth and Karl Rahner, through the many writers who contributed in the 1970s, 1980s and 1990s. I will attempt to identify the key claims concerning the content and use of Trinitarian theology that are presently being offered, so that these can be evaluated against the history as we begin to explore it.

It is perhaps worth stating my thesis at the outset: I see the twentieth-century renewal of Trinitarian theology as depending in large part on concepts and ideas that cannot be found in patristic, medieval, or Reformation accounts of the doctrine of the Trinity. In some cases, indeed, they are points explicitly and energetically repudiated as erroneous – even occasionally as formally heretical – by the earlier tradition. This is a historical judgement; it may be that recent writers are right in their accounts of the content and use of Trinitarian doctrine, but if so, we need to conclude that the majority of the Christian tradition has been wrong in what it has claimed about the eternal life of God. This book is not particularly devoted to arguing that thesis, though: it is a series of readings of central texts on the doctrine of the Trinity, each of which is an attempt to be faithful to the writer's own ideas and concerns. The claimed thesis, I submit, arises naturally out of such readings without very much need for further argument.

Twentieth-Century Trinitarianism: Origins

By the end of the nineteenth century, the doctrine of the Trinity was perceived either as wrong or, at best, as useless orthodoxy. Most Christian theologians were schooled in a liberal tradition, finding its classic exponents in Adolf von Harnack and Albrecht Ritschl. Both, in different ways and for different reasons, saw speculation concerning the nature of God as a foreign accretion to Christianity, which should be discarded.[3] More conservative theologians, such as the Princeton school of Hodge and Warfield, still taught the doctrine in a carefully traditional form, but could find little use for it.[4] Borrowing an image from a novelist contemporary to Hodge and Ritschl, the doctrine seemed to be no more than one of six impossible things to be believed

---

[3] Ritschl and von Harnack are discussed in more detail below, pp. 196–8.

[4] I argue below (pp. 190–1) that Hodge in particular saw clearly the need to demonstrate that the doctrine was useful (in response to Schleiermacher), but found himself unable to do this.

before breakfast each morning: abstruse; obscure; and of no practical import.

Karl Barth: God and revelation

The great Swiss-German theologian Karl Barth (1886–1968) was schooled in this liberal theology – indeed, he studied under von Harnack for a time. Famously, his experiences in the pastorate and his disillusionment with his teachers' uncritical support for militarism at the outbreak of World War I led him to reject his liberal heritage. For a while, his theology was mostly occupied with accounts of what was wrong with his inherited tradition, but he eventually (after a false start) produced one of the most massive, and influential, theological contributions of the twentieth century, the *Church Dogmatics*.[5] The doctrine of the Trinity plays at least two crucial roles in that work: it identifies God; and it grounds revelation.

Barth was heir to a theological tradition that for some centuries had been downplaying the uniqueness of the Christian account of God. On the one hand, a tradition of philosophy taught that there was a common content to the word 'God', shared (it was assumed) by all religions. Specifically Christian ideas, such as the doctrine of the Trinity, were regarded as secondary to this common core of belief. This began as a response to the realization by European intellectuals that there were other religious traditions in the world, particularly to the discovery of the different religious traditions of great civilizations such as China. To claim that these traditions were simply wrong in their highest values and most basic beliefs seemed unpalatable, and the early accounts that came back made it appear that there was some commonality with European Christianity (largely because the early travellers interpreted what they encountered using the concepts they had to hand). It was therefore very attractive to postulate a set of

---

[5] There are many good books on Barth. For an excellent introduction with helpful suggestions for further reading, see John Webster, *Karl Barth* (London: Continuum, 2nd edn, 2004). For more detailed biography, see Eberhard Busch, *Karl Barth: His Life from Letters and Autobiographical Texts* (London: SCM, 1976). On Barth's doctrine of the Trinity, E. Jüngel's *God's Being Is in Becoming: The Trinitarian Being of God in the Theology of Karl Barth* (trans. J. Webster; Edinburgh: T&T Clark, 2004) is an enormously influential treatment; Alan Torrance, *Persons in Communion: An Essay on Trinitarian Description and Human Participation* (Edinburgh: T&T Clark, 1996) goes far beyond Barth, but is extremely instructive on him; see also Alan Torrance, 'The Trinity', in *The Cambridge Companion to Karl Barth* (ed. John Webster; Cambridge: CUP, 2000), pp. 72–91.

beliefs concerning the divine that were common to all human civilizations.[6] This was further reinforced in the nineteenth century by a
strand of Roman Catholic fundamental theology, which suggested
that the truth of God's existence and unity was a datum of natural theology, available to all people.

On the other hand, since Schleiermacher, theology had been recast
as a scientific analysis of human religious feeling.[7] For theology to be
a possible or interesting discipline when conceived like this, however,
at least some religious feeling must be common to all humanity;[8]
equally, (analysis of) our religious feeling must be an adequate source
of true knowledge about the divine;[9] these two claims taken together
give strong impetus to believe that the accounts of the divine given by
differing religious traditions should differ only in inessentials.

Barth was, famously, not interested in natural theology; he also
took decisive leave of the intellectual tradition of Schleiermacher. He
insisted on the priority and particularity of revelation in identifying
the God of the Christian tradition – he chose, that is, to write a *church*
dogmatics. As Barth himself says, 'The doctrine of the Trinity is what
basically distinguishes the Christian doctrine of God as Christian . .
. in contrast to all other possible doctrines of God.'[10] The Trinity is, of
course, not the only candidate to do this distinguishing work – a little earlier, P.T. Forsyth, following Isaak Dorner, had lit upon the
claim that God is 'Holy Love' as the distinguishing definition of the

---

[6] For a classic example of this, see Edward, Lord Herbert of Cherbury, *De Veritate*
(London, 1633; trans. Meyrick H. Carré; Bristol: University of Bristol Press, 1937),
and the 'five common notions' therein developed. I discuss this work further
below, pp. 176–7.

[7] I note below (pp. 186–7) that recent scholarship on Schleiermacher is not convinced that this is a fair representation of his own programme; that it accurately
reflects a reorientation in theological method that has often sought validation
from Schleiermacher is not in doubt, however.

[8] Schleiermacher assumes that it is in order to construct an apologetic context for
Christian theology, and arranges the religious traditions of the world into a hierarchy on the basis of a Christian estimation of the adequacy of their response to
this common experience (see *The Christian Faith*, §§7–9 (pp. 31–44)); Rudolph Otto
names the problem with some exactness in the early pages of *The Idea of the Holy*
(Harmondsworth: Penguin, 1959), commenting, 'whoever knows no such
moments in his experience, is requested to read no further . . .' p. 22.

[9] Ludwig Feuerbach's observation that, in the absence of other good reason to
believe in the existence of a benevolent God, this assumption is necessarily
groundless, seems to me to be devastating for this style of theology.

[10] K. Barth, *Church Dogmatics* (14 vols; Edinburgh: T&T Clark, 1956–75) (hereafter
CD), 1.1, p. 301.

God of the Christians;[11] the majority liberal tradition would point to something like 'universal beneficent Fatherhood' as doing the same work; Charles Hodge had repeated, with great satisfaction, the formula of the Westminster Catechism.[12] Barth himself, in his discussion of the divine perfections in *CD* 2.2, offers 'the One who loves in freedom' as an identification of God. Why look to the doctrine of the Trinity?

Two things need to be said in answer. First, and less importantly, this is not necessarily an either/or decision. Barth claims that to be the One who loves in freedom is necessarily to be triune;[13] Dorner had made a similar argument about 'Holy Love' in his own dogmatic system. Second, Barth's decision to prioritize the Trinity as description reflects a central theme of his theology, his intense focus on the person of Jesus Christ as the key to every epistemological door. In his early reaction against liberalism, his endlessly repeated point had been the sheer otherness and unknowability of the God of the Bible; as he himself notes with some humour, when the time came for him to say something positive he had created a certain difficulty for himself.[14] His answer was the realization that the God who is totally other, and unknowable and unreachable by any human argument, observation, or analogy, is nonetheless sovereignly able to make himself known, and does so in Jesus Christ.

In adequate speech about God, then, God is not so much spoken about as speaking – God makes himself known. For Barth, this works out in his account of revelation in at least two ways. On the one hand, he finds a triune structure to the event of revelation – in his own summary, 'God reveals God by means of God'.[15] God speaks; God is spoken; and God is the only possible source of the capacity for human hearing. On the other hand, Barth offers a complex account of the 'Word of God', finding a threefold form in which the Word is at once Jesus Christ (primarily), the Bible, and the

---

[11] On Forsyth and Dorner, see below, pp. 191–6.

[12] 'Probably the best definition of God ever penned by man, is that given in the "Westminster Catechism": "God is a Spirit, infinite, eternal, and unchangeable, in his being, wisdom, power, holiness, justice, goodness, and truth."' Charles Hodge, *Systematic Theology* (3 vols; Peabody, MA: Hendrickson, 2003), 1:367.

[13] 'Since God is Father, Son and Holy Ghost, i.e., loves in freedom . . .' *CD* 2.1, p. 323.

[14] See his introduction to Heinrich Heppe's *Reformed Dogmatics* (ed. Ernest Bizer; trans. G.T. Thomson; Grand Rapids, MI: Baker, 1978).

[15] *CD* 1.1, pp. 295–333.

preaching of the Bible.[16] Identifying the preaching of the Word with divine speech is merely a repetition of a strand of the Reformed tradition, of course,[17] but Barth's reason for doing it is not an assertion of the authority of the pulpit, so much as an insistence that if God is adequately spoken of, then necessarily only God can be the speaker.

Where Barth did perhaps depart more decisively from the Reformation inheritance is his denial of any existence of the Second Person of the Trinity, the divine Son, that is not also the existence of Jesus Christ, the man from Nazareth. In Barth's famous phrase, there is no *Logos asarkos*, no divine Word that is unfleshed. The difference from the tradition needs to be stated with a certain precision, however (Barth was a far more traditional Reformed theologian than is usually recognized): the seventeenth-century Reformed theologians would speak, not of a *Logos asarkos*, but of a *Logos incarnandus* – the Word who was to become incarnate. Barth's objection was that this was a second moment in God's life: God, who already existed, determined himself to be the One who saves his covenant people.[18] Barth wants to insist that there is no second moment in God's life: God's being is his act, and his act is to determine himself to be the One who saves in and through Jesus Christ.[19]

---

[16] *CD* 1.1, pp. 88–124.

[17] Most famously, in the title added to the Second Helvitic Confession: *Praedicatio verbi Dei est verbum Dei* – 'The preaching of the Word of God is the Word of God'. For a helpful, if brief, review of this theme in Calvin, Bullinger, and their Reformed successors, see Philip W. Butin, 'Preaching as a Trinitiarian Event', in *Trinitarian Theology for the Church: Scripture, Community, Worship* (ed. Daniel J. Trier and David Lauber; Nottingham: Apollos, 2009), pp. 204–24.

[18] The idea of the covenant of redemption – the pretemporal agreement of Father and Son (and Spirit) to act to save (some of) the sinful human beings who would exist within creation – was somewhat controversial within traditional Reformed thought, but highlights well this tendency to imagine a 'second moment' of God's life.

[19] Again, the extent to which even this claim is a departure from the dogmatic tradition needs to be carefully elucidated. On the one hand, concern to protect divine freedom and aseity (or what Barth would have regarded as unacceptably abstract accounts of these two things) led to a repeated insistence that God's acts in creation and redemption – not excluding the incarnation – remain external to the being of God, voluntary rather than necessary; on the other hand, the claim that God's being is *actus purissimus sine ulla potentia* demands an identity of being and act. In my estimation, Barth is right to think that he is doing something different from the earlier tradition, but very few of his interpreters – Bruce McCormack stands out as an exception – grasp the logic of the earlier tradition well enough to state what the difference is with adequate precision. See McCormack, 'Grace and Being: The Role of God's Gracious Election in Karl Barth's Theological Ontology',

Barth is emphatic that in this God remains free – he is, fundamentally, the One who loves in freedom. God does not need creation to be perfect and complete, but in Jesus Christ God has chosen to be perfect and complete with, and not without, creation. This is not a second moment; this is God's determination of his own eternal life and being. There is nothing behind the God who chooses to be for us in Jesus Christ, no prior existence or being. God elects himself to be this God, and his election is sovereign over his own life also, and so he is this God without qualification or reserve.[20] There is an important sense, then, in which the history of Jesus Christ is God's own history. Barth spells out what this means with great power in the lengthy narratives of *CD* 4.

All of this is an account of the use to which Barth put the doctrine of the Trinity in his wider theology; in his technical account of the

---

in *The Cambridge Companion to Karl Barth* (ed. Webster), pp. 92–110, esp. pp. 101–4; see also McCormack, 'Election and the Trinity: Theses in Response to George Hunsinger', *SJT* 63/2 (2010): pp. 203–24.

[20] Does this mean that God chooses to be Trinity? This point has proved somewhat controversial amongst eminent interpreters of Barth in recent English-language theology, with Paul D. Molnar and George Hunsinger arguing for an ontological priority of Trinity over election, and Bruce McCormack arguing that, although Barth was somewhat inconsistent on this point (changing his view around 1938, and lapsing sometimes into his former view), from *CD* 2.2 onwards, Barth saw only a logical priority of Trinity over election. McCormack's own construction suggests that Barth did not go far enough; we should see a logical priority of election over Trinity ('The decision for the covenant of grace is the ground of God's triunity . . .' McCormack, 'Grace and Being', p. 103). See variously, McCormack, 'Election and the Trinity'; Hunsinger, 'Election and the Trinity: Twenty-Five Theses on the Theology of Karl Barth', *Modern Theology* 24/2 (2008): pp. 172–98; Molnar, *Divine Freedom and the Doctrine of the Immanent Trinity: In Dialogue with Karl Barth and Comtemporary Theology* (London: T&T Clark, 2002) and 'The Trinity, Election and God's Ontological Freedom: A Response to Kevin W. Hector', *IJST* 8/3 (2006): pp. 294–306; also Kevin W. Hector, 'God's Triunity and Self-Determination: A Conversation with Karl Barth, Bruce McCormack and Paul Molnar', *IJST* 7/3 (2005): pp. 246–61. The debate is impossible to summarize here, but my own view is that two issues are being unhelpfully conflated: what Barth said; and what should be said, theologically. McCormack is probably more nearly right in his exposition of Barth, in my estimation, but – for all the unquestionable brilliance of the theological synthesis McCormack is engaged in constructing, one of the most exciting projects in systematic theology today – I think that Molnar's and Hunsinger's attempts to insist on something like a traditional account of divine aseity are appropriate; my reasons for this judgement will become clear to any attentive reader of this book. See also Moltmann's contention that Barth erroneously gives God's sovereignty precedence over his Trinitarian nature. Jürgen Moltmann, *The Trinity and the Kingdom of God* (trans. M. Kohl; London: SCM, 1981), pp. 139–41.

Trinity, in *CD* 1.1 §9, he is self-consciously rehearsing the tradition (in its Western form – he places great stress on the *filioque* clause)[21] with one exception. Presumably following Dorner,[22] he refuses to use the word 'person' of Father, Son, and Holy Spirit, offering instead 'mode of being' (*Seinsweise*). Whatever the merits of the decision to depart from traditional terminology, and the term chosen as a replacement – and it could be argued that both are unhappy – it is clear that Barth's motive for this departure is only to preserve with complete clarity the doctrine of the Trinity that he had discovered in the tradition:

> It is well to note at this early stage that what we to-day call the 'personality' of God belongs to the one unique essence of God which the doctrine of the Trinity does not seek to triple but rather to recognise in its simplicity . . .
>
> 'Person' as used in the Church doctrine of the Trinity bears no direct relation to personality. The meaning of the doctrine is not, then, that there are three personalities in God. That would be the worst and most extreme expression of tritheism . . .[23]

Barth offers a lengthy genealogy of the use of 'person' (*sic, persona; πρόσωπον*) in technical Trinitarian discourse, highlighting both the habit of offering precise philosophical definitions that have little or nothing to do with 'personality' (so Boethius; Thomas Aquinas), and the regular expressions of hesitation about the term (Augustine; Anselm; Calvin). Decisively, however, in the nineteenth century the concept of 'person' became explicitly and inseparably identified with 'personality', rendering it unusable in theological discourse. Theologians both Roman Catholic (Anton Günther) and Protestant (Richard Grützmacher) fell into the trap of 'ascrib[ing] a separate I-centre with a separate consciousness and will and content to Creator,

---

[21] See *CD* 1.1 pp. 477–84.

[22] Barth does not reference Dorner, but it is difficult to believe that he had not read Dorner's *System*, and the coincidence in choice of terminology is striking. Moltmann has suggested that Barth's use of Dorner implies a modalism by 'guilt of association'; see *The Trinity*, p. 139, and p. 241 n.21. However, as Paul Collins has noted (*Trinitarian Theology West and East: Karl Barth, the Cappadocian Fathers, and John Zizioulas* [Oxford: OUP, 2001], p. 116), 'it does not necessarily follow that Barth accepted the context in which Dorner placed the term'; further, Moltmann's suggestion that Dorner was guilty of modalism is unconvincing; see my comments on Moltmann and Dorner below.

[23] *CD* 1.1 pp. 350–51.

Son and Spirit respectively'. In Barth's view, the continued use of the word so invites this error that, *in order to believe what the church has always believed*, we must speak in novel ways.[24]

There is no question that Barth brought the doctrine of the Trinity back into the centre of theological discourse. The reception of his theology, however, suggests that most of those who have followed have found the conservative tendencies of his stated doctrine of the Trinity to be at odds with his radical deployment of the doctrine. Robert Jenson, for instance: '. . . it is Barth who taught twentieth-century theology – or the lively parts of it – the importance and point of trinitarian discourse . . . But his contribution to required new trinitarian *analysis* is not so great as might be expected, nor does he carry us to full liberation from a past-determined interpretation of God. There is room for further reflection.'[25]

Karl Rahner and John Zizioulas: economy and personhood

The two most significant contributions to what Jenson sees as the 'required new trinitarian analysis' come from the Roman Catholic theologian Karl Rahner and the Greek Orthodox bishop John Zizioulas. Rahner's great contribution was to insist on the importance of the economy of salvation for Trinitarian reflection; Zizioulas's was to bring concepts of personhood and relationality into centre stage.

Rahner's book, simply entitled *The Trinity*, appeared in 1967;[26] the key ideas, however, had already been developed in more occasional writings over the previous decade.[27] Rahner begins his analysis with

---

[24] *CD* 1.1 pp. 355–8, quotation from p. 357. Barth's critics seem to ignore this semantic justification for his change of terminology, preferring to find hidden theological commitments – whether it be an over-commitment to rationalist constructions as opposed to biblical ideas (so Leonard Hodgson, *The Doctrine of the Trinity: Croall Lectures*, 1942–3 [London: Nisbet, 1943], p. 229), an inheritance from German idealism (Moltmann, *The Trinity*, pp. 139–42), or something equally speculative.

[25] Robert W. Jenson, *The Triune Identity: God according to the Gospel* (Philadelphia: Fortress, 1982), p. 138.

[26] Karl Rahner, *The Trinity* (trans. Joseph Donceel; Tunbridge Wells: Burns & Oates, 1970). It is surprising how little attention Rahner's Trinitarian thought has received from his major interpreters; there are several book-length studies of his theology which barely mention the theme. For a good overview of his thought, however, see Karen Kilby, *Karl Rahner: Theology and Philosophy* (London: Routledge, 2004).

[27] See particularly 'Remarks on the Dogmatic Treatise "De Trinitate"', in *Theological Investigations*, vol. 4 (London: DLT, 1966), pp. 77–104, which essay originally appeared in a *Festschrift* for Bischof A. Stohr in 1960.

the striking remark that 'should the doctrine of the Trinity have to be dropped as false, the major part of religious literature could well remain virtually unchanged.'[28] In Rahner's analysis, the reason for this is twofold: first, the doctrine of the Trinity has, since Thomas Aquinas, been separated from, and subordinated to, the doctrine of God; second, the doctrine of the Trinity has become detached from salvation history. Rahner's proposed solution to this second problem has become both famous, and axiomatic for virtually all recent Trinitarian theorizing, under the name 'Rahner's rule': 'The "economic" Trinity is the "immanent" Trinity and the "immanent" Trinity is the "economic" Trinity.'[29]

Rahner offers this formulation as a way of defending the point that the doctrine of the Trinity is a 'mystery of salvation' – if it were not, 'it would never have been revealed'.[30] In Rahner's view, the doctrine had, in (Roman Catholic) dogmatics, become an isolated claim about the interiority of God which had no connection to the human experience of salvation. The slogan, current since at least St Augustine, that *opera Trinitatis ad extra indivisa sunt* ('the external acts of the Trinity are undivided'), seems to demand that every divine act in the economy of salvation is an act of the One God, who internally happens to be triune, but who acts in a simply unitary way in the world. However, Rahner believes that this must be wrong, since God only reveals useful truth.

In the divine economy of salvation, we see the incarnate Son relating to the Father in the Spirit; this is the 'economic' Trinity in Rahner's terms, and this gives the lie to the (standard interpretation of) the old claim about the indivisibility of divine acts. The Son, only, is incarnate in the economy, not the Father nor the Spirit. The fact of incarnation is, of course, a triune act ('The Holy Spirit will come upon you, and the power of the Most High will overshadow you; therefore the child to be born . . . will be called Son of God'; Luke 1:35 NRSV), but still, 'he is incarnate' is a claim that can be made of the Second Person of the Trinity only, not of the Father or of the Spirit. So, we see an 'economic' Trinity, a history of relations between Father and Son, in the unity of the Spirit, that takes place within the created order. This, claims Rahner, is identical to the 'immanent' Trinity, the interiority of the divine life in all eternity.

---

[28] *The Trinity*, pp. 10–11.
[29] *The Trinity*, p. 22.
[30] *The Trinity*, p. 21.

What does this assertion of identity mean? For Rahner, there appears to be a certain ambiguity: at times, the claim is epistemological: we can be confident that what God appears to be like in the economy is in fact what God is like in reality. So Rahner can say, 'it is a fact of salvation history that we know about the Trinity because the Father's Word has entered our history and has given us his Spirit' (p. 48). At other times, however, it appears that a far stronger, ontological, claim is being made, in which the economic Trinity constitutes the eternal life of God: 'the Father is the incomprehensible origin and the original unity, the "Word" his utterance into history, and the "Spirit" the opening up of history into the immediacy of its Fatherly origin and end. And precisely this Trinity of salvation history . . . is the "immanent" Trinity' (p. 47).

This ambiguity has been noticed by several commentators. Some have, as a result, dismissed Rahner's 'rule' as a superficially impressive, but actually meaningless, statement;[31] others have collapsed the ambiguity, usually with an insistence that Rahner was not sufficiently radical to see that the logic of his position demanded an insistence that the life of God simply is the life of the world.[32] It would seem, however, that the importance of Rahner's rule in recent theological discussion is not its precise logical signification so much as its helpful gesturing towards the narratives of gospel history as key data – perhaps the only data – to which the doctrine of the Trinity must be responsible.

Rahner's technical Trinitarian theology is, like Barth's, self-consciously traditional and orthodox. He notes the same problems with the word 'person' that Barth had found,[33] but does not believe that the word can be set aside.[34] His concern is with the derivation and use of the doctrine, not with its formal statement. The church – for Rahner, the magisterium of the Roman Catholic Church – has taught rightly

---

[31] See, e.g., Randal Rauser, 'Rahner's Rule: An Emperor without Clothes?' *IJST* 7 (2005): pp. 81–94, or Bruce D. Marshall, *Trinity and Truth* (Cambridge: CUP, 2000), pp. 263–5. Yves Congar suggests that the rule should be uni-directional – the economic Trinity is the immanent Trinity, but not vice versa. *I Believe in the Holy Spirit*, vol. 3 (New York: Seabury, 1983), pp. 13–15.

[32] So, e.g., Catherine Mowry LaCugna, *God for Us: The Trinity and Christian Life* (New York: HarperCollins, 1991), pp. 221–3, or Moltmann, *The Trinity*, pp. 158–61.

[33] '. . . when nowadays we hear of "three persons" we connect, almost necessarily, with this expression the idea of three centres of consciousness and activity, which leads to a heretical misunderstanding of the dogma.' Rahner, *The Trinity*, pp. 56–7.

[34] See Rahner, *The Trinity*, pp. 56–7, 73–6.

about the dogma of the Trinity, but theologians in explicating the teaching have detached it from its proper source, in the gospel history, and so separated it from its proper relation with other doctrines, as the fundamental truth of salvation.

That said, Rahner's invitation to read the gospel histories as accounts of inner-triune relations has invited others to go further than he would in reinterpreting technical Trinitarianism. In particular, it is very tempting to read the gospel narratives as describing relations between persons who are precisely distinct 'centres of consciousness and activity'; when the incarnate Son prays, 'yet, not my will but yours be done' (Luke 22:42 NRSV), the assumption that the Son has a different centre of consciousness and volition from the Father is invited.[35]

John Zizioulas, metropolitan bishop of Pergamum, has been as influential as Rahner on the late twentieth-century Trinitarian revival, and has explicitly made and celebrated this move to a more natural (in contemporary idiom) reading of the language of 'person' in the Trinity in his book *Being as Communion*.[36] Zizioulas argues in the first part of this book that the Cappadocian fathers developed a novel ontology, which connected being with personhood and relationship. The second half of the book offers an ecclesiology which Zizioulas claims flows naturally from his doctrine of the Trinity; this ecclesiology (a very hierarchical version of episcopalianism, with an insistence on the maleness of the clergy) has been largely ignored by Zizioulas's followers, and his claim that it flows naturally from his Trinitarian doctrine quietly passed over.[37]

Zizioulas bases his claim on an account of the history of Trinitarian doctrine in which at a decisive moment – in the lead-up to the Council of Constantinople – there was a quiet revolution in language use. St Basil, primarily, and St Gregory Nazianzen and St Gregory Nyssan

---

[35] The patristic tradition, in its settled form after the monothelite controversy, generally read the text as a collision between the human will of the Incarnate One and the one divine will which is fully and identically present in both Father and Son. On this, see my 'Christology, Scripture, Divine Action, and Hermeneutics', in *Christology and Scripture: Interdisciplinary Perspectives* (ed. Angus Paddison and Andrew T. Lincoln; London: T&T Clark, 2007), pp. 156–170.

[36] John D. Zizioulas, *Being as Communion: Studies in Personhood and the Church* (hereafter *BaC*) (London: DLT, 1985). For some critical engagement, see *The Theology of John Zizioulas: Personhood and the Church* (ed. Douglas H. Knight; Aldershot: Ashgate, 2007), and Miroslav Volf, *After Our Likeness*, pp. 73–123.

[37] An honourable exception is Miroslav Volf, who finds his way around the problem by making a significant alteration to the received ecumenical doctrine of the Trinity, as I shall explore later in this chapter.

with him, took the classical language of Greek ontology – *ousia,*
hypostasis, etc. – and redefined it in personal and relational terms. The
basic nature of reality was no longer substance, but relationship.
Cause was, fundamentally, now not a physical category but a personal one.

The first step along this line to which Zizioulas points is the articu-
lation of the doctrine of *creatio ex nihilo.*[38] This is important for two reasons. First, it begins a stress on the freedom of God which will run
through Zizioulas's theology; second, it removes any physical, or
indeed metaphysical, data from the questions of ultimate cause and
fundamental ontology. The world is neither ultimate nor fundamental; no component of its existence is eternal. It was freely brought into
being by God, and so its being is contingent and derivative.

Second, and in an explicit polemic against the Western tradition of
Trinitarian theology, Zizioulas insists that the recognition of the
Father as the source or cause ($\alpha\iota\tau\iota\alpha$) of the Trinity is a decisive move.[39]
Once again, this allows him to make claims about freedom and ontol-
ogy. With regard to freedom, asserting the (personal) Father as cause
insists that, at the most fundamental level, causation is something free
and personal, not something mechanical and fixed. With regard to
ontology, Zizioulas's construction permits him to claim that *ousia* –
'substance' – never exists except in personal (hypostatic) form. Again
at the most fundamental level, ontology is about particular personal
existence, not the general nature of a substance – and freedom is a
property of the person, the *hypostasis,* not of the *ousia.*

The third move that Zizioulas sees as central is the gradual separation of *hypostasis* from being a synonym of *ousia* and its alignment
instead with *prosopon.*[40] This, Zizioulas argues, is the decisive moment:
an ontological word – the fundamental ontological word, according to
the second point above – becomes identified with a personal word.
The basic nature of reality is now no longer about the 'stuff' from
which things are made, but about the persons who made it, and their
relatedness.

The result of these three moves is a stress on the personal, volitional nature of God's existence:

---

[38] *BaC* pp. 39–40.
[39] *BaC* pp. 40–42. Zizioulas has recently defended his position against criticisms by
Alan Torrance and others; see 'The Father as Cause: Personhood Generating
Otherness', in John D. Zizioulas, *Communion and Otherness* (ed. Paul McPartlan;
London: T&T Clark, 2006), pp. 113–54.
[40] *BaC* pp. 36–9.

... the being of God is not an ontological 'necessity' or a simple 'reality' for God – but we ascribe the being of God to His personal freedom. In a more analytical way this means that God, as Father and not as substance, perpetually confirms through 'being' His *free* will to exist. And it is precisely His trinitarian existence that constitutes this confirmation: the Father out of love – that is, freely – begets the Son and brings forth the Spirit . . .[41]

Notice here that volition is possessed by God the Father, not by the Holy Trinity indifferently. Zizioulas's account of the personal nature of deity seems to imply that each of the *hypostaseis* is fully personal, possessed of their own will, intellect, and so on, in precisely the way that Barth and Rahner warned against. This accusation has been levelled at Zizioulas before;[42] his defence turns on the claim that he has never described God as 'three individuals, three "axes of consciousness" on which natural or moral qualities concur . . .'[43] this, however, needs specification: Turcescu's term 'axes of consciousness' may be unhappy or misleading, but it seems clear that Zizioulas locates the capacity of volition with the person, not with the essence – so the quotation above, which could be multiplied almost endlessly from Zizioulas's writings. One result of this is a shift in reference of the divine names: throughout Zizioulas's work, they are taken as referring to the persons, not to the *ousia*. Consider the following:

If God the Father is immortal, it is because His unique and unrepeatable identity as Father is distinguished eternally from that of the Son and of the Spirit . . . If the Son is immortal, He owes this primarily not to His substance but to His being the 'only-begotten' . . . The life of God is eternal because it is personal . . . Life and love are identified in the person . . .[44]

---

[41] *BaC* p. 41; emphasis original. This point is basic to Zizioulas's thought throughout his career; see the various essays in *Communion and Otherness* for examples.

[42] See especially L. Turcescu, '"Person" vs "Individual", and Other Modern Misreadings of Gregory of Nyssa', *Modern Theology* 18 (2002): pp. 527–39; there is a response by A. Papanikolaou, 'Is John Zizioulas an Existentialist in Disguise? A Response to Lucian Turcescu', *Modern Theology* 20 (2004): pp. 601–7. See also Alan Brown, 'On the Criticism of Being as Communion in Anglophone Orthodox Theology', in *Theology of John Zizioulas* (ed. Knight), pp. 35–78, and Zizioulas's own comments in *Communion and Otherness*, pp. 171–7. I believe these defences can be answered, or rather that the more important aspects of the criticism can be maintained. (I have no desire to cast Zizioulas as an existentialist, but I do think his reading of the Cappadocians is wrong in some specific, but important, particulars.)

[43] *Communion and Otherness*, p. 171.

[44] *BaC* pp. 48–9.

Finally, according to Zizioulas there is one word, at least, which refers univocally to both God and (some) creatures: 'person'. More pointedly, there is a class, a genus, 'persons', into which both God and (again, some) creatures might be indifferently placed. Thus stated, the charge is blunt, but I believe it can be upheld. It should be qualified by an acknowledgement that Zizioulas only ever claims true personhood for human beings as an eschatological reality. Most often, he correlates his understanding of personhood with the biblical and traditional language of creation in the 'image of God'. However, even if it is only at the eschaton, it seems that for Zizioulas humans may be, by grace, persons in exactly the same sense that Father, Son and Spirit are personal by nature.[45] It is interesting that even when writing about the apophatic tradition of theology, so important in aspects of the Greek tradition, Zizioulas will not surrender this point.[46] Given the significance of questions about how language refers to the divine in the Cappadocian debate with Eunomius,[47] this is an important point.

Zizioulas's analysis has been accepted and built upon by many of the contributors to the recent revival in Trinitarian theology. Much of the development has been ethical, particularly ecclesiological. God's own life is a loving communion of persons; so, then, the life of the church should be the same, and the distinctively Christian approach to wider questions of social ethics will be informed decisively by these recognitions.[48] This Miroslav Volf describes as enjoying 'the status of an almost self-evident proposition' in recent theology.[49] The consequences hinted at above, of accepting some of the names of God, at

---

[45] There is an illuminating comment on this matter in an exchange of letters appended to one of the essays in *Communion and Otherness*. Philip Sherrard had asked about the immortality of the angels; Zizioulas responds that angels are naturally immortal, but this is irrelevant; unless they become persons through the grace of Christ they will 'fall into the anonymity of the place of the dead' (p. 283). He goes on to claim that 'nature cannot exist in itself but only as a relationship-person' (p. 283). The univocity of personal and relational language seems clear.

[46] This is particularly clear in the brief consideration given to ontology in *BaC*. Zizioulas makes all the necessary assertions: 'we are unable to use the concepts of the human mind . . . for signifying God . . .'; God *'is beyond affirmation and negation'* (emphasis original) (both p. 90), but then goes on to suggest that categories of 'love' and 'communion' can bridge this gap, because God is love (pp. 89–92).

[47] See pp. 97–116 below.

[48] For the broader point see, e.g., Volf, 'The Trinity is Our Social Program', or David S. Cunningham, *These Three Are One: The Practice of Trinitarian Theology* (Oxford: Blackwell, 1998).

[49] Volf, *After Our Likeness*, p. 191.

least, as univocal,[50] and of tending to locate the perfections of God as applying to the persons, not to the undifferentiated Godhead, are also commonly visible.

Twentieth-Century Trinitarianism: Patterns

In different ways the work of Barth, Rahner, and Zizioulas has been taken forward by a vast array of writers within late twentieth-century theology. Here, I intend to cover the most important, and to try to give some shape to the landscape, to expose the broad themes which, in different ways, appear repeatedly in different thinkers.[51]

The Trinity and history: Pannenberg, Moltmann, and Jenson

Barth's insistence that there is no second moment in God's life, and therefore that the history of Jesus Christ is who God has elected to be, and Rahner's insistence on finding the core data for the development of Trinitarian theology in the gospel narratives, both invite a radical reconstruction of traditional accounts of the relationship of God with history. God is not the timeless eternal sovereign Creator who begins and supervenes history from without; rather, God chooses to be God with, not without, the created order, and its history is his story.[52]

Wolfhart Pannenberg's[53] theological programme was focused on history from the outset. An early edited volume, *Revelation as*

---

[50] So, for obvious example, the collection edited by Colin Gunton and Christoph Schwöbel, *Persons Divine and Human* (Edinburgh: T&T Clark, 1991).

[51] My selection of themes owes something, at least, to Stanley Grenz's *Rediscovering the Triune God: The Trinity in Contemporary Theology* (Minneapolis: Fortress, 2004), which offers an insightful and informed book-length survey of much the same ground as I am covering in this chapter.

[52] It might be tempting to find some background in either Hegelian dialectics or process theology for this move. I do not suppose that any thinker, particularly any theologian, of the late twentieth century can be simply unaffected by Hegel, and it may be that either Hegel or the process thinkers contribute significantly towards creating an intellectual context in which radical reconceptions of God's relationship to history can be essayed; however, as I have tried to indicate, there is sufficient motivation and resource in the history of theology's own development to explain the turn to history; and generic accusations of 'Hegelianism', unless supported by close textual evidence, are not helpful to the task of understanding theological development.

[53] My reading of Pannenberg has been shaped by a close and insightful engagement offered by my student, Jason Sexton.

History,[54] indicated that discussions around the relationship of theology and history had been a crucial part of his intellectual development through his twenties, and it has remained central for him through his life. History is a process, leading to an eschatological consummation when the ultimate truth of things will be not just revealed, but in some sense established. God's Lordship will be unambiguously actual in the End, but before the End there is an ambiguity about it, and it is not just that we do not clearly see God as Lord of all creation, but that the fact of God's Lordship remains provisional until it is finally demonstrated to have always been the case in the End, although it is anticipated in the coming of Jesus, itself an anticipation of the eschaton.[55]

Pannenberg's early thought was not un-Trinitarian, but the doctrine of the Trinity was neither the focus nor the basis of what he was doing. In writing his three-volume *Systematic Theology*, however, he took a conscious decision to attempt to make Trinitarian doctrine central to every area of his thought.[56] Given his constant focus on the fact of history, it is no surprise that Pannenberg took up the invitation of Barth and Rahner[57] to find the basis of the doctrine in the history of the incarnate Son's relationship with the One he called Father.[58] Pannenberg, an assiduous student of the history of theological discussion, is of course aware that the statements within the gospels which he finds as definitive of the Trinitarian relationships were read by an older tradition as reflecting the relationship of the human Jesus of Nazareth to God,[59] but he is simply dismissive of this reading.

---

[54] Wolfhart Pannenberg, ed., *Revelation as History* (trans. David Granskou; London: Sheed & Ward, 1979).

[55] See Wolfhart Pannenberg, *Systematic Theology*, vol. 1 (trans. Geoffrey W. Bromiley; Edinburgh: T&T Clark, 1991) (hereafter *ST*), p. 229 for a concise statement of this theme.

[56] This decision is signalled in Pannenberg's 1981 contribution to the famous 'How My Mind Has Changed' column in the *Christian Century*, where he suggests his career has been a slow approach to the doctrine of God, moving from 'the unknown God who came close only in Jesus Christ' to a doctrine of God which 'constitute[s] the final task of Christian theology' and which 'will be more thoroughly trinitarian than any example I know of'. Pannenberg, 'God's Presence in History', *ChrCent* 98 (1981): pp. 260–63, quotations from p. 263.

[57] Pannenberg's doctrine of the Trinity in the *ST* is developed in extensive dialogue with Barth – see, e.g., *ST* 1:303–5; he offers a lengthy discussion of Rahner's rule in *ST* 1:327–33; however, his account of the history of the location of the doctrine in dogmatics in the medieval period is already visibly, if silently, dependent on Rahner; *ST* 1:280–83; compare Rahner, *The Trinity*, pp. 16–18.

[58] *ST* 1:308–15.

[59] *ST* 1:309–10.

Pannenberg's conclusion to his reading of the biblical history indicates how much he has been able to draw from it, and his awareness of going beyond the traditional accounts:

> Relations among the three persons that are defined as mutual self-distinction cannot be reduced to relations of origin in the traditional sense. The Father does not merely beget the Son. He also hands over his kingdom to him and receives it back from him. The Son is not merely begotten of the Father. He is also obedient to him and he thereby glorifies him as the one God. The Spirit is not just breathed. He also fills the Son and glorifies Him in his obedience to the Father, thereby glorifying the Father himself. In so doing he leads into all truth (John 16:13) and searches out the deep things of Godhead (1 Cor. 2:10–11).[60]

The biblical language describing relations in the economy has become, here, definitive of the immanent Trinity. Pannenberg is beginning here to show how taking Rahner's and Barth's methodological moves seriously leads necessarily to a move away from the self-consciously traditional doctrines of the Trinity that they both offered.[61]

Pannenberg pushes his point further, however. If this history is intrinsic to what it is for God to be God – Rahner's rule, in Pannenbergian language – then 'creation is brought into the relations of the trinitarian persons and participates in them.'[62] Pannenberg makes this claim having already accepted the traditional assertion that the three persons of the Trinity are constituted by their relations with each other,[63] and he does not shy away from the necessary logical result: the life of Father, Son, and Spirit is now dependent on the world. As he puts it: 'Through the Son and Spirit, however, the Father, too, stands in relation to the history of the economy of salvation. Even in his deity, by the creation of the world and the sending of his Son

---

[60] *ST* 1:320.

[61] 'Karl Barth demanded that we base the doctrine of the Trinity on the revelation of God in Jesus Christ. He did not succeed in meeting his own demand, but Karl Rahner has taken it up and sharpened it with his thesis of an identity between the immanent and the economic Trinity.' *ST* 1:328.

[62] *ST* 1:328.

[63] 'We may thus say . . . what trinitarian theology from the time of Athanasius has said about the trinitarian relations, namely, that they constitute the different distinctions of the persons. The persons simply are what they are in their relations to one another . . .' *ST* 1:320. Pannenberg goes on to suggest that the older view erred in thinking that the relations between the persons could be reduced to simple relations of origin: filiation and spiration.

and Spirit to work in it, *he has made himself dependent upon the course of history.*[64] Pannenberg credits Jüngel with the original development of this point, and then points to Moltmann's *Crucified God* as the classical exposition.

It is important to notice here that there is still a Barthian primacy of the divine decision – the Father 'has made himself dependent'. In this, God is still sovereign, and is other than the creature; my dependence on the world is given; God's is chosen. Further, Pannenberg invokes God's Lordship over time in explaining what he means: Moltmann is right to 'link the consummation of salvation history in eschatology with the consummation of the trinitarian life of God in itself'; and it is true that 'the deity of God is . . . dependent upon the eschatological coming of the kingdom'; thus, from our time-bound perspective, it appears as if God is becoming, and will only be in the eschaton. God, however, is eternal, and his sovereign decision is that this eschatological becoming will always have been the authentic and inviolable basis of his life.[65]

I have already indicated that Pannenberg makes reference to Jürgen Moltmann in his development, and it is to Moltmann himself I now turn.[66] Moltmann began his career with an emphasis on eschatology rather than history – his first celebrated book, *Theology of Hope*, insisted on the eschatological context of all Christian theology.[67] With *The Crucified God*,[68] however, he insisted on the gospel history, supremely (as the title suggests) the passion of Christ, as an event in the divine life,[69] and so began developing an account of the Trinity similar to

---

[64] *ST* 1:329, my emphasis.

[65] *ST* 1:.330–31.

[66] The most perceptive introductions to Moltmann on the Trinity in English are Richard Bauckham's pair of books, *Moltmann: Messianic Theology in the Making* (Basingstoke: MMS, 1987) and *The Theology of Jürgen Moltmann* (Edinburgh: T&T Clark, 1995); although these books do not cover a significant period of Moltmann's work, they trace with great insight the development of his Trinitarian thought, which occurred early.

[67] Moltmann's own summary of the book's thesis has become famous: 'From first to last, and not merely in the epilogue, Christianity is eschatology, is hope'. *Theology of Hope: On the Ground and Implications of a Christian Eschatology* (trans. J.W. Leitch; London: SCM, 1967), p. 16.

[68] Jürgen Moltmann, *The Crucified God: The Cross of Christ as the Foundation and Criticism of Christian Theology* (trans. R.A. Wilson and John Bowden; London: SCM, 2001) (the German original was published in 1972, the first English translation in 1974).

[69] In *Experiences of God* (trans. Margaret Kohl; London: SCM, 1980), Moltmann suggests that, in working through an adequate theology of the cross, he found the crucial question facing him to be, 'what does Christ's cross really mean for God himself?' p. 15.

Pannenberg's later account, but more self-consciously radical.[70] Towards the end of the book he will announce that 'the material principle of the doctrine of the Trinity is the cross of Christ.'[71] His major work on the Trinity, *The Trinity and the Kingdom of God*, stands in clear continuity to this earlier work, in (for instance) taking as its starting point 'the passion of God'.[72]

The Trinity and the Kingdom of God is more careful than its predecessor in several regards. The earlier book at least invites the reading that God becomes Trinity through the cross.[73] For Moltmann, the basic problem with this claim is not its compromising of divine freedom, but its compromising of divine victory over evil. He is simply happy that God's life is affected, changed, by creation[74] – although he wishes to hold to a certain divine priority, less than Barth or Pannenberg wanted, in which God creates the creatures who are then able, through the freedom he has given them, to frustrate and change his own life. However, given the centrality of theodicy, of finding an adequate answer to the problem of suffering, to so much of what Moltmann is doing, the idea that making the cross central to God's life makes evil necessary to God being God is one with which he struggles. That said, his desire to make the cross central to the doctrine of God seems so strong as to continually draw him back to such problematic assertions: '[t]he pain of the cross determines the inner life of the triune God from eternity to eternity.'[75]

Again, in the earlier book the question of the unity of Father and Son (and Spirit) is, at least, obscure, when judged according to the classical canons of orthodoxy. Moltmann will speak of Trinity as

---

[70] In my estimation, Moltmann is more radical and innovative (or, put differently, less concerned to be responsible to the tradition) than Pannenberg; my point here is, however, that he celebrates, rather than minimizing, his divergences from the earlier tradition. He announces his desire for a 'revolution in the concept of God', for instance, language it is difficult to imagine Pannenberg using. *Crucified God*, p. 155.

[71] *Crucified God*, p. 249.

[72] Jürgen Moltmann, *The Trinity and the Kingdom of God: The Doctrine of God* (trans. Margaret Kohl; London; SCM, 1981) (hereafter, *TKG*).

[73] For a clear statement of the problem, and Moltmann's moves in answer, see Bauckham, *Moltmann*, pp. 106–9.

[74] There is an illuminating discussion of what can and cannot be meant by divine freedom in *TKG* pp. 52–6. The summary statement has it nicely: 'Through his [sic, God's] freedom he does not only speak as Lord, but listens to men and women as their Father', p. 56.

[75] *TKG* p. 161.

'event', and the cross as 'an event concerned with a relationship between persons in which these persons constitute themselves in their relationship with each other.'[76] This claim raises two rather telling questions: on the one hand, read straightforwardly, it seems to imply that God becomes Trinity at the cross; on the other, it suggests that there is something contingent about God's life as Trinity. Father and Son could conceivably have been otherwise; perhaps, even, three persons could have been four or two. It is certainly not intrinsic to divine existence that the Father begets the Son and the Son is begotten of the Father. Responding to this charge is perhaps the main theme of *TKG*, where Moltmann explores two major themes: a perichoretic social Trinity as an answer to Lordship; and the relationship of economic to immanent Trinities.

Moltmann is deeply concerned that a traditional monotheism, speaking of a single divine subject (such as Barth's), is profoundly disruptive of proper political and social theory. In this, he draws extensively on an important essay published in 1935 by Erik Peterson, which contended that it was a Greek infection of early Christianity that spoke of God as a single omnipotent power, and legitimized imperialism and absolute monarchy in the political realm.[77] Peterson was writing in response to attempts to claim theological legitimacy for Nazism, and so in a noble cause, but his conclusions have not stood the test of time.[78] Nonetheless, Moltmann takes it as a methodological principle that the monarchy of God (or indeed of the Father, in Zizioulan terms) is an unacceptable doctrine. Instead, in *TKG*, he develops an avowedly 'social' doctrine of the Trinity: three persons, mutually interrelated, mutually constitutive, with no hierarchy. He draws much on the ancient doctrine of *perichoresis* (interpenetration) in this, although he radically reinterprets the doctrine in so doing: for the later Greek fathers, who coined the term *perichoresis*, expressed the depth of ontological identity of Father, Son, and Holy Spirit: each necessarily fully and mutually filled and was filled by the others, as

---

[76] *Crucified God*, p. 254. Cf. the whole section on pp. 243–58.
[77] Erik Peterson, *Der Monotheismus als politisches Problem: Ein Beitrag zur Geschichte der politischen Theologie im Imperium Romanum* (Leipzig: Jakob Hegner, 1935). Moltmann was drawing on this work at least as early as 1971, in an essay in which he described it as 'magnificent'. Jürgen Moltmann, 'Political Theology', *ThTo* 28 (1971): pp. 6–23, p. 11.
[78] See Randall Otto, 'Moltmann and the Anti-Monotheist Movement', *IJST* 3/3 (2001): pp. 293–308, pp. 294, 306–7, for some details of the (rather devastating) scholarly critique.

each is an instantiation of the same ineffable substance. For Moltmann, *perichoresis* rather becomes an account of how seemingly rather ontologically diverse beings might find unity. Moltmann's critics are concerned that perichoresis is not adequate for this task: the unity established seems more like that of a family (an image Moltmann uses); togetherness rather than oneness.[79] (It was said of Nestorius's doctrine of the incarnation that, despite all his protestations of unity, everything metaphysically important remained two and separate; for Moltmann's Trinity, despite all the rhetoric of unity, it is difficult not to conclude that everything metaphysically important does not remain three and separate.)

In *TKG* Moltmann takes Rahner's rule to an extreme point: 'I found myself bound to surrender the traditional distinction between the immanent and the economic Trinity, according to which the cross comes to stand only in the economy of salvation, but not within the immanent Trinity.'[80] The standard complaint concerning such a move is that it surrenders God's aseity, and so freedom: God becomes caused by the world, if created events are events in the life of God. Moltmann faces this squarely, and essentially accepts the charge, whilst somewhat recasting it. Freedom, he suggests, is not the first word to be spoken of God; love is.[81] In love, God gives himself, binds himself, to the creation.

Is there any distinction between immanent and economic Trinity for Moltmann? He allows a certain distinction in the context of doxology: worship moves from the re-narrating of God's life with the world, to praise offered to God that names 'the transcendent conditions which make this experience (of salvation) possible'.[82] There is thus some account of transcendence remaining in Moltmann's thought, it seems – an account which perhaps links to his embracing of a belief in the ontological priority of the future not unlike Pannenberg's. The ontological presuppositions that underlie these

---

[79] A survey of some of the critics of Moltmann's understanding of *perichoresis*, and a careful account of the issues, can be found in Thomas H. McCall, *Which Trinity? Whose Monotheism? Philosophical and Systematic Theologians on the Metaphysics of Trinitarian Theology* (Grand Rapids, MI: Eerdmans, 2010), pp. 164–6.

[80] *TKG* p. 160.

[81] This is particularly obvious in Moltmann's criticism of Barth on creation; Barth wishes to affirm the freedom of God to create or not to create; Moltmann happily denies this, suggesting it is a failure to believe in the primacy of God's out-going love.

[82] *TKG* p. 153.

seemingly conflicting assertions of Moltmann's are not clear, at least to me.

The same emphatically cannot be said about the third writer I wish to treat here. Robert Jenson, an American Lutheran, is explicit throughout his work that he is essaying a radically revised meta-physic, which is deployed in order that an account of God's life which is thoroughly determined by the gospel narrative may be offered.[83] Jenson is deeply rooted in the Lutheran tradition, and it is possible to understand his theology as a development of key themes in that tra-dition. In contrast to patristic orthodoxy, the post-Reformation Lutherans speculated that, after the resurrection, the human nature of the incarnate Son could share in (some of) the perfections of the divine nature. The theological impetus for this move was in their debates about the Eucharist with the Reformed: the Lutherans wanted to affirm a real presence of the body and blood of Christ in the conse-crated elements on the altar; the Reformed denied this, insisting that a human body (and human blood) could only be in one place; Jesus Christ (in his human nature) was now at the right hand of the Father, and so could not be on the altar – or indeed on all the altars. By pos-tulating that divine transcendence of locality is transferred to the human nature, the Lutherans were able to rebut this argument.

Robert Jenson inherits this argument and develops it by asserting a symmetry: not only can the human nature share in the perfections of the divine nature, but so too the divine nature can share in the peculiar characteristics of the human nature. This move has been made with some regularity since the mid-nineteenth century (kenotic Christ-ologies almost always make a move at least similar to this, for instance), but Jenson wants to go further in exploring the inner logic of the move by pressing at what is meant by 'nature'. He is not content to allow the meaning inherited from Greek metaphysics to be decisive, but instead wants the term to be reconstructed to allow it to be used, and the gospel narrative to be told without reserve. (Jenson is commit-ted to retaining the ecumenically accepted formulas, including the Decree of the Council of Chalcedon, so does not regard putting aside the word 'nature' as unhelpful as an option.) 'Nature', for Jenson, is an indicator of participation in a community. 'That Christ has the divine nature means that he is one of the three whose mutuality is the divine life, who live the history that God is. That Christ has human nature

---

[83] My reading of Jenson also owes something to perceptive comments by students and former students, notably Russell Rook, Marion Gray, and David Sonju.

means that he is one of the many whose mutuality is human life, who live the history that humanity is.'[84] Like Zizioulas, Jenson feels a need to escape from metaphysical accounts that prioritize the 'whatness' of things in order to speak adequately of the Trinity, and he looks to concepts of community and history to do this work.

The overarching concept for Jenson's new metaphysic is not community or history, however, but *narrative*. The triune God is a story, a story of community, of mutuality and conversation between Father, Son, and Holy Spirit. And the story which the triune God is, is the gospel story. Jenson means this without any qualification or reserve: 'the second identity of God is directly the human person of the Gospels'.[85] Barth's denial of a *Logos asarkos*, Rahner's insistence on the identity of the immanent Trinity with the economic Trinity, and Pannenberg's and Moltmann's desire to see God's life as open to the gospel history, all reach their most extreme, and most coherent, expression in Jenson's theology. God is the gospel history; the Jewish man Jesus is the Second Person of the Trinity; the eternal generation of the Son is the event of incarnation.[86] The triune God of history is the history of God. Jenson's greatness – and in my estimation he is one of the greatest theologians working today – is that he sees with astonishing clarity just how thoroughly classical theology will have to be revised if 'Rahner's rule' is to be taken seriously, and does not at any point shrink from the revision, because he believes that to speak faithfully of the gospel, this revision is necessary.

The Trinity and the life of the church: Leonardo Boff and Miroslav Volf

A second pattern in late twentieth-century Trinitarianism is a pressing interest in the usefulness of the doctrine of the Trinity in discussing the life of the church. I have already sketched Zizioulas's attempt to

---

[84] Robert W. Jenson, *Systematic Theology, vol. 1: The Triune God* (Oxford: OUP, 1997), p. 138.

[85] Jenson, *ST* 1 p. 137; in a footnote to this phrase Jenson reinforces his point by quoting Bultmann: 'The man Jesus is, as the Revealer, the Logos.'

[86] 'In the triune life, what ontologically precedes the birth to Mary of Jesus who is God the Son, the birth, that is to say, of the sole actual second identity of that life, is the narrative pattern of *being going to be* born of Mary. What in eternity precedes the Son's birth to Mary is not an unincarnate *state* of the Son, but a pattern of movement within the event of the Incarnation, the movement to incarnation, as itself a pattern of God's triune life.' Jenson, *ST* 1 p. 141, emphases original.

derive a functional ecclesiology from his Trinitarian doctrine, and suggested that many who follow him want to adopt a similar method, although they also want to arrive at rather different results. Here we turn to examine two representative thinkers who do this in different ways.

Of course, any categorization like this is an over-simplification, or an imposition of a neat schema on evidence that is rather more messy. The primary influence on my first theologian in this section, the Brazilian Leonardo Boff, is not Zizioulas but Moltmann. Boff is a liberation theologian, who contributed significantly to the development and self-articulation of the movement in his early work. Like all liberation theologians, he maintains a particular interest in social ethics, and Moltmann's work on the political implications of his social Trinitarianism was obviously attractive to Boff. When he came to write his own treatment of the subject, patriarchal family relationships and authoritarian governments *are* both linked to inadequate Trinitarian understandings that stress the monarchy of the Father.[87] Boff surveys the history of the doctrine to its scholastic development, describing the resultant dogma as 'highly formal', and suggesting it seems very removed from the lived experience of salvation and liberation.[88] He looks at strategies of reinvigoration, exploring both the embracing of triple subjectivity and Barth's rejection of the term 'person', before criticizing everything that has come before as 'based either on the category of *substance* (nature or essence) or on that of *person* (subject, subsistant)', hence 'their dominant tone of thought is either metaphysical or personalist.'[89] The problem, for Boff, is that society and history are not the controlling factors.

On this basis he turns to Moltmann, and his notion of a community of persons, bound together by *perichoresis*. This vision of freely chosen, freely given, mutual, and equal community then gets used as a model against which the practices of community within the church, and indeed within wider society, can be judged. He writes, 'a society that takes its inspiration from trinitarian communion cannot tolerate class differences, dominations based on power (economic, sexual or ideological) that subjects those who are different'.[90] Similarly, '[t]he trinitarian vision produces a vision of a church that is more communion than hierarchy, more service than power, more circular than

---

[87] Leonardo Boff, *Trinity and Society (Liberation and Theology, vol. 2)* (Tunbridge Wells: Burns & Oates, 1998), pp. 13–14.

[88] Boff, *Trinity*, p. 111.

[89] Boff, *Trinity*, p. 118.

[90] Boff, *Trinity*, p. 151.

pyramidal, more loving embrace than bending the knee before authority.'[91]

This vision of the church is sufficiently radically different from that of Zizioulas to arouse interest: how is it that both claim to be deriving their vision of the church from the doctrine of the Trinity? The answer lies in differing accounts of the ordering (*taxis* is the traditional Greek word) of the triune relations. For Zizioulas, the monarchy of the Father, as cause of the Son and the Spirit, leads to a monarchical view of the role of the bishop, and a strongly hierarchical, and tightly ordered, church. For Boff, *perichoresis* is the decisive principle, and it is completely mutual and symmetrical: 'This perichoretic communion does not result from the Persons, but is simultaneous with them, originates with them. They are what they are because of their intrinsic, essential communion. If this is so, it follows that everything in God is triadic, everything is *Patreque, Filioque* and *Spirituque*. The coordinate conjunction "and" applies absolutely to the three Persons: and is always and everywhere.'[92] The vision, therefore, is of endless mutuality of relationship between equals, rather than an ordered hierarchy of cause and origin.

This same point, that differences in Trinitarian doctrine lead to very different accounts of ideal human society, is also found in my next writer, the Croatian theologian Miroslav Volf. In his magisterial *After Our Likeness: The Church as the Image of the Trinity*,[93] Volf first contrasts views on the church of Zizioulas and of the present pope, then Cardinal Ratzinger. He gives reasons for preferring Zizioulas's approach, and claims to be following closely in what follows. When he develops his own ecclesiology from Trinitarian dogma, however, he pictures a classically congregationalist church polity (he quotes John Smyth, the founder of the English Baptist movement, repeatedly) where the gathering and covenanting together of believers establishes the church, and ministry arises from within the gathered congregation, dependent on it for calling and recognition. This is sufficiently far from Zizioulas's ecclesiology to cause us to pause: the claim that the doctrine of the Trinity is generative for ecclesiology and ethics is in danger of being cast into doubt if such wildly divergent implications can be drawn from the same doctrine.

---

[91] Boff, *Trinity*, p. 154.

[92] Boff, *Trinity*, p. 146.

[93] Miroslav Volf, *After Our Likeness: The Church as the Image of the Trinity* (Grand Rapids, MI: Eerdmans, 1998).

Logically, this difference can be explained in one of three ways: either Zizioulas and Volf are in fact employing different doctrines of the Trinity; or there is an error in argument from Trinity to church in at least one of these two texts; or, despite appearances, ecclesiological programmes cannot in fact be derived from Trinitarian dogma, and the assumption that they can is a methodological flaw shared by both Zizioulas and Volf.

One of the great strengths of Volf's book is his recognition that it is simply not trivial to move from a Trinitarian account of divine persons in relation to an ecclesial or political account of human persons in relation. As he says:

> Today, the thesis that ecclesial communion should correspond to trinitarian communion enjoys the status of an almost self-evident proposition. Yet it is surprising that no-one has carefully examined just where such correspondences are to be found, nor expended much effort determining where ecclesial communion reaches the limits of its capacity for such analogy. The result is that reconstructions of these correspondences often say nothing more than the platitude that unity cannot exist without multiplicity nor multiplicity without unity . . . (p. 191)

Volf offers serious theology that does intend to move beyond the platitudes. He attempts to examine carefully the analogies that can be drawn between divine and human personhood, and their limitations. However, his passion for a particular ecclesiology (which I confess I share) forces him in an unacceptable direction. It is clear from the texts that the first of my three options above is the relevant one. Volf makes a significant alteration to the received ecumenical doctrine of the Trinity, which alteration allows him to embrace the Free Church ecclesiology that he commends. The alteration can be described rather simply: Volf attempts to differentiate between the relations of origin and the eternal relations of love in the Godhead. That is, the begetting of the Son by the Father, and the procession of the Spirit from the Father (and the Son?) are to be distinguished from the ongoing, decisive relationships in the triune God. On this basis, there is no priority of the Father, but simply a mutuality between the three hypostases, as straightforward a mutuality as Boff offers, if not quite so endlessly paraded and celebrated. As a result Volf can support the Free Church ecclesiology to which he is committed.[94]

---

[94] Volf is open about this move on pp. 216–17 of *After Our Likeness*, although he does not highlight just how radical his proposal is.

This might already suggest a problem for the core claim I am exploring here, that Trinitarianism is ecclesially and ethically generative. It seems that the minutiae of scholastic Trinitarian discussion, the sort of arid debates which most recent Trinitarian theologians want to pass over as rapidly as possible, determine the ethical implications of the position, not just at the level of minor nuances, but at the level of major and basic commitments. Volf proclaims his loyalty to Zizioulas's Trinitarian programme, yet by a seemingly minor technical variation, he effectively completely inverts all the ecclesiological implications of it, generating a radically different vision of the life of the church. It might be that this is the reality, that the difference (transposing the argument into the political realm) between democracy and fascism (say) is determined by the most abstruse of theological differences, but this feels to me uncomfortable; I would rather believe that the error of fascism is demonstrable on the basis of fundamental positions in anthropology, and does not rely on subtle distinctions in theology proper.

Perhaps, however, Volf's distinction is not general? The evidence suggests otherwise: Volf suggests, fairly, that this separation is shared by his *doktorvater* Moltmann,[95] and I have already indicated that Boff takes a very similar view. When Volf himself claimed, in a ringing slogan, that 'the Trinity is our social program!', he presumably assumed that a doctrine of the Trinity was something generally accessible to Christian believers, not something which was obscure and abstruse, and yet which took us in fundamentally different social and political – and ecclesiological – directions depending on precisely where we split the scholastic hair.

However, I think the point can be pressed further than this. Volf's doctrine of the Trinity in *After Our Likeness* is explicitly a deviation from the received ecumenical doctrine. Simply, Volf is choosing to adjust the orthodox doctrine of the Trinity because he does not like the ecclesiological (and social, and political) implications of the received doctrine. Moltmann is less clear about the implications of making the same move, perhaps because his grasp of the patristic debates is less sure; Boff takes refuge in an appeal to apophaticism, dismissing the classical language in which Zizioulas invests so much as merely figurative: 'Expressions such as "cause" referring to the Father, "begetting" referring to the Son [*sic*], and "breathing-out" applied to the

---

[95] Volf, nn. 108–12 on pp. 216–17, referencing Moltmann, *TKG* pp. 165–6 and 175–6, and various sections of *The Spirit of Life*.

Holy Spirit [*sic*] . . . are analogical or descriptive and do not claim to be causal explanations in the philosophical sense. The inner meaning of such expressions shows the diversity that exists in the divine reality on the one hand, and the communion on the other.'[96] In each case, however, the approved and acceptable ethical outcomes cannot flow from a patristic doctrine of the Trinity: the dogma needs massaging, relativizing, or even simply reversing, before it can generate 'acceptable' political content for today. I conclude that, unfortunately, the ecumenically received doctrine of the Trinity, to which Zizioulas witnesses (on the key point of the relationships of origin being inseparable from the ongoing relationships of love),[97] is politically unhelpful in modern western liberal terms; political utility is only achieved if the received form of the doctrine of the Trinity is radically adjusted.

What are we to do then? Boff witnesses helpfully to the fact that these proposals that attempt to find a social ethic, or an ecclesiology, in the doctrine of the Trinity are all – Zizioulas not excepted – a departure from the classical tradition(s). (Boff follows many contemporary readings – including Zizioulas's own – in finding different classical traditions: a Greek tradition, which stresses the Father as cause, and a Latin tradition, which stresses the unity of the divine nature as the basis of the Trinity;[98] as will become clear, I think this is mistaken.) He identifies a 'modern' tradition of Trinitarianism which starts from three persons understood as distinct subjects, and finds unity through the doctrine of *perichoresis*.[99] Zizioulas makes much less play of *perichoresis* than Boff or Moltmann, but shares the understanding of the persons as distinct subjects. It is this move that makes the attempt to derive a social theory from the doctrine of the Trinity so attractive: the triune persons are very like us, in their personhood at least, so their perfect relations might be a model for our attempts to imagine what well-lived relationships might look like. The question of the historical validity of seeing personhood as univocal, or at least as very closely analogical, when applied to divine persons and human people is therefore a vital one for a historical exploration of the doctrine today.

---

[96] Boff, *Trinity*, p. 235.
[97] As will become very clear when I treat the fourth century in chapter 4, I think Zizioulas gets other aspects of the classical doctrine rather badly wrong.
[98] Boff, *Trinity*, pp. 78–83, or p. 234 for a summary statement.
[99] Boff, *Trinity*, pp. 83–4, 234–5.

Analyzing the Trinity: Plantinga, Leftow, and Rea

The astonishing reinvigoration of analytic philosophy of religion in the second half of the twentieth century has given rise to a third pattern of Trinitarian theorizing, one that has been carried on largely separately from the intertwined discussions I have so far considered, but which is instructive not least because it shares certain presumptions and themes.

'Analytic' philosophy of religion is a largely Anglophone tradition that sees striving for conceptual and logical clarity as central to its task. Key terms will receive precise definition, and arguments will be carefully tested for logical validity, often reduced to symbolic form to highlight and explore the logical moves being made. Since the 1970s, there has been an explosion of work in this area that has been devoted to clarifying and (generally) supporting the traditional core doctrines of Christianity, including the doctrine of the Trinity.

In analytic terms, the problem is that the traditional doctrine seems logically incoherent and so necessarily false when stated clearly. In the words of an ancient statement of faith still recited in many liturgies, the *Quicumque vult* (or 'Athanasian creed' as it is, somewhat misleadingly, known), 'the Father is God, the Son is God, and the Holy Spirit is God; and yet there are not three Gods, but one God.' The analytic problem is not the truth of this claim, but its sense: does it, in fact, mean anything?

In his recent *Which Trinity? Whose Monotheism?*[100] Thomas McCall suggests that there are three basic analytic approaches to this problem: 'social Trinitarianism', developed first by Cornelius Plantinga and Richard Swinburne; 'relative identity', developed primarily by Michael Rea; and 'Latin trinitarianism', most fully defended by Brian Leftow.[101] Social Trinitarians start from the analogy of persons in relation, insisting that the three divine *hypostases* are fully personal in the modern sense of the term, possessed of distinct centres of consciousness;[102] they then attempt to develop an account of the unity possible

---

[100] Thomas H. McCall, *Which Trinity? Whose Monotheism? Philosophical and Systematic Theologians on the Metaphysics of Trinitarian Theology* (Grand Rapids, MI: Eerdmans, 2010).

[101] McCall, *Which Trinity?* pp. 11–55.

[102] This point is explicit in, e.g., Cornelius Plantinga, 'Social Trinity and Tritheism', in *Trinity, Incarnation, and Atonement: Philosophical and Theological Essays* (ed. Ronald J. Feenstra and Cornelius Plantinga; Notre Dame: UoND Press, 1989), pp. 21–47, p. 22.

to three such persons. This generally involves a willingness to sacrifice traditional accounts of divine unity (particularly accounts of divine simplicity), coupled with a series of suggestions or analogies for a closeness of relationship that might be characterized as unity, not unlike those offered by Moltmann or Boff.

Leftow summarizes his own Latin trinitarianism thus: 'there is just one divine being, God. The three divine persons are at bottom just God: they contain no constituent distinct from God. The Persons are in some way God three times over.'[103] He develops this using the term 'trope', which he defines as 'an individualized case of an attribute'.[104] Human beings instantiate humanity, but we also have our own nature (as Leftow has it, 'Cain's humanity was not identical with Abel's: Abel's perished with Abel, but Cain's did not').[105] This is not true of divine persons: 'While Cain's humanity ≠ Abel's humanity, the Father's deity = the Son's deity = God's deity.'[106] Divine unity is clearly here safeguarded; the question concerns modalism: how, on this view, does one deny that the Father is identical to the Son, and therefore that the Father suffered on the cross? Leftow offers suggestions and analogies to argue that this is possible, but his critics do not find them convincing.

These two views have been debated for some years, with the proponents of each suggesting that theirs is more successful, and some writers arguing that in fact neither offers an adequate account of the Trinity.[107] Michael Rea's theory of relative identity is a newer departure. He invites us to consider a lump of marble used as a pillar and carved in the form of a statue. The object is both pillar and statue; it is possible to imagine it ceasing to be one without ceasing to be the other (erosion over the years might destroy the statue, but not the pillar; removal and placement in a museum might mean it ceased to be a pillar but remains a statue). This is 'relative identity' – the lump of marble is both pillar and statue; the two are distinct identities, and yet numerically there is clearly one thing.[108] Similarly, Rea suggests that

---

[103] Brian Leftow, 'Modes without Modalism', in *Persons: Human and Divine* (ed. Peter van Inwagen and Dean Zimmerman; Oxford: OUP, 2007), pp. 357–75, p. 357.

[104] Leftow, 'Modes', p. 358.

[105] 'Modes', p. 358.

[106] 'Modes', p. 358.

[107] See, e.g., Dale Tuggy, 'The Unfinished Business of Trinitarian Theorizing', *RelS* 39 (2003): pp. 165–83.

[108] See Michael C. Rea, 'The Trinity', in *The Oxford Handbook to Philosophical Theology* (ed. Thomas H. Flint and Michael C. Rea; Oxford: OUP, 2009), pp. 403–29, pp. 417–21.

God is Father, is Son, and is Spirit – three distinct identities, but one God. This appears very neat, but critics have challenged its coherence.

There is much to applaud in this analytic tradition: the relentless focus on conceptual clarity is clearly an academic virtue, and one that has sometimes been lacking in the recent theological debates about the doctrine of the Trinity (most obviously, perhaps, in the endless repetition without analysis of 'Rahner's rule', discussed above). That said, some common themes emerge: Plantinga's social Trinity bears obvious comparison with Moltmann or Boff, for instance, and there is a parallel philosophical discussion of the meaning of the term 'person'. More basically, analytic discussions of the Trinity seem generally to proceed with a remarkable confidence about the success of language in referring to the divine. The theological question of analogy is, as far as I can observe, never raised, and the assumed answer would always seem to be that language refers univocally to the divine and the created. (If it does not, the core project of analysis would be impossible.)

Conclusion and Prospect

I have tried, in this chapter, to give a flavour of the energy and the main themes of contemporary Trinitarian theology. Rahner's rule and the desire to find the doctrine of the Trinity in the gospel narratives, and Zizioulas's focus on the personal nature of God, have alike become almost axiomatic for all the writers I have considered. In every case some language, at least, is held to refer univocally to the divine and the created. There is generally a willingness to entangle the life of God with the history of the world, and often even a celebration of this move. These are the ideas which I claimed at the start were absent from, or even formally condemned by, all earlier accounts of the Trinity. The truth of that claim can only be judged by a reading of earlier accounts. First, though, I turn to the basis of all doctrine, the biblical text.

2.

'In your light, we see light': The Trinity in the Bible

There are two aims to this chapter, which only partly overlap. On the one hand, I will explore the extent to which Trinitarian doctrine, or at least its inchoate precursors, can be found in the Christian Scriptures; on the other hand, I will explore some of the claims made in the development of Christian theology for biblical support for the doctrine of the Trinity. That these two aims do not precisely cohere is a pointer to what will be the chief problem raised in this chapter: when it comes to the interpretation of the Bible, L.P. Hartley's opening claim from *The Go-Between* is quite true. 'The past is a foreign country; they do things differently there.' The history of the early development of the doctrine of the Trinity is largely a history of biblical exegesis, but exegesis of a kind that is unconvincing, obscure, or seemingly arbitrary to the modern reader. If we are to understand the arguments that went on, we need to understand the exegetical rules – and the debates over those rules – that governed those arguments.

Assuming, however, that we continue to find the exegesis of the church fathers unconvincing even when we understand their reasons for it, a second question is raised: was their conclusion – that their developed Trinitarian dogma was a legitimate, even required, deduction from the Bible – correct? Put another way, are there convincing exegetical arguments for the doctrine of the Trinity, even if they were unknown to the fathers? True conclusions are regularly reached from false premises, after all, and might have been in this case, even if traditional claims about the supervenient guidance of the Holy Spirit in these core dogmatic decisions are regarded as unconvincing.

The Old Testament

It is a fact as obvious as it is uncomfortable (for the modern scholar) that biblical support for the doctrine of the Trinity has as often been drawn from the Old Testament as from the New. The fourth-century debates that set the ecumenical doctrine of the Trinity involved much exegesis of disputed texts, and the texts were as likely to be drawn from Proverbs or the Psalms as from Romans or John. We cannot consider the history of the doctrine of the Trinity without studying this tradition of exegetical support; nor can we simply presume that modern readers will accept, or even understand, the exegetical arguments being offered. There is a need to start, therefore, by addressing the question of hermeneutics, the theories of interpretation that underlie our readings of biblical texts.

We tend to assume today that a text means what the author intended it to mean. If this is right, it will be very difficult to find any treatment of the doctrine of the Trinity in the Old Testament. Before the coming of Christ, the writers could not have thought in these terms, and whatever a text like 'You are my son; today I have begotten you' (Ps. 2:7 NRSV) might mean, its use in debates over whether the generation of the Logos from the Father is a volitional and time-bound act, or an essential and eternal one, is completely inappropriate. This was not the case, however, for the fourth-century theologians whose arguments gave us the ecumenically received doctrine of the Trinity. This is not a claim that their use of the text was in any sense loose or ungoverned by proper interpretative practices; instead, they had a different account of which interpretative practices were proper. They worked with a different hermeneutic.

It is perhaps becoming easier for theologians to grasp this point than it has been for a century or so, just because practices of biblical hermeneutics are more in flux today than they have been for several decades. The old hegemony of the historical-critical method has, rightly or wrongly, been broken, and many interpretative practices now vie for the scholar's attention.[1] Some of these are best understood as supplements to the historical-critical method, not challenging it, but adding to its insights. An example of this might be social-scientific criticism, which

---

[1] The first eleven chapters of *The Cambridge Companion to Biblical Interpretation* (ed. John Barton; Cambridge: CUP, 1998) offer a good survey of the options, and demonstrate just how central to the discipline of biblical studies negotiating this profusion of interpretative options has become.

adds to the tools of history those of the social sciences in its attempt to comprehend the context which gives rise to the writings. Others, however, more directly challenge the traditional methods, some on the basis of broader currents in academic reading practices, others on the basis of explicitly theological concerns.

In the first group we might list a series of politicized and postmodern approaches that question the supposed neutrality and innocence of the ideal historical critic. No reader approaches any text in a neutral and uncommitted manner, and so every proposed reading is a politicized and partial appropriation of the text for purposes and causes that belong to the interpreter, not the text. Feminist readings highlight not just the patriarchy of the text, but the patriarchy of dominant modes of interpretation, which have erased women's concerns and actions from the text, and have ignored potentially subversive aspects of the text that might have challenged the readers' own easily assumed patriarchy. Political and post-colonial readings demonstrate that the text has been, sometimes despite its own radically subversive nature, co-opted to lend sacred support to the maintenance and extension by violence of oppressive regimes.

In the second group, canonical criticism has perhaps had the most investigation and lasting effect. This takes its cue from more theoretical criticisms of historical-critical reading practices, such as Roland Barthes' confident assertion of 'The Death of the Author' (a celebrated essay that asserts that the notion of an 'Author', to whom a text belongs, and whose voice must be recovered to understand the text, is both recent in origin and fundamentally mistaken, being perpetuated by critics whose claims to have privileged insights into the 'Author's' psyche allowed them to control the meaning of a text).[2] Such theoretical considerations suggest that the text has a certain fluidity, and that its meaning can be determined by its later reception. A text such as Psalm 2, then, can properly be interpreted as a part of the Christian canon, and the echoes of Christology that Christian readers hear in it are – in this reception – not improper. (It can also be properly interpreted as part of the lectionary of the synagogue, where its Davidic overtones become decisive to its meaning; multiple meanings as a result of multiple receptions of a particular text are not a problem on

---

[2] Roland Barthes, 'La mort de l'auteur', en Barthes, *Oeuvres Complètes, Tome 2: 1966–1973* (ed. Éric Marty; Éditions de Seuil, 1994), pp. 491–5; ET: 'The Death of the Author', in Roland Barthes, *Image-Music-Text* (ed. and trans. Stephen Heath; London: Flamingo Paperbacks, 1984), pp. 142–8.

this understanding.) More directly theological interpretative strategies, which take their cue from a conviction that the Bible is properly understood theologically, as an aspect of divine revelation, are also currently explored.[3]

Of course, none of these recent developments is identical to patristic exegetical practice, and their acceptance is neither uncontested, nor adequate to demonstrate the appropriateness of patristic readings. They do, however, help the contemporary reader to begin to understand that the older 'pre-critical' reading practices were not wild and uncontrolled, still less intellectually vacuous, but were (at least intending to be) the careful and serious application of rules of good interpretation that merely happen to be rather different from those rules to which we have recently grown used. With this in mind I turn to a brief examination of patristic hermeneutics.

Christianity has had a concept of 'Scripture' – authoritative sacred text – from the beginning of the movement. Initially, both the concept and the texts were inherited from Palestinian Judaism. In the earliest Christian documents we have – the letters of Paul – we can find multiple examples of Scripture being cited as an authority that is to be accepted, and that is capable of settling an argument.[4] The gospel accounts routinely portray Jesus as regarding the text similarly; Acts suggests that quotation of Scripture was a common rhetorical move in both the evangelism and the deliberations of the earliest Christians. There seems no good reason to doubt any of this evidence. Within the apostolic period, at least certain apostolic writings were being cited as Scripture alongside the received Jewish texts (2 Pet. 3:15–16; see also 2 *Clem.* 14:2), as inspired and so authoritative, with perhaps the implication that they were being read formally in Christian worship.[5]

---

[3] Kevin J. Vanhoozer, ed., *Dictionary of Theological Interpretation of the Bible* (Grand Rapids, MI: Baker, 2005) is perhaps the best single guide to these developments.

[4] Longenecker's list of direct quotations and their introductory formulae remains a helpful guide here, showing forty-five quotations in Romans alone; nine in Galatians; twenty-two in the Corinthian letters; etc. Richard N. Longenecker, *Biblical Exegesis in the Apostolic Period* (Grand Rapids, MI: Eerdmans, 1975), pp. 108–11. For a good general introduction to Paul's use of Hebrew Scripture, see James W. Aageson, *Written Also for Our Sake: Paul and the Art of Biblical Interpretation* (Louisville, KY: WJKP, 1993); for a sophisticated recent contribution to the debate, see Christopher D. Stanley, *Arguing with Scripture: The Rhetoric of Quotations in the Letters of Paul* (London: T&T Clark International, 2004).

[5] 'Probably the implication is that they [*sic*, Paul's letters] are suitable for reading in Christian worship'. Richard Bauckham, *2 Peter and Jude*, WBC (Waco: Word, 1983), p. 333.

The formal settling of the canon was to come several centuries later, but the evidence we have suggests that, with one or two exceptions, the list of books accorded the status of Scripture was relatively stable and settled from very early on.[6] Hermeneutical practices were varied in the early centuries – Origen of Alexandria (c.185–254) is perhaps the first Christian writer both to reflect self-consciously on how to interpret the Scriptures, and to put his ideas into practice in the disciplined production of commentaries. It is clear that most reading practices were decisively Christological, however: the person, and story, of Jesus Christ was seen as the key to understanding the various scriptures. Scripture was seen primarily as God's revelation, and what God had revealed was the gospel of Jesus Christ.[7]

As best as we can determine, this began with the circulation of *testimonia*, lists of particular texts from the Hebrew Scriptures that could be correlated with events or claims about Jesus (Ps. 2:7, above, is an obvious example). The assumed (if not articulated) interpretative claim that 'the Scriptures teach the faith of the church' could cut both ways: on the one hand, a scriptural citation could settle an argument; on the other, the meaning of a text could be determined by the need to make it conform to the beliefs of the church. As we shall see, the deity of Christ was widely assumed from as early in the history of the Christian movement as we can penetrate, so Scriptures were sought that could illuminate and support this claim.

The next significant move beyond the *testimonia* is most visible in the writings of Justin Martyr (c.100–c.165). Justin sought to defend the reasonableness of the Christian faith against both Jewish and pagan Roman opponents. He did so by constant appeal to Scripture. He seems to have been well versed in contemporary Jewish methods of allegorical interpretation, and deployed them freely; his distinctive contribution, however, was what we might call 'the argument from prophecy': he repeatedly cited prophecies from the Hebrew Scriptures, and sought to show how they had been fulfilled in Jesus Christ,

---

[6] See H. von Campenhausen, *The Formation of the Christian Bible* (trans. J.A. Baker; Minneapolis: Fortress, 1972) or Bruce Metzger, *The Canon of the New Testament* (Oxford: Clarendon, 1987).

[7] On patristic hermeneutics, see variously: D. Dawson, *Allegorical Readers and Cultural Revision in Ancient Alexandria* (Berkeley: UC Press, 1992); R.P.C. Hanson, *Allegory and Event* (Minneapolis: John Knox, 1959); M. Simonetti, *Biblical Interpretation in the Early Church* (trans. J. Hughes; Edinburgh: T&T Clark, 1994); Frances Young, *Biblical Exegesis and the Formation of Christian Culture* (Cambridge: CUP, 1997).

thus demonstrating the significance of Jesus in God's dealings with the world, and that the Christian church, not the Jewish synagogue, was the true inheritor of God's promises to Abraham, Moses, and David.[8]

The attentive reader of the Hebrew Scriptures, however, was still faced with a problem: there is much in the text that is neither testimony nor prophecy; how was this material to be read and understood within the church? As noted above, the first writer to give a comprehensive theoretical response to this was Origen of Alexandria, early in the third century.[9] Origen believed that Scripture spoke of Christ, in whole and in part; he also believed in the plenary verbal inspiration of Scripture – that every word, indeed every letter and vowel-point, was intended by God and meaningful. He was therefore faced with the challenge of showing how such unpromising (from this perspective) texts as the Levitical law codes, the genealogies of 1 Chronicles, or the sometimes homely advice of Proverbs could speak the gospel. His answer was to allegorize.[10] Texts had a literal meaning, without question, but also a spiritual meaning, which spoke directly of the gospel realities of Jesus Christ. The details of Origen's allegorizing were controversial even in his own day,[11] and need not concern us here;[12] rather, what is of interest is the driving concern to find Christian meaning in the Hebrew Scriptures.

---

[8] For more on Justin's exegesis see W.A. Shortwell, *The Biblical Exegesis of Justin Martyr* (London: SPCK, 1965) and Craig D. Allert, *Revelation, Truth, Canon and Interpretation: Studies in Justin Martyr's Dialogue with Trypho* (Supplements to *VC* 64) (Leiden: Brill, 2002). Allert offers an extensive bibliography both of more general texts on either Justin or patristic interpretation, and of articles dealing with the subject.

[9] Origen describes and justifies his exegetical method in Book 4 §§1-3 of *De principiis*. (The best text is that of Henri Crouzel and Manlio Simonetti in *Sources Chrétiennes* 252–3; 268–9; 312, which contains the Latin text of Rufinus, the Greek text preserved in the *Philokalia*, and other Greek fragments: *Origène: Traité des Principes* [5 vols; Paris: Les Éditions du Cerf, 1978-84]. The relevant sections of Book 4 are found in vol. 3 [SC 268], pp. 368-99; it happens that these sections were preserved in their entirety in the *Philokalia*, and so we have a good Greek text. There are extensive notes to the text in vol. 4 [SC 269], pp. 151–234.)

[10] The precise nature of Origen's allegorical method, and its theological justification, have been the subject of some dispute. See Karen Jo Torjesen, *Hermeneutical Procedure and Theological Method in Origen's Exegesis, Patristiche Texte und Studien* 28 (Berlin: de Gruyter, 1986), pp. 5–11 for a brief guide to the debate.

[11] See Adolf von Harnack, *Der kirchengeschichtliche Ertrag der exegetischen Arbeiten des Origenes, Erster Teil: Hexateuch und Richterbuch*, TU 42.3 (1918), p. 8.

[12] Torjesen offers several extensive and careful readings of Origen's actual exegetical practice in her book. See particularly the section on the *Song of Songs*, pp. 54–62.

The debates which led to the formulation of the doctrine of the Trinity occur a century after Origen, although they occur amongst theologians who are still debating his legacy, both in terms of their theological formulation and in terms of their exegetical practice. It is common to suggest that two major streams of interpretative practice can be identified in the fourth century: an Alexandrian tradition, which preserved Origen's fascination with Christological allegory; and an Antiochene tradition, which was far more concerned with the historical meaning of the text. This is not wholly misleading: the greatest of the Antiochene commentators, John Chrysostom, will insist that a text cannot be understood unless we know its author, the context of composition, and so on.[13] That said, Chrysostom remains committed to the Christological meaning of Old Testament texts, and was not unhappy to use allegory to find it from time to time.[14] There is a debate in the fourth century over the level of allegorical speculation that may justly be employed in biblical exegesis, but all patristic interpreters are united in seeing the primary meaning of the biblical text as Christological, and in finding hermeneutical methods that allow them to maintain and practise this belief. With this in mind, I turn to their use of some key Old Testament texts, to illustrate how they found Trinitarian doctrine within the Old Testament.

Proverbs 8 and Wisdom 7

'The LORD created me at the beginning of his work, the first of his acts of long ago.' So speaks the personified figure of Lady Wisdom in Proverbs 8. Who is this mysterious figure of 'Wisdom'? The early Christian readers of Proverbs seem united in finding a literal, rather than metaphorical, account of an act of divine generation here, and so generally identify her as the *Logos*,[15] born of the Father in all eternity. The theme is reinforced by verses from Wisdom 7:

---

[13] See, e.g., *Hom. Act.* 1.3 or *Hom. Rom.* arg. 1. (The best editions seem still to be Migne's; these references can be found in PG 51:71–2 and PG 60:392.) The point is explored helpfully in Judit Kecskeméti, 'Exégèse Chrysostomienne et Exégèse Engagée', *StPatr* 22 (1989): pp. 136–47.

[14] See Gilberte Astruc-Morize et Alain Le Boulluec, 'Le sens caché des Écritures selon Jean Chrysostome et Origène', *StPatr* 25 (1993): pp. 1–26 for a demonstration of this, with an explicit comparison to Origen.

[15] Irenaeus and Theophilus of Antioch, both in the second half of the second century, each essay an interpretation where Wisdom is the Spirit, so a text such as Prov. 3:19 ('The LORD by wisdom founded the earth; by understanding he established the heavens') could be read by Theophilus as a proto-Trinitarian account of

For wisdom is more mobile than any motion;
because of her pureness she pervades and penetrates all things.
For she is a breath of the power of God,
and a pure emanation of the glory of the Almighty;
therefore nothing defiled gains entrance into her.
For she is a reflection of eternal light,
a spotless mirror of the working of God,
and an image of his goodness.
Although she is but one, she can do all things,
and while remaining in herself, she renews all things;
in every generation she passes into holy souls
and makes them friends of God, and prophets;
for God loves nothing so much as the person who lives with wisdom (NRSV).

These verses were repeatedly cited by Origen, for whom the figure of Lady Wisdom was identified with the Logos, and these texts spoke of the generation of the Son by the Father.[16] Lewis Ayres has suggested that this text, understood this way, is important in the early anti-Arian writers, notably Alexander's and Athanasius's earlier works: an argument is made that a person is never without their wisdom, and so the Son is always with the Father, from all eternity.[17] In a fragment of disputed authenticity, Pamphilus cites Origen as linking Wisdom 7:25 to (what was to become) the core Trinitarian claim of the *homoousios*, the Son's being 'of the same substance' as the Father: 'Both these comparisons ["vapour" and "emanation"] most clearly prove that there is a sharing of substance by the Son with the Father. For "emanation" seems to be of one substance [*homoousios*] with that body from which it is either an "emanation" or a "vapour".'[18]

---

creation, the Father creating by means of his Spirit, 'wisdom', and his Son, 'understanding'. Prestige suggests, however, that the wisdom = Logos identification was already so strong that this interpretation could not hope to take hold. G.L. Prestige, *God in Patristic Thought* (London: SPCK, 2nd edn, 1952), pp. 91–2.

[16] So, e.g., *Princ.* 1.2.2 or *Comm. Jo.* 1.19, where in both cases the Wisdom text is primary, but Proverbs is cited as a supporting or explanatory statement. Wisdom 7 occurs very frequently in Origen's Christological writings. For Origen's use of Wisdom 7, see R.M. Grant, 'The Book of Wisdom at Alexandria: Reflections on the History of the Canon and Theology', *TU* 92 (= *StPatr* 7) (1966): pp. 462–72, pp. 465–8. Grant also suggests that Clement was already using this text Christologically prior to Origen (pp. 464–5).

[17] Lewis Ayres, *Nicaea and Its Legacy: An Approach to Fourth-Century Trinitarian Theology* (Oxford: OUP, 2004), pp. 40–52.

[18] Translation from Grant, 'The Book of Wisdom', p. 468. Grant argues for the authenticity of the fragment, as does Crouzel (Henri Crouzel, *Théologie de*

Whether this is Origen or the interpolation of a later writer, it is evidence of how the wisdom texts in both Wisdom and Proverbs were being read to support the development of Trinitarian dogma in its technical formulations. Of course, counter-readings were advanced by those with differing Trinitarian commitments, but the ways in which Old Testament texts could be interrogated to support the Trinitarian cause is clear.

Isaiah 53

Christological readings of Isaiah 53 are hardly uncommon even in contemporary Christian exegesis; however, in the patristic period a seeming detail of the text that is not even visible in modern English translations became a rich and sustained source of Trinitarian and Christological speculation. Speaking of the Servant's death, the text declares:

> By a perversion of justice he was taken away.
> Who could have imagined his future? (Isa. 53:8)

The Hebrew is more literally translated, 'By an oppressive judgement he was taken away; who can speak of his generation?',[19] and this sense of the second half of the verse was preserved in the Septuagint (the standard Greek translation of the Hebrew Scriptures, which most of the Fathers used).[20] From the unspeakableness of the Servant's generation, the fathers quickly derived its ineffability, and so found here an account of the unknowable eternal generation of the Son by the Father.

In Justin Martyr, the unspeakable generation of the Servant seems to be taken as a reference to the virgin birth;[21] by the fourth century,

---

l'image de Dieu chez Origène [Paris: F. Aubier, 1956] p. 99). Ayres suggests the fragment has probably been tampered with to bring it into line with later orthodoxy – *Nicaea*, p. 24, citing Williams, *Arius*, pp. 134–7.

[19] מֵעֹצֶר וּמִמִּשְׁפָּט דּוֹרוֹ מִי יְשׂוֹחֵחַ   (BHS)

[20] ἐν τῇ ταπεινώσει ἡ κρίσις αὐτοῦ ἤρθη· τὴν γενεὰν αὐτοῦ τίς διηγήσεται; (Rahlfs).

[21] *Dial.* 43; 63; 76; 89. Childs seems to take the passage in ch. 76 as being about the eternal generation, but that is a misreading. B.S. Childs, *The Struggle to Understand Isaiah as Christian Scripture* (Grand Rapids, MI: Eerdmans, 2004), p. 36. For a thorough discussion of Justin's use of this passage in the Dialogue, see Christoph Markschies, 'Jesus Christ as a Man before God', in *The Suffering Servant: Isaiah 53 in Jewish and Christian Sources* (ed. Bernd Janowski and Peter Stuhlmacher; trans. Daniel P. Bailey; Grand Rapids, MI: Eerdmans, 2004), pp. 225–323, pp. 262–7.

however, it has become a reference to the Logos's origin in the Father –
read this way even by theologians keen to stress the subordination of
the Son to the Father, such as Eusebius of Caesarea.[22] On the pro-Nicene
side, Basil of Caesarea cites this text against Eunomius as a proof of the
unknowability of God's essence – if the mode of generation of the
divine Son is unknowable according to Scripture, and this is an act of
the divine essence, then the essence of God is clearly unknowable.[23] By
the fifth century we can find writers taking this text in both ways simultaneously: the prophet bears witness both to the marvellous virgin birth
of the Lord, and to his ineffable divine generation.[24]

It is striking to the modern reader, but entirely characteristic of
patristic exegesis, that so minor a detail of the text – one that is probably a misreading, indeed – can become so fertile a source for theological exploration and definition. As we shall see in chapter 4, Basil's
argument concerning the unknowability of the divine essence is
absolutely central to the development of fourth-century Trinitarian
orthodoxy; whilst this text is very far from his only biblical support,
we once again see an Old Testament text being read out of context
(when judged by modern standards), and astonishingly woodenly, as
a support for crucial technical theological positions.

The Psalms

As a final example, we might consider two texts in the Psalms. The
kingship psalms are of course routinely cited as references to the true
heir of David's throne, Jesus Christ. The wedding hymn, Psalm 45, for
instance, is read by many early writers as a lengthy exposition of the
perfections of Christ. Indeed, it is already read as referring to Christ
by the author of Hebrews in the New Testament (Heb. 1:8–9, quoting
Ps. 45:6–7). The fathers found a Trinitarian reference in the very first
verse of the Psalm. Where the English has 'My heart overflows with a
goodly theme' (NRSV), the Greek versions spoke of a 'good word
[*logos*]'[25] which was taken by several early writers, including Eusebius

---

[22] See Eusebius's commentary on Isaiah in Eusebius *Werke, Neunter Band: Der Jesajakommentar, Der Griechischen Christlichen Schriftsteller* (ed. Joseph Ziegler; Berlin: Akademie-Verlag, 1975), pp. 336–7. I am not aware of any English translation of this work.

[23] Basil, *C.E.* 1.12, *SC* 299, p. 212.

[24] So Augustine, *Serm.* 184 (Migne, PL 38:996–7) or Cyril of Alexandria *Comm. Is.*
(Migne, PG 70:9–1190, in loc.).

[25] Septuagint: ἐξηρεύξατο ἡ καρδία μου λόγον ἀγαθόν; the Hebrew has דָּבָר טוֹב
רָחַשׁ לִבִּי.

of Caesarea, Alexander of Alexandria, Ambrose, and Augustine,[26] to be a reference to the generation of the Logos by the Father.

The anointing of the king in verse 7 is used to defend proto-Trinitarian doctrine as early as Justin Martyr (*Dial.* 63) and Irenaeus (*Haer.* 3.6.1). The repeated 'God' in this verse was seemingly read as a vocative (although the Septuagint has it as nominative), perhaps referring back to the implied vocative in the previous verse ('Your throne, O God . . .').[27] So Irenaeus reads, 'therefore, O God, your God has anointed you', which he naturally parses as God the Father anointing God the Son. Augustine makes the same point (*Enarrat. Ps.* 45:19). Further, the 'oil of gladness' with which the king is anointed is understood by many writers to be the Holy Spirit.[28]

The fathers found the Trinity in many other texts in the Psalms. Psalm 36:9 is particularly interesting:

> For with you is the fountain of life;
> in your light, we see light (NRSV).

Many patristic authors took this to be an account of the multiplicity within the divine life. Evagrius of Pontus and Theodoret of Cyr both take 'fountain' to refer to Christ,[29] Theodoret cross-referencing to Jeremiah 2:13, where God is spoken of as a 'fountain of living water', and so finding an assertion of the unity in deity of the Father and the Son in the two texts. Augustine, in a sermon on the text 'this is eternal life, that they may know you, the only true God, and Jesus Christ whom you have sent' (John 17:3 NRSV), similarly invokes the fountain image to discuss the oneness of Father and Son. The second clause, 'in your light . . . ', is profoundly important in fourth-century Trinitarian reflection. Origen references the phrase when narrating the rule of faith at the beginning of *De principiis*: 'Such then is the meaning of the saying, "In your light shall we see light"; that is, in your

---

[26] See Blaising and Hardin, *Psalms 1 – 50*, pp. 343–4 for references.

[27] Interestingly, Theodore of Mopsuestia reads the text as a repeated nominative, 'God, your God, has anointed you . . .' but then contrasts it with the previous verse ('Your throne, O God, will last for ever'). He reads this as a clear ascription of deity to the king, whereas v. 7 asserts his humanity; therefore Theodore finds the incarnation taught in the text. *Comm. Ps.* 45:8.

[28] So Cyril of Jerusalem, Basil of Caesarea, and John Chrysostom. See *Psalms 1 – 50*, ACCS Old Testament 7 (ed. Craig A. Blaising and Carmen S. Hardin; Downers Grove: IVP, 2008), p. 349 for references.

[29] For both references, see *Psalms 1 – 50* (ed. Blaising and Hardin), p. 284.

word and wisdom, which is your Son, in him shall we see you, the Father.'[30]

Thus interpretation becomes part of the common stuff of fourth-century Greek Trinitarian theology, perhaps because of the influence of Origen, and the text is even referenced in the creed of Nicaea, and in the Niceano-Constantinopolitan Creed ('God from God, light from light . . .'). In his famous *Theological Orations*, preached in Constantinople as a manifesto for his mission in promoting the Cappadocian version of Nicene orthodoxy there,[31] Gregory of Nazianzus summed up his Trinitarian doctrine using this image: 'This is the meaning of David's propehtic [*sic*] vision: "In thy light we shall see light." We receive the Son's light for the Father's light in the light of the Spirit.'[32] The most significant invocation of the text, however, is a reported comment. Theodoret quotes Athanasius as suggesting that the text was decisive at Nicaea:

> The bishops, having detected the Arians' deceitfulness in this matter, collected from Scripture those passages that say of Christ that he is the glory, the fountain, the stream, and the express image of the person; and they quoted the following words: 'In your light we shall see light'; and likewise, 'I and the Father are one.' They, then, with still greater clearness, briefly declared that the Son is of one substance with the Father; for this, indeed, is the signification of the passages that have been quoted.[33]

There is good reason to believe that there were extra-biblical reasons for the Fathers to find light imagery so congenial a way of discussing the divine;[34] nonetheless, the suggestion of Athanasius that this text, alongside John 10:30, was the decisive scriptural warrant for the *homoousion* is a striking example of just how significant interpretation of the Old Testament was for the development of Trinitarian doctrine.

---

[30] Origen, *Princ.* 1.1.1.

[31] The term 'manifesto' is Ayres's. Lewis Ayres, *Nicaea and Its Legacy: An Approach to Fourth Century Trinitarian Theology* (Oxford: OUP, 2004), p. 244. I offer an extended reading of the *Theological Orations* below, pp. 111–116.

[32] *Or.* 31.3, trans. from Ayres, *Nicaea*, p. 248.

[33] *Hist. eccl.* 1.7, NPNF trans.

[34] See Ayres, *Nicaea*, pp. 248–9, and the works referenced there; also John McGuckin, 'Perceiving Light from Light in Light: The Trinitarian Theology of St Gregory the Theologian', *GOTR* 39 (1994): pp. 7–32.

Old Testament Theology

I have of course offered no more than a small sample of the rich theological readings of the Old Testament in early Christian writers; whilst this tradition of exegesis is historically important, much of it is hardly convincing today. (Although nor should it be completely dismissed; to take only one example, however unconvincing the details of readings of individual verses, a Christian writer producing an Old Testament theology today might well take the promises to the Davidic king in the kingship psalms as having Christological import.)[35] Has the doctrine of the Trinity anything to do with the Old Testament under contemporary critical readings? The question concerns the nature of monotheism in ancient Israel, and it is one that has been a matter of some dispute in recent scholarly literature.

'Monotheism' itself is not a biblical category (the term is first used in 1660 by the Cambridge Platonist Henry More);[36] MacDonald has shown ably how the word has gained a very particular philosophical cast in its history of usage, and how that has affected – perhaps infected – scholarly discussions of Israelite monotheism.[37] His own study of Deuteronomy suggests that an account of 'monotheism' which sees it as an intellectual claim concerning metaphysical reality – the recognition of the truth of the proposition that there is only one deity – fails to capture the message or rhetorical force of the biblical text. Rather, such texts as the *Shema* (Deut. 6:4–9) reflect a repeated call to the difficult task of exclusive loyalty to God alone, and God's uniqueness is more soteriological than metaphysical.[38] God alone saves the people, and so the people should be loyal to God's laws and commands.

This is important for my discussion in two ways. First, belief in only one God is here as much or more about *fiducia* (commitment), as *notitia* (knowledge) or *assensus* (intellectual assent).[39] Old Testament monotheism, on this account, is not a careful claim as to the numbers of deities; rather it is an exclusive devotion that must be learned and

---

[35] So, albeit hesitantly, Walter Brueggemann, *Theology of the Old Testament: Testimony, Dispute, Advocacy* (Minneapolis: Fortress, 1997), pp. 619–21.

[36] So Nathan MacDonald, *Deuteronomy and the Meaning of 'Monotheism'* (Tübingen: Mohr Siebeck, 2001), pp. 6–7.

[37] MacDonald, *Deuteronomy*, pp. 6–52.

[38] See his conclusion: *Deuteronomy*, pp. 209–21.

[39] These three together make up the classical Reformed scholastic account of the nature of saving faith: one must know the facts of the gospel (*notitia*), believe them to be true (*assensus*), and trust one's life to them (*fiducia*).

won, and remains constantly precarious. This perhaps makes it easier to understand how Trinitarian devotion could develop so rapidly
after the ascension of Jesus: there was no need to overcome a developed and defended metaphysical conception of deity.[40] Second,
MacDonald's account suggests that, for all its flaws, something like
Sanders's account of the Old Testament as 'monotheizing literature'[41]
would seem to be invited: the text constantly calls its readers
towards the difficult and costly task of worshipping God alone.[42] The
operative definition of the divine, therefore, is not metaphysical but
doxological: God is the one to whom worship may properly be
given.[43]

It is not even easy to come to a conclusion on whether the Hebrew
Scriptures assert that only the one true God exists. On the one hand,
'the gods of the peoples are idols' (Ps. 96:5); on the other hand – one
chapter later, in canonical order – 'All gods bow down before him' (Ps.
97:7). An older 'history of religions' approach saw the Old Testament
as one example of a general religious maturing towards monotheism,
visible repeatedly in history, which in Israel's case was reached with
Hezekiah's reforms and the Deuteronomic writings of the seventh century BC;[44] however, when one considers that apocalyptic literature,
universally dated late, contains some of the most vivid depictions of
the heavenly court (e.g. Dan. 7:9–14), offers some of the most straightforward assertions of the reality of national spiritual principles that
work against God (e.g. Dan. 10:12–14), and continues the early practice

---

[40] This is not to minimize just how radical the extension of worship to the ascended
Jesus was in a first-century Jewish context, on which see later in this chapter.

[41] James A. Sanders, *Canon and Community: A Guide to Canonical Criticism*
(Philadelphia: Fortress, 1984), pp. 51–2. Sanders defines the verb 'to monotheize'
as 'to struggle within and against polytheistic contexts to affirm God's oneness'
(p. 52). See Richard Bauckham, *Jesus and the God of Israel* (Grand Rapids, MI:
Eerdmans, 2008), pp. 82–94 for some discussion of what this might look like.

[42] This is to stray a little into the much-disputed question of the point in Israel's history where 'monotheism' became normative: was this exclusive demand revealed
at Sinai and in the desert, or is it a much later discovery that is then written back
across Israel's history? I take it that Christian theology's primary responsibility is
to the text that we have been given, and therefore that I do not need to come to a
view on this question.

[43] Larry Hurtado in a number of works has helpfully indicated the importance of
this recognition for understanding the rise of devotion offered to Jesus. For a
rapid summary, with references, see his *Lord Jesus Christ: Devotion to Jesus in Early
Christianity* (Grand Rapids, MI: Eerdmans, 2003), pp. 42–53.

[44] For a classic example, see the discussion in Walther Eichrodt, *Theology of the Old
Testament*, vol. 1 (London: SCM, 1961), pp. 220–27.

of eliding descriptions of God's messengers into the identity of God himself (e.g. Zech. 1:18–21; 3:1–2), then this account must fail.[45]

We might instead suggest a diverse and confused witness, a cacophony of voices making diverse and often contradictory claims. Theological work, however, has tended to desire a united, even if complex, testimony from the pages of Scripture. John Goldingay offers a plausible construction of an overarching Old Testament view, suggesting the existence of created spiritual principles to whom God assigns the other nations, of a series of 'aides' through whom God is pleased to act ('the angel of the LORD' and the like), and of a specific figure or office, the 'accuser' or 'satan', who serves God by bringing charges before the heavenly court.[46] As part of that discussion, he raises the interesting question of the occasional slipperiness of the identity of a divine emissary. This is a repeated feature of the patriarchal narratives of Genesis: an angel of the Lord can suddenly be the Lord; as noted above, the same apparent confusion is there in Zechariah's visions. Goldingay links this to personified divine attributes in the Psalms. When the psalmist writes, 'righteousness and peace will kiss each other' (Ps. 85:10), Goldingay suggests that righteousness and peace are being represented as 'personal entities'. Were this an isolated example, we might dismiss it as an overly literal reading of a poetic image, but he makes a convincing claim not just that this is a regular feature of the text, but that the range of attributes that are personified like this is both narrow and stable.[47] When the early Christian theologians seized on the image of light in the Psalms as proof that there was a personal reality, identified with God, yet coming forth from God, they might have appealed to the wrong image in the wrong text, but the idea they were defending is in fact there, on Goldingay's reading.

This is not, of course, a doctrine of the Trinity; it is not even proto-Trinitarianism; it is, however, a suggestion that a measure of plurality within the life of the one God is not an alien and difficult thought for Old Testament religion. Hurtado notes that in much scholarship addressing the beginnings of devotion offered to Jesus, there is an overriding assumption that the monotheistic inheritance of Judaism needed to be broken in some cataclysmic philosophical shift before Jesus could be worshipped;[48] on the evidence of the Old Testament

---

[45] See also MacDonald's discussion of the existence of other divine beings in Deuteronomy.

[46] John Goldingay, *Old Testament Theology, vol. 2: Israel's Faith* (Milton Keynes: Paternoster, 2006), pp. 43–58.

[47] Goldingay, *Old Testament Theology 2*, pp. 49–50.

[48] Hurtado, *Lord Jesus Christ*, pp. 42–7.

texts, this assumption appears to be incorrect. (Although there are of course developments in Jewish religious thought between the end of the Old Testament texts and the time of Christ, to which I will turn in the next section.)

Can we say more than that about the Trinity in the Old Testament? Recent canonical and theological readings have wanted to recover a willingness to read the text as Christian Scripture (without denying that it is also, and properly, read as Jewish Scripture in the synagogue). If authorial intent is not the key determiner of meaning, as many recent hermeneutical proposals suggest, and if canonical context can demand that Scripture be read through the lens of Christian dogma, then we ought to be able to see Trinitarian themes in the Old Testament. (Indeed, if after sufficient experimentation we cannot, then we might be forced to accept that the project of theological interpretation has failed.) Francis Watson has offered a particularly striking example of what this might look like in a reading of the first creation narrative in Genesis 1.[49]

Watson notes first that there is throughout the text a privileging of speech as the primary mode of divine creativity: 'God said, let there be . . .' is the repeated refrain. Under this, however, three distinct modes of divine creative action are visible: transcendent command ('God said, "Let there be light," and light was'); bodily involvement ('God said, "Let there be a firmament . . ." And God *made* the firmament . . .'); and mediation by indwelling ('God said, "Let the earth put forth vegetation . . ." The earth brought forth vegetation . . .'). Divine action toward the creation, on this account, is at once utterly transcendent, profoundly involved, and immanent in the sense of God exercising his power through the granting of potency to created intermediaries. As Watson notes, in the texts these modes all intermingle in the creation of the land creatures (vv. 24–5), and occur elsewhere singularly or in pairs. He reads this as an account of triune divine action, indivisibly united, but representing the particular modes of relation of the three persons: transcendent command; bodily presence; and immanent indwelling.

It would be hard to claim that this reading is demanded by the text, but it is at least faithful to the text, and profoundly attentive to the particular details of the text; as such, it is difficult to dismiss as allegory or eisegesis; perhaps this is an example of what good theological

---

[49] Francis Watson, *Text, Church, and World: Biblical Interpretation in Theological Perspective* (Edinburgh: T&T Clark, 1994), pp. 140–45.

interpretation should look like, and how a witness to the doctrine of the Trinity might be found in the Old Testament.

The Intertestamental Period

There is an older scholarly consensus on developments in Israel's monotheism between the return from exile and the time of Jesus, which is still fairly regularly rehearsed. Hurtado suggests it is traceable to the work of Bousset, and that his presentation has generally been repeated, rather than refined or advanced, in later work.[50] This seems to me to be a fair summary. The consensus view, then, was that a strict philosophical monotheism that existed before the exile was softened after the exile, on the basis of increased interest in semi-divine mediators – notably angels, personified attributes (such as Wisdom), and (we should add, although Bousset does not consider them himself) exalted patriarchs. The argument for the increased interest in these figures is textual; the hypothesis offered to explain the increasing interest notices a developing stress on the transcendence of God, and so a perceived need for intermediary beings: God was more remote, and less available, and so a pantheon of intermediaries filled the gap.

Hurtado accepts that there is some evidence for increased speculation concerning the numbers and orders of angels in post-exilic Jewish thought, but denies that there is any evidence for an increased sense of divine transcendence and remoteness, still less for these angels operating as intermediaries. He cites 2 Baruch 48, which contains a lengthy prayer asserting that 'innumerable hosts' serve God in different offices; the prayer, however, is addressed unreflectively directly to God. Why, then, the development of these vast speculative ranks of angels? Hurtado notes that the political reality of post-exilic Israel was existence as a minor and remote province of one vast empire or another, each governed by an extensive bureaucracy of officials reporting to higher officials. In this context, what more natural and direct way of narrating God's sovereignty over the whole earth than by picturing great hierarchies of ministering spirits?[51]

---

[50] Larry Hurtado, *One God, One Lord: Early Christian Devotion and Ancient Jewish Monotheism* (London: T&T Clark, 2nd edn, 1998), p. 22, referencing W. Bousset, *Die Religion des Judentums im späthellenistischen Zeitalter* (ed. H. Gressmann; Tübingen: JCB Mohr, 3rd edn, 1926).

[51] Hurtado, *One God*, pp. 22–7.

Of course, given the discussion of Old Testament monotheism above, this is all rather beside the point anyway. The question on the table is less the number of heavenly beings than the appropriate recipients of worship. Heaven may be full of angels and archangels; so long as, like the angel that appeared to John, the seer of Revelation, they refuse as scandalous any proposed offer of worship,[52] the form of monotheism which I have suggested (following MacDonald) is found in the Old Testament is not endangered. Bousset's further suggestion that the worship of angels became a part of post-exilic Jewish devotion is, however, crucial in this context. Hurtado again soberly surveys the evidence offered:[53] there are some texts that might suggest angel worship, but they are few in number and all are at best obscure; there are repeated prohibitions of the worship of angels, but these hardly prove that the practice was commonplace; there are some esoteric or magical incantations that involve angelic names, which, however, cannot be taken as evidence for anything more than a hinterland, perhaps small, of superstition; finally, there are Christian accusations that Jews worshipped angels, which are best explained as Christian theological constructions of Jewish devotion, which would not have been accepted or recognized by Jews themselves.

All that said, there has been a persistent interest in the ways in which this apparent increased interest in the population of heaven forms a useful background for understanding the birth of Christology. The first point I would make is that it seems that the wrong question has too often been asked: if we assume, as Bousset apparently did, that the problem faced by the New Testament writers was basically logical, or theological, making room for Jesus in a carefully articulated philosophical monotheism, then we will not understand what went on; rather, we need to realize that the crucial question is worship – as has been argued variously and convincingly by Hurtado and Bauckham.[54] In the narrative of John's visions, the angel refused worship, but Jesus accepted it; how is this not a violation of the fundamental command to monolatry, and the fundamental prohibition of idolatry?

Phrased like this, speculation about the names, titles, and status of exalted patriarchs, or about the various ranks of angels, is rather beside the point. More interesting is the instability over the identity of

[52] Rev. 19:10; compare, importantly, Rev. 1:17–18.
[53] Hurtado, *One God*, pp. 28–35.
[54] See my later discussion, pp. 54–5.

certain divine agents; if the angel of the Lord refuses to receive worship, the Lord does not, and the fact that the two may be confused in biblical narrative is suggestive. More helpful again, perhaps, are the developing references to 'personified divine attributes' – notably Wisdom and the Logos. In terms of divine identity, God's Wisdom occupies an ambiguous position as at once one with God and the first of God's works. As we have seen, this practice of 'hypostasizing' divine attributes stands in direct continuity with central texts from the Old Testament – notably certain psalms – and it is clearly widespread in the intertestamental period.

I suppose, however, the answer to my question is simpler than this: from as early as we can determine, the early Christians worshipped Jesus, and did so with remarkable consistency despite their differences and divergences over so many other issues. This was not the result of extensive deliberation, but a reflexive response which can be explained very simply: they believed that in Jesus they had met the God of Israel face to face, so to speak. The fact that Second Temple Judaism did not have a worked-through philosophical monotheism made the response easier: there was no theoretical barrier to such a confession of divine identity. Complex arguments about divine identity were a response to this basic doxological response, not the cause of it. In the canonical writings of the New Testament we find the contours of this response, to which I will come; we also find a further store of texts, perhaps less contentious than the Old Testament ones, which have been cited as proofs that the doctrine of the Trinity is revealed in Scripture.

The New Testament 1: Exegetical Demonstrations of Trinitarian Doctrine

There is a remarkable level of continuity in the exegetical appeals made by developers and defenders of Trinitarian doctrine from the patristic period down to (conservative) defenders of the doctrine of the Trinity today. This is not surprising: any standard account of biblical authority will affirm, whatever else is also affirmed, that the propositional claims concerning God's life made or necessarily implied by biblical texts are adequate guides to the truth of God's life. Given this, certain texts are simply obvious places to appeal, and all of them were identified and discussed by the fourth century, at least. As we have seen, in the case of Old Testament texts, two factors have created a dislocation between patristic and modern exegesis: the modern suspicion of the strikingly literalistic reading practices once common; and the modern assumption that texts mean what their authors thought they meant.

Neither of these applies with the same force, however, in the New Testament, at least in this area. Literalistic reading practices become more problematic as the texts in view become more poetic or allusive; this is certainly an issue with aspects of New Testament interpretation, notably parables (should Luke 16:23–26 be read as an accurate description of eschatological judgement, or is it merely culturally determined background to the main point of the parable?) and apocalyptic material (Revelation, of course, but also Mark 13, and parallels). Almost none of the important Trinitarian texts have serious problems of this sort attached, however. On the second point, it has seemed easier to believe that the authors of the New Testament could have been intending to write about the eternal relation of the divine Son to the Father, and so there has been less pressure to abandon classical exegetical defences of Trinitarian doctrine from the New Testament.[55]

The gospels present the relationship between Jesus and the One he calls 'Father' as unique and central. This is presented as core to Jesus' own awareness of his identity from an early age (Luke 2:49), and is confirmed by the Father's testimony from heaven at his baptism (Matt. 3:17). Jesus mediates the Father's works and words to the world in various ways (John 5:30; 15:15), and offers prayer to the Father. He acknowledges that 'the Father is greater' than he is (John 14:28). That said, he shared in the Father's glory before creation (John 17:5), and claims to be 'one with' the Father (John 10:30). He is the visibility of the Father (John 14:9), has received 'all things' from the Father, and knows the Father intimately and uniquely (Matt. 11:27). The writer of the fourth gospel asserts the pre-existence of Jesus, his oneness with the Father, and his deity (John 1:1–2).

In all of this there is a complex relationship of intimacy, union, shared knowledge and action, and subordination. There is also wit-

---

[55] Of course, there has been a shift. Earlier generations of theologians would have thought that, since God is the primary author of Holy Scripture, Scripture could be assumed to teach, or at least to assume, a fully worked-through account of the Trinity; modern writers, even 'conservative' ones, will not hold that Paul and John understood the Trinity, and so will have an account which is somewhat more nuanced, that they grasped that Jesus is the incarnation of the divine, and that he was eternally and inseparably one with the Father, although they had no developed conception of how this worked through. The older way was more coherent.

ness to a change of state ('the Word became flesh . . .' John 1:14), a witness which is reinforced by Pauline reflections (e.g. Phil. 2:5–11). One of the crucial exegetical questions in the development of Trinitarian doctrine is the untangling of what belongs to the pre-existent nature, and what belongs to the state of subordination: when Jesus says, 'the Father is greater than I', or when he prays to the Father, is this a reflection of his pretemporal relationship with the Father, and so something that is always true, or does it reflect the subordination inherent in the incarnation, but not natural to who he is?

A further line of argument turns on the divine works. A work that belongs to God alone, such as creation, can be referred to the Son (John 1:3; Col. 1:16; Heb. 1:2–3); if we turn to the work of redemption, it can be referred to Father, Son, or Holy Spirit, or to all three acting together (1 Pet. 1:2). The same might be said of a string of works that are properly referred to God alone: revelation; providential ordering; judgement; eschatological fulfilment . . . There is a series of exegetical arguments, therefore, of the form 'Only God can do x; but the Son and/or the Spirit are shown as doing x; therefore the Son/Spirit is/are God.' There is no account here, yet, of a divine triunity, but there is an exegetical pressure to include reference to the Son – and sometimes the Spirit – when God is spoken of.

The third line of argument is similar, and turns on divine titles. The Son is named as God (John 1:1; 20:28; Rom. 9:5; Titus 2:13; Heb. 1:8-9); both Son and Spirit are given the title 'Lord' (for the Spirit, see 2 Cor. 3:17), the English translation of a Greek word, κυριος, used to translate the name of God revealed to Moses at the burning bush (YHWH). Similarly, both the Son and the Holy Spirit can be blasphemed against (Luke 12:10). If a divine title is properly applied to the Son or the Holy Spirit, then it is an indication that Son and Spirit somehow share in the divine identity or glory.

New Testament responses to this very pressure give us our last argument. A series of proto-credal or liturgical formulae can be discerned in the text which suggest that it is natural to speak twice or thrice over when speaking of God. On the basis of the claim that the text is authoritative revelation, indeed, this is not just natural, but necessary. The two most obvious are the un-self-conscious doubling of the *Shema* – the fundamental confession of Old Testament monotheism/monolatry (Deut. 6:4-5) – in 1 Corinthians 8:6, and the triadic baptismal formula in Matthew 28:19, but we could add many others (to take only a few of the most striking triadic patterns: 1 Cor. 12:4–6; 2 Cor. 13:13; Gal. 4:6; Eph. 4:4–6; Rev. 1:4–5). To speak of God in formal confession or in worship seems to need mention of Jesus, and often of the Spirit.

These four arguments do not amount to an exegetical defence of the doctrine of the Trinity worked out in the fourth century; they do, however, create exegetical pressure to find a way of speaking about God that includes, rather than excluding, speech about Jesus and the Spirit. The development of Trinitarian doctrine is largely a response to this pressure, and is also largely a lengthy exegetical debate, trying to find something to say that is responsible to all the texts that were being adduced by defenders of various different positions.

The New Testament 2: Witness to the Historical Development of Christian Worship

The debate was also shaped by the fact that it seemed normal and natural for the primitive church to worship Jesus. This brings me back to the comments I made above about the nature of monotheism in the Second Temple period: monolatry is the key reality, not a philosophical insistence on monotheism. This fact makes it even more astonishing that, as far as we can determine, amidst all the variety of primitive Christianity, the worship of Jesus as divine was simply ubiquitous. The evidence is there already in the New Testament, even in the earliest strata, the Pauline letters: prayer is offered to the Father 'through Jesus Christ' (Rom. 1:8), and to the Father and Jesus together (1 Thess. 3:11–13); benedictions can be uttered in either name (Rom. 16:20), or in the name of Jesus with no mention of the Father (1 Cor. 16:23).

What evidence we have of more formal worship practices reinforces this. In 1 Corinthians 16:22, a direct appeal to Jesus in Aramaic, *marana tha*, 'Our Lord, come!' is repeated without translation in a letter to a Greek-speaking church. The best understanding would seem to be that this is a piece of Aramaic liturgy so common that it is familiar even in a Greek church, and it is addressed directly to Jesus. When we recall that 1 Corinthians must be dated less than four decades after Jesus' crucifixion, we are presented with evidence that the worship of Jesus in formal liturgy was well established within three decades of his death. I have already mentioned the triadic baptismal formula, to which may be added the witness of Acts that baptism in the name of Jesus alone was also common (Acts 2:38; 8:16; 10:48). Those passages of the New Testament usually considered to be fragments of common Christian hymnody (e.g. John 1:1–18; Phil. 2:5–11; Col. 1:11–15) reinforce this picture of the centrality of worship offered to Jesus, as do the Christological reinterpretations of the Psalms (e.g. in Heb. 1), psalms which would have been sung or chanted in early Christian worship.

Larry Hurtado has collected the evidence for this impressively, and notes that in the period he surveys (AD 30–170) Jesus was a central figure for all groups, and that all groups regarded him as divine. Hurtado says:

> Amidst the diversity of earliest Christianity, belief in Jesus' divine status was amazingly common. The 'heresies' of earliest Christianity largely presuppose the view that Jesus is divine. That is not the issue. The problematic issue, in fact, was whether a genuinely *human* Jesus could be accommodated . . .
>
> Additionally, in spite of the diversity, it is equally evident that Jesus was *central* in all forms of earliest Christianity, proto-orthodox or others, that we can describe with any confidence. This centrality of Jesus, and the uniqueness of his status in the various religious convictions of earliest Christians, also demanded, almost unavoidably, a new view of God.[56]

The early Christian community worshipped Jesus, and was committed by those writings which it read in worship and regarded as Scripture to the belief that God could not be named adequately without speaking of Jesus (and the Holy Spirit). A doctrine of God that made sense of these practices and commitments would take centuries to work out, but that should not blind us to the reality and seriousness of the doxological practices and the exegetical commitments that shaped the community far more than its formulated doctrine.

---

[56] Hurtado, *Lord Jesus Christ*, p. 650. On this point see also Richard Bauckham's work on divine identity, especially the various papers collected in *Jesus and the God of Israel: God Crucified and Other Studies on the New Testament's Christology of Divine Identity* (Milton Keynes: Paternoster, 2008).

3.

'Always with him are his Word and Wisdom': Early Patristic Developments in the Doctrine of the Trinity

The crucial components in the ecumenical doctrine of the Trinity were settled in the fourth century, in the arguments surrounding Arius and Eunomius (amongst others). These debates were largely exegetical, appealing to the text of Scripture (and to a lesser extent to the worshipping practices of the church) for justification of points. Whilst there was a general respect for the writings of earlier theologians, it would be wrong to present the fourth-century discussions as particularly focused on building on earlier arguments. They did, however, draw on a technical vocabulary, on traditions of exegesis, and on certain modes of negotiating the intellectual inheritance of Greek philosophy, all of which had been established by earlier writers in the patristic period. This chapter is largely intended, therefore, to set the context for the decisive debates, which will be discussed in the next chapter. There is not, of course, space here to describe every idea and writer, and I will focus on those that led more directly to the fourth-century settlements.

That said, it would be wrong to conclude that the developed doctrine of the fourth century was something entirely novel. As we have seen, from as early as we can discern, Jesus was named alongside the Father as divine in Christian discourse. In the immediate sub-apostolic period, virtually every witness we have to Christian devotional and confessional practice suggests that a threefold naming of God was so normal as to be reflexively assumed. With regard to devotion, the second-century martyrologies are of particular interest: routinely, they end with a doxology which is straightforwardly Trinitarian in form. In the brief account of the martyrdom of saints Carpus, Papylus and Agathonicé (c.170?), for instance, there are repeated references to the 'glory of the Lord Jesus', and the account ends with a Trinitarian doxology: 'to the Father, the Son, and the Holy Spirit, now and for ever and for all the ages to come. Amen.'[1] A similar phrase ends the account of the trial in the 'Acts of the Scillitan Martyrs', which can be dated with confidence to 17 July 180.[2] Martyrologies are central documents of Christian devotion in the period, and the routine practice of ending them with a triadic formula suggests strongly that speaking of the threefold name, Father, Son, and Holy Spirit, was essential to, and normal within, Christian devotion.

We do not have so early a reference to confessional practices, but by the end of the second century we have witness to a remarkably widespread and constant practice of announcing the 'rule of faith'. This is a brief formula, seemingly not yet set in particular words (and so not a creed), but constant in pattern, which several writers use as an authoritative summary of Christian belief.[3] Within a generation we can find recognizably the same 'rule of faith' used by Irenaeus (born in what is now Turkey and working in France), Tertullian (in Carthage, in North Africa), Origen (in Egypt) and elsewhere. In each case, the confession is triadic, asserting belief in Father, Son, and Spirit.

Histories of doctrine, focused as they are on the development of coherent and convincing ideas, can unfortunately present the development of the doctrine of the Trinity as a fourth-century novelty. Certainly the technical terminology and conceptuality necessary to give a tight account of how it is possible to speak of one God existing in three hypostases is only developed in the fourth century, but we should see this not so much as the development of a new confession, as the discovery of the necessary theology to give firm intellectual grounding to an idea that is so deeply engraved in Christian devotion and confession as to be inescapable. The early Christians worshipped

---

[1] See Herbert Musurillo, trans., *The Acts of the Christian Martyrs* (Oxford: Clarendon, 1972), pp. 27–9; quotation from p. 29.

[2] See Timothy David Barnes, *Tertullian: A Historical and Literary Study* (Oxford: Clarendon, 1971), pp. 60–62 for a translation.

[3] The 'rule of faith' or *regula fidei* is a proto-credal pattern of Christian teaching found in several second- and third-century writers. The precise words are not fixed, but the pattern is sufficiently similar to hypothesize that it is something formal. For some discussion of the sources and form, together with a brief history of scholarship, see Eric F. Osborn, 'Reason and the Rule of Faith in the Second Century AD', in *The Making of Orthodoxy: Essays in Honour of Henry Chadwick* (ed. Rowan Williams; Cambridge: CUP, 1989), pp. 40–61.

the Trinity from the first; the tale of the development of Trinitarian theology is an account of how they came to find a satisfying way of speaking of the One they worshipped.

In stark contrast to the abundant discussion of the fourth-century debates, there are not very many good accounts of the development of the doctrine of God prior to the fourth century for the general reader; the readings below rely in the main on primary sources – often enough available in the original languages only – and specialist secondary literature, which is not always in English. Dünzl's book is mostly focused on the fourth century, but offers two helpful chapters on the earlier period;[4] Behr's account is much fuller, and often extremely helpful,[5] but it is somewhat idiosyncratic in places – perhaps distorted by his desire to conform the history to later judgements of orthodoxy.[6] Prestige remains the best guide to the pre-Nicene period, a judgement which emphasizes the quality of his work, but also the paucity of successors in the eighty years since he wrote.[7]

The Early Development of Christian Theology

It is difficult to trace the earliest developments of Christian reflection with any precision. We have a small number of early texts which, in the absence of any other evidence, we tend to assume represent the mainstream of Christian reflection in the first half of the second century; this assumption might not, however, be true, and (as with the New Testament writings) the dating of some of the texts is imprecise in any case. Indeed, drawing a hard line between the writings included in the New Testament and some of the other early material is anachronistic: whilst there was, very early, a sense that some of the apostolic writings should be classed as 'Scripture' (see, e.g., 2 Pet. 3:15–16), and a broad acceptance that the four gospels, Acts, and many

---

[4] Franz Dünzl, *A Brief History of the Doctrine of the Trinity in the Early Church* (trans. John Bowden; London: T&T Clark, 2007). See pp. 11–41.

[5] John Behr, *Formation of Christian Theology, vol. 1: The Way to Nicaea* (Crestwood, NY: SVS Press, 2001).

[6] Most striking is his relegation of Tertullian to a footnote or two. The emphasis on Hippolytus (and/or, we should add, his school) in combating modalistic monarchianism is a welcome corrective to older accounts, but Tertullian's *Prax.*, despite its evident origins in the New Prophecy, simply cannot be written out of the picture.

[7] G.L. Prestige, *God in Patristic Thought* (London: SPCK, 2nd edn, 1952; original edn, 1936).

of the letters should be included, there was doubt for some centuries over Revelation, 2 and 3 John, 2 Peter, Jude, and Hebrews; conversely, many in the early period received as authoritative such writings as the *Shepherd of Hermas*, the *Didache*, the epistle of *Barnabas*, or *1 Clement*. Current scholarly judgements about the dating of various writings suggest that some of these may have been written prior to the last of the New Testament books, further indicating the fuzziness of the border.

All that said, there is a fairly well-established tradition of dividing the early patristic writings into several periods, a tradition which, for all its imprecision, remains useful. The earliest writings – the *Didache*, *Shepherd of Hermas*, the letters of Ignatius of Antioch – are mostly concerned with the internal management of the church, and tell us little about the development of Trinitarian doctrine. They do, however, reinforce the point that Christian devotion, from the earliest time we can trace, assumed the deity of Christ, and that speaking of God in triadic formulas was normal and natural. Consider, for brief example, Ignatius to the Romans: 'It is better for me to die in Christ Jesus than to be king over the ends of the earth . . . Suffer me to follow the example of the passion of my God' (Ign. *Rom.* 6). Some typical triadic doxologies from the end of martyrologies have already been quoted above.

In the face of repeated persecution and the deaths of many martyrs, Christian thinkers produced apologetic writings around the middle of the second century, pleading for general tolerance of the faith, or for clemency in specific cases. The Apologists strove to emphasize the continuities between (what they perceived as) the best of Graeco-Roman culture and the faith of the Christian church. One of the charges they faced was atheism (Christians were known to refuse to take part in religious ceremonies which were both important cultic means of uniting the disparate peoples of the empire, and also intended to honour the gods whose favour was believed to establish the prosperity of the state), and so they explored at length what the church believed about God, and how it might be aligned in presentation with the traditions of Greek philosophy, in order to make it comprehensible to their persecutors.

The description of the pre-existent divine Son as the 'Logos' ('Word') in the Johannine prologue provided one easy point of continuity. The first recorded philosophical use of the term 'Logos' is in Heraclitus, one of the earliest of the Greek philosophers, who is most remembered for his slogan 'everything is flux'. The world, Heraclitus believed, is endlessly changing because there is ceaseless competition between various opposed eternal principles. There is, however, in Heraclitus's system, an underlying order, generally unattainable, that made sense of the whole. This he called the Logos.[8] The concept became almost ubiquitous in Greek philosophy, with a wide variety of shades of meaning. Thus, for the Stoic tradition, the Logos was the immanent principle of order within the world (roughly as it had been for Heraclitus), which they identified with God; for the middle Platonists, the Logos was the overflowing generative power of the divine, through which the material world was ordered.[9] This conception was adopted by the Jewish philosopher Philo, and deployed freely in his philosophical exegesis of the biblical texts.[10]

The extent to which this background influenced the language of the fourth gospel is debated, and not to my purpose here;[11] the point is that this coincidence of language, whatever its origins, enabled the Apologists to speak of Christian belief in the incarnate Son in language that would be recognizable to their surrounding culture. Justin Martyr's language about the origin of the Logos provides an interesting case-study of how this was worked out. He cites Proverbs 8:21–25, and identifies the figure of Wisdom with the Logos; in expounding the passage, which in Justin's translation speaks of wisdom being both 'created' (v. 22) and 'begotten' (v. 25), he quietly drops the language of

---

[8] On Heraclitus see Daniel W. Graham, 'Heraclitus: Flux, Order, and Knowledge', in *The Oxford Handbook of Presocratic Philosophy* (ed. Patricia Curd and Daniel W. Graham; Oxford: OUP, 2008), pp. 169–88. The Logos is discussed on p. 176.

[9] A good, if brief, survey of the varieties of meaning, with helpful references to primary texts, may be found in F.E. Peters, *Greek Philosophical Terms: A Historical Lexicon* (New York: NYUP, 1967), pp. 110–12.

[10] Philo's development of the *logos* concept in his biblical commentaries does not appear to have had a direct influence on the Apologists, in that the evidence that they were aware of Philo's work is very far from convincing. On this see David T. Runia, *Philo in Early Christian Literature* (Minneapolis: Fortress, 1993), pp. 94–116. Runia's argument turns on the fact that we have no convincing evidence for Philo's works being known outside of Alexandria in this period, and on the extensive spread of Hellenistic Judaism. In the absence of direct citation, it thus seems more probable that the occasional terms or themes that appear philonic in the Apologists are in fact merely generically Jewish.

[11] Many commentaries on the fourth gospel provide an excursus on the subject, one of the most helpful being found in George R. Beasley-Murray, *John*, WBC (Waco: Word, 1987) pp. 6–10. See also useful entries s.v. in *New International Dictionary of New Testament Theology* (ed. Colin Brown; Exeter: Paternoster, 1975–86) and *Theologisches Wörterbuch zum Neuen Testament* (ed. G. Kittel; Stuttgart: Kolhammer, 1933–79).

creation, and speaks only, but three times, of the Logos being begot-ten/generated (the Greek word is ἐγέννησεν).[12] He will use images that are very reminiscent of Platonic ideas of the emanation of the Logos from the divine – light from light; fire causing fire; etc. – but again refuses to use the language of emanation, preferring (once again) begetting.[13] He insists, drawing on the example of fire, that this beget-ting does not lessen the begetter in any way. The Logos, he says, is 'a second God', although he qualifies this by saying distinct in number, not in will.[14]

Theophilus of Antioch similarly uses the word 'beget/generate' to describe the Logos's relation with the Father, and, like Justin, sees the Old Testament theophanies as appearances of the Logos. He borrows technical Stoic vocabulary,[15] to speak of the Logos who was 'always innate [the Stoic term ἐνδιαθέτος] in the heart of God' and of the moment when God 'generated this Logos, making him external [the Stoic term προφόρικος], as the firstborn of all creation.'[16] Notice in this that generation is a second moment: the Logos is always with God, but the act of generation occurs as a precursor to the act of creation. Justin had not addressed the question of the time of the origin of the Logos; another apologetic writer, Athenagoras, has a similar concep-tion of the eternal immanent presence of the Logos within the Father to that of Theophilus.[17] Like Justin, Theophilus is keen to insist that the act of generation does not deprive the Father of anything: '[h]e did not deprive himself of the Logos but generated the Logos and constantly converses with his Logos.'[18]

This is all rather inchoate, but very suggestive. Justin is clearly already convinced that 'generation' is the right language to describe the Father's relationship to the Logos; his philosophical sources invite him to speak of 'emanation' and – more strikingly – his biblical sources offer 'creation', but he appears to avoid both terms intention-ally. The identification of the Old Testament theophanies with the

---

[12] *Dial.* 129.

[13] See, e.g., *Dial.* 61 and 128.

[14] *Dial.* 56.

[15] For the Stoic distinction between the external and internal *logos* see, e.g., *Stoicorum Verterum Fragmenta* (4 vols; ed. J. von Arnim; Lipsiae [sic, Leipzig]: Teubner, 1903–24), 2:135.

[16] *Autol.* 2.22. Translation quoted from Robert M. Grant, *Theophilus of Antioch: Ad Autolycum* (Oxford: Clarendon, 1970), p. 63.

[17] Athenagoras, *Leg.* 10.

[18] *Autol.* 2.22.

Logos can perhaps be read as suggestive of an awareness of the elision of language between the 'angel of the Lord' and God himself in several of the texts (which was discussed in chapter 2 above), and a willingness to locate the Logos in this indeterminate state as being both God's representative and somehow identical with God – a location that the Johannine prologue invites in its opening phrases. The Stoic language of the becoming-external of the eternally innate Logos is harder to read in proto-Trinitarian terms, and the point will eventually be quietly forgotten by most of the tradition, and condemned when it appears in developed form in Marcellus of Ancyra. There is no attempt in the Apologists to give an account of the life of God in Trinitarian terms, but there is a struggling with language about the relation of the Logos to God that indicates that the Trinitarian questions are already open.

Irenaeus of Lyons

Around the same time as the Apologetic writers, but engaged in a different task, Irenaeus of Lyons also offered significant, if similarly inchoate, Trinitarian development. Irenaeus's place and date of birth are uncertain; the latter we might locate with some certainty between AD 130 and 140;[19] the former we might suppose, with less confidence, was somewhere in modern Turkey, since we can place him as a teenager listening to Polycarp in Smyrna.[20] He was well educated in Christian writings and in Greek philosophy, and probably spent time in Rome before travelling on to Lyons, to a church only a few decades old. During the persecution of 177, Pothinus, bishop of Lyons, died, and Irenaeus succeeded him. There is a tradition that he himself was martyred under Septimus Severus in 202–3, but this is uncertain.

Irenaeus's great project was to oppose the various syncretistic amalgamations of Christianity with Greek philosophy that he lumped

---

[19] So J. van der Stretten, 'Saint-Irénée fut-il martyre?' in *Les Martyrs de Lyon (177)* (ed. J. Rougé et R. Turcan; Paris: CNRS, 1978), pp. 145–52. The book gives useful context to Irenaeus's writings at several points.

[20] Eusebius, *Hist. eccl.* 4.14, citing a letter of Irenaeus. There is no reason of which I am aware to doubt the veracity of this citation. Polycarp was martyred 155–6, so Irenaeus cannot have been more than a teenager when he encountered him. Whilst his family may have moved during his childhood, we have no evidence of this, so locating the family home near Smyrna at this point in his life is plausible.

together under the name 'Gnostic'.[21] His primary target is a group known as Valentinians, although he wants to suggest that they exist in a 'family tree' of erroneous ideas, which becomes a part of his polemic (essentially, he contrasts the apostolic succession of truth passed from Jesus and the Twelve through the bishops with a heretical succession of falsehood that he traces back to Simon Magus).[22] Smith has argued that the essence of all Gnosticism was 'anticosmic dualism', i.e. the connected beliefs that, on the one hand, the world of matter and the world of spirit are fundamentally opposed, and on the other, that therefore the world of matter is evil, pointless, or worthless.[23] Whether this is adequate as an account of everything that gets called 'Gnosticism' might be disputed; it is certainly at the heart of that to which Irenaeus was opposed.

The fundamental Gnostic problem, then, was cosmogony: how did the world come to be? In this they were borrowing and adapting an extensive discussion from the contemporary schools of Greek philosophy, which were profoundly concerned with giving an account of the origins of imperfection in the world. Plato had introduced the idea that the origin of the world was in a single first principle;[24] why, then, is there apparent disorder and chaos in the world? What has gone wrong with the perfect unfolding of a rational principle? Another chance phrase of Plato's offered an answer: the origin of the world can be described as the imposition of order on a pre-existent disordered

---

[21] It has recently become fashionable to question the existence of a unitary Gnosticism (for the classic statement, see Michael A. Williams, *Rethinking 'Gnosticism': An Argument for Dismantling a Dubious Category* [Princeton: PUP, 1996]). Inevitably, counter-proposals have arisen, some stressing the utility and precision of the term (e.g. Carl B. Smith, *No Longer Jews: The Search for Gnostic Origins* [Peabody: Hendrickson, 2004]); others locating the problem in ideologically conditioned scholarly practices in the modern academy (e.g. Karen L. King, *What Is Gnosticism?* [Cambridge, MA: Belknap, 2003]). The debate is complex, and not to my purpose. Birger A. Pearson, *Ancient Gnosticism: Traditions and Literature* (Minneapolis: Fortress, 2007) offers a well-informed non-technical introduction to the movement which highlights the diversity; Manlio Simonetti, *Testi Gnostici in Lingua Greca e Latina* (Vincenza: Fondazione Lorenzo Valla, 1993) is a valuable collection of fragments and works, with useful commentary.

[22] This is developed in Book 1 of *Haer*. See Irénée de Lyon, *Contre les Hérésies: Livre 1, SC 263–4* (édition critique par Adelin Rousseau et Louis Doutreleau; Paris: Cerf, 1979). The most recent full English translation is, unhappily, in the *ANF*; for a recent English translation of the relevant part here, however, see Robert M. Grant, *Irenaeus of Lyons* (London: Routledge, 1997), pp. 88–105.

[23] Smith, *No Longer Jews*, pp. 13–17.

[24] See, e.g., *Tim.* 28.

substratum, the imposition of form on unformed matter.[25] This proposed two answers to the question of the disorder of the world to
Plato's successors in Irenaeus's day: monism, with some account of
decline or imperfection; or dualism. These in fact tend to the same
answer when worked through.

The monist account, represented classically by Plotinus, but also
developed by Alexander of Lycopolis and others, postulates a series
of emanations from a perfect first principle. Each emanation, being
slightly further from the origin, is slightly less perfect, until the fur-
thest emanation – material being – becomes marked by a radical
imperfection. The dualist account sees creation as the imposition of
order on an eternally existing chaotic substance, 'matter'. Material
beings, then, exist as the somewhat precarious organization of a naturally chaotic element, and have an innate tendency to drift back
towards chaos and imperfection – a thermodynamically inevitable
increase of entropy, in modern terms. (Notable middle Platonic dualists include Plutarch and Atticus.) Either way, then, matter was a common answer to the question of what is wrong with the world. For
monists, matter was less real than spirit, and so the material world
was prone to error or distortion; for dualists, matter was recalcitrant,
resistant to the organizing principle of spirit, and so prone to error or
distortion. For the Gnostic traditions that Irenaeus wrote to oppose,
this was radicalized into the fundamental dualism of spirit and matter described by Smith. Matter is now not imperfect, but evil; not
somewhat recalcitrant to spirit, but utterly inimical to spirit; not at
several removes from perfection, but simply opposed to perfection.

This of course creates a problem: assuming a standard ancient anthropology, which sees both material and spiritual aspects in human beings,
how does this amalgam of good and evil happen? More bluntly, whence
creation? The standard response of the various Gnostic teachers that
Irenaeus was most concerned with was a combination of the Platonic
accounts of emanation and formation. A series of, increasingly less perfect, spiritual beings emanates from the perfect spiritual being; eventually, far enough down the series, comes a being who is prepared to get
her (this being was usually represented as female) hands dirty and work
with the evil stuff of matter. The typical reason for this seems to concern
knowledge: each being in the spiritual hierarchy desires to understand
perfection; the higher beings grasp perfection intuitively; the lower
beings have to reason to understand perfection; finally comes a being

---

[25] *Tim.* 30.

who can only understand perfection by making imperfect models of it, hence creation. The Valentinian system had thirty beings in the hierarchy (which they called the *pleroma* [Gk, 'fullness']), with Sophia the lowest being who creates; the Basilidean system had eight, with the lowest two, Power and Sophia, combining to produce the first heaven, and its angels. There is then a series of increasingly lower heavens, 365 in all; the chief angel of the lowest heaven is the God of the Jews, who creates the material world.[26] These systems are complex, and their detail need not concern us; the crucial points are the evil of the material world, and the concomitant extensive distancing of the world from the Most High God by a postulation of a series of intermediaries.

The Gnostic traditions Irenaeus wrote to oppose were supporting their views with appeals to Christian Scripture;[27] Irenaeus, however, perceives that there is a deep variance between this account of matter as evil and both the rule of faith, and the practices of worship, of the church. We cannot confess the incarnation if matter is evil, as it would be unthinkable for God to unite himself with matter;[28] equally, practices of devotion which centre on the Eucharist, on physical eating and drinking, implicitly but stridently demand that materiality is not identified as evil. Irenaeus thus also rejected the distancing of God from the world, and the patterns of intermediaries proposed by the Gnostics. Instead, he suggested, the Father works in the world through his 'two hands', the Son and the Spirit. And the Son and the Spirit are one with the Father, not separating the Father from the world, but being the immanent presence of the Father within creation. Irenaeus's answer to Gnosticism, then, is to develop a proto-Trinitarian theology.[29]

Irenaeus is already heir to a triadic confession of belief. His account of the 'rule of faith' begins with belief 'in one God, the Almighty

---

[26] For these details, with references to sources, see Pearson, *Ancient Gnosticism*, pp. 136–8 (for Basilides) and 148–89 (for Valentinianism).

[27] For a helpful analysis of many examples see Gerard P. Luttikhuizen, *Gnostic Revisions of Genesis Stories and Early Jesus Traditions, Nag Hammadi and Manichaean Studies* 58 (Leiden: Brill, 2006).

[28] As at least some of Irenaeus's opponents realized, and so taught a docetic account of the incarnation, in which Christ only appeared to have a material body.

[29] Eric Osborn, *Irenaeus of Lyons* (Cambridge: CUP, 2001) is the best recent introduction to Irenaeus's theology. Grant, *Irenaeus* is also useful, as are some older studies: Gustav Wingren, *Man and the Incarnation: A Study in the Biblical Theology of Irenaeus* (trans. R. Mackenzie; Edinburgh: Oliver & Boyd, 1959) and Albert Houssiau, *La Christologie de Saint Irénée* (Louvain: Publications Universitaires de Louvain, 1955).

Father . . . in one Christ Jesus, the Son of God, who became incarnate
. . . and in the Holy Spirit . . .'[30] and Christians are baptized into the
threefold name.[31] As noted in chapter 2 above, he identifies the figure
of Wisdom in Proverbs 8 with the Spirit rather than the Son. God
made all things 'through himself, that is, through his word and wisdom'; again, 'he himself in himself . . . made all things; by his untiring
word he made all things that have been made.'[32]

These last two citations point to Irenaeus's struggling towards an
expression of something close to classical Trinitarianism. He is so concerned to deny Gnostic accounts of mediation that he wants to insist
that the principles of mediation, the Son/word and the Spirit/wis-
dom, are identical with God. His celebrated metaphor of the 'two
hands of God' is the primary way he asserts this, as in *Adversus haere-
ses* 4.20.1, discussing creation:

> Angels did not make or form us, for angels could not have made an
> image of God, not any other but the true God, nor any power far dis-
> tant from the Father of all things. God needed none of these to make
> whatever he had foreordained to make, as if he did not have hands of
> his own. For always with him are his Word and Wisdom, the Son and
> the Spirit, through whom and in whom he made everything freely and
> independently, to whom he also speaks when he says 'Let us make man
> after our image and likeness' [Gen. 1:26], taking the substance of the
> creatures from himself as well as the pattern of the things he adorned.[33]

The image is used elsewhere, but this text captures the import of it.
God contains within his own life the necessary mediators of his creative (and salvific) power. There is no need for endless speculations
about emanations, angels, and spiritual beings. God is close and present to the world – the material world – which he created, loves, and
called 'very good'.

Two more comments need to be made. First, the image of God's
hands could be misleading in its impersonality. Irenaeus ascribes distinct personal action to both Son and Spirit: the Spirit speaks through
the prophets (*Epid.* 6), and is the comforter promised by Jesus in John

---

[30] Irenaeus, *Haer.* 1.10.1 (my trans.).

[31] *Epid.* 3. Irénée de Lyon, *Démonstration de la prédication apostolique*, SC 406 (trans. A. Rousseau; Paris: Cerf, 1995).

[32] *Haer.* 2.30.9 and 2.2.4, respectively; both trans. from Osborn, Irenaeus, p. 90.

[33] Trans. from Grant, *Irenaeus*, p. 150.

14 (*Haer.* 3.17.3); the Son is of course personally active in the creation when he becomes incarnate, but also before – he is always the one who reveals the Father, although he is never present prior to the incarnation.[34] How do we understand three personal presences who are somehow one being? Irenaeus does not speculate – perhaps he does not even see it as a problem (his thought is generally allusive and rich in imagery, rather than full of careful logical precision) – but he feels compelled to assert that these things must be true.

Second, like Justin before him, Irenaeus gives an account only of an economic Trinity; as we have seen, he asserts that the Son and Spirit are 'always with him [the Father]', which perhaps gestures towards some sense of an immanent Trinity, but more likely the question simply never occurs to him. The God he knows is present and active in the world; who God is in all eternity, 'before' creating the world, is a question that it never occurs to him to ask. It is perhaps no surprise that Irenaeus, so long ignored, has been feted as a key Trinitarian thinker in the recent 'Trinitarian revival'; his stress on the economy fits recent Trinitarianism far better than it did classical Trinitarianism.

Tertullian, Hippolytus, and Modalistic Monarchianism

Tertullian was a native of Carthage in North Africa, who wrote extensively around the beginning of the third century, and who converted during his life to an ascetic and charismatic movement later to be repudiated by the church called Montanism, or 'the New Prophecy'. Much more than that it is difficult to be certain about.[35] Amongst his works are several extended controversial texts, in which, like Irenaeus, he refined his doctrine of God through opposing the errors of others. One of his opponents, Hermogenes, held to Platonic ideas similar to those discussed above, believing that God created the universe out of unformed matter; another was Marcion who, although no Gnostic, held to the ideas that the God of the Hebrew Scriptures was a different being from the Father of Jesus Christ, and that Christ only

---

[34] Houssiau, *Christologie*, traces this with some exactness; see pp. 79–104.

[35] Barnes, *Tertullian*, is still the crucial source, for his demolition of the ancient myths concerning Tertullian's biography. Barnes plausibly dates all Tertullian's works to 196–212 (pp. 32–56), and suggests that he began writing young, perhaps born c.170, and therefore died young, perhaps martyred (pp. 58–9). Neither conjecture can be proved, of course; one can die young through accident or natural causes, and many authors begin their writing careers later in life.

appeared to take on flesh, as he could have no true union with matter, which is evil.

Hippolytus is an even more shadowy figure, although a celebrated one, whose statue stands in the Vatican library to this day. The works attributed to him include a *Refutation of All Heresies* and a book, *Contra haerisin Noeti;*[36] he was bishop in Rome, and involved in controversy with another bishop in Rome, Callistus, a fact which has led some to regard him as an 'anti-pope'. We can be fairly certain that he was martyred in AD 235; beyond that, understanding the details of his life and controversies has been difficult. A recent proposal from Brent, however, seems to me to make sense of much of the evidence.[37] He argues that the dispute between Hippolytus and Callistus predates the existence of a single and recognized pre-eminent bishop in Rome, with instead each being the leader of a particular school of presbyters, and that the works attributed to Hippolytus are works from his school, but not necessarily all from his own pen.[38]

The Noetus whom Hippolytus wrote against was a representative of a reactionary theological position that has been called 'modalistic monarchianism', but is more commonly referred to as 'modalism' today. It is a view most commonly identified with Sabellius,[39] but it was taught by Noetus of Smyrna, who seemingly indirectly influenced Hippolytus's long-term opponent, Callistus.[40] These writers solved the Trinitarian question by insisting on the absolute monarchy (i.e. sole rule) of God as the controlling doctrine; the Son clearly shares

---

[36] The best edition of the *Refutatio* (sometimes referred to as the *Elenchos* after its Greek title) is that of Miroslav Marcovich, Patristiche Texte und Studien 25 (Berlin: de Gruyter, 1986). The *Refutatio* is perhaps best regarded as 'school of Hippolytus'; see Brent, *Hippolytus, passim*. The *Noet.* can be found in R. Butterworth, *Hippolytus of Rome: Contra Noetum: Text Introduced, Edited, Translated*, Heythrop Monographs 2 (London: Sheed & Ward, 1999).

[37] Allen Brent, *Hippolytus and the Roman Church in the Third Century: Communities in Tension before the Emergence of a Monarch-Bishop*, Supplements *to VC* 31 (Brill: Leiden, 1995).

[38] Having accepted Brent's argument on this point, I will however generally refer to 'Hippolytus' as the author of the works of the school; anything else seeming intolerably clumsy.

[39] Sabellius is almost unknown other than for giving his name to this heresy. Callistus apparently formally excommunicated him (Hippolytus, *Haer.* 9.7). His name seemingly resurfaced in the disputes around Paul of Samosata (see the next section of this chapter) and so, in the East, he became the figurehead for the modalistic position.

[40] The claim is made, credibly, by Hippolytus, *Haer.* (= *Refutatio/Elenchos*) 9.7ff.; see also 10.26.

in the divine rule, so there can be no ontological distinction between Father and Son. They are different modes of presentation of the same divine being, who is sometimes called Father, and sometimes called Son. The theology appears at this point to have been rather undeveloped, but found its force in an aggressive reassertion of monotheism in the face of the tendency in the Logos theology to speak of two divine beings – even, as we have seen with Justin, of two Gods.

The response in Hippolytus's *Refutatio omnium haeresium* is to insist on the genuine distinction of the Father and the Logos, who is brought forth first by God and is the primary agent of creation. He alone is 'from the Father' and is 'the substance of the Father'. Indeed, he 'is God'. All else that exists is created through the Logos, and can cease to exist; the Logos by contrast is eternal. The Logos spoke through and controlled the prophets, and in due time, the Logos was sent by the Father to come as a true human being to reveal God to the world and to exemplify a well-lived human life. (All of this may be found in 10.33.)

The differing starting points of the *Refutatio* and its opponents are worthy of notice. Hippolytus, following the practice of Justin and other Apologists, begins with a philosophical account of the nature of God, which leads to reflection on creation and incarnation. The monarchians, it seems, began with the claim that the Jesus of the gospel narratives was indeed God, and worked back from there to a straightforward theory of identity. Hippolytus does not even mention the name 'Jesus' in his construction, being primarily interested in speaking of the eternal relationship of Father and Son.

Hippolytus's *Contra haeresin Noeti* appears to be a mediating work, withdrawing somewhat from the bold claims of the *Refutatio* in order, perhaps, to find common ground with the modalists. A theory not dissimilar to Theophilus's account of the innate Logos becoming the external Logos at the incarnation is in evidence, although the Father always knew his Logos, and the Logos was made known to and through the prophets. The starting point is thus (explicitly – see 9.1) biblical revelation, but it is not the exclusive focus on the gospel story that the *Refutatio* ascribes to the modalists; rather, it is a broad account of the narrative of Scripture from creation, through the calling of Abraham and Sarah and the election of Israel, to the coming of Christ and the awaited final consummation.

Tertullian's most significant work for the development of Trinitarian doctrine was directed against 'Praxeas'. This book is of enormous significance in Latin Trinitarian theology, not least in

introducing virtually all the technical terminology that would
become standard, including the word 'Trinity' (Lt., *trinitas*).[41]
'Praxeas' in Greek means something like 'busybody', and the lack of
any other reference to a writer of that name has led to the suggestion
that it is in fact a pseudonym. The best interpretation, although not
completely certain, is that Tertullian had in mind Callistus.[42]
Whether this is right or not, clearly 'Praxeas' held modalistic monarchian views; the logical implication of this position, horrific to
Tertullian, is 'patripassianism', the claim that the Father suffered on
the cross. Further, Tertullian wrote this work whilst a Montanist, and
it is clear that his Montanist views were not irrelevant to his desire
to oppose Praxeas (who is pictured as interfering to prevent the
bishop of Rome accepting Montanism[43]).

Tertullian's response is first[44] to insist exegetically on real differentiation between the Son and the Father, turning to familiar passages in
John 1, Proverbs 8, and Psalms 2 and 45. The divine monarchy is not
compromised by the existence of the Son, since Father and Son share

---

[41] Of course, most of the words had been used before, including *trinitas*: Tertullian
is seemingly the first to apply it to the doctrine of God, but he had previously used
it, seemingly in a standard usage, to describe the erroneous anthropology of
Valentinus. For an exhaustive review of the evidence of the previous use of most
of Tertullian's theological vocabulary, see René Braun, *Deus Christianorum:
Recherches sur le vocabulaire doctrinal de Tertullian* (Paris: Études Augustiniennes,
2nd edn, 1977).

[42] For a recent argument to this effect, see Brent, *Hippolytus*, pp. 525–35, which looks
at possible biographical coincidences between 'Praxeas' and Callistus, and at theological similarities. R.E. Heine, 'The Christology of Callistus', *JTS* NS 49 (1998):
pp. 56–91 argues that Praxeas was a historical individual, connected to Callistus,
and that Tertullian attacks both Praxeas and Callistus under cover of Praxeas's
name. This accounts for some divergence in the views ascribed to Praxeas by
Tertullian. See pp. 58–60. My interest is in Tertullian, so the identity of his opponent is not crucial to my argument.

[43] Tertullian, *Prax.* 1.5. The best edition is in CCSL 2; Ernest Evans offers an edition
with English translation in *Tertullian's Treatise against Praxeas: The Text Edited, with
an Introduction, Translation, and Commentary* (London: SPCK, 1948); I believe this to
be the most recent English translation, and am following it in my quotations.

[44] *Prax.* is not well ordered in contemporary systematic terms, and I am here sum-
marizing my construction of the argument, rather than sequentially working
through the text. For useful guides to the theology of the text, see Evans,
Tertullian's Treatise, pp. 18-82; Theodorus Veroeven, *Studiën over Tertullianus'
Adversus Praxean* (Amsterdam: Noord-Hollandsche Uitgevers Maatschappij,
1949). Kevin McCruden, 'Monarchy and Economy in Tertullian's *Adversus
Praxean*', *SJT* 55 (2002): pp. 325–37 says little that is not already in Evans and
Veroeven, but is perhaps more accessible.

one will and intention (*Prax.* 4, citing John 5:19). He has a similar account to Theophilus of the eternal interior existence of the Logos, coupled with a 'going forth' at the beginning of creation; for Tertullian this explains the language of the creation of Wisdom in Proverbs 8 (*Prax.* 5–7). He introduces the language of 'person' (*persona*) to speak of Father, Son, and Spirit; elsewhere in his corpus he has used the word to refer to a human individual 'with no psychological or metaphysical or juristic reference';[46] in *Adversus Praxean*, the new Trinitarian usage of *persona* is similarly underdetermined: any existence of a substance is a thing (*res*); a *persona* is a self-conscious thing. This lack of metaphysical subtlety is rather characteristic as we work through the text: for Tertullian, a substance (*substantia*) is, roughly, something that exists. Early in the treatise, the individual substance of the Son is stressed, to stress that the Son is another alongside the Father, and not merely some property or mode of the Father's being; by the time Tertullian has finished his construction, the substance of Son is – unphilosophically – 'of the Father's substance' (*de substantia patris*; §4); Father, Son and Spirit are 'one substance, in which three are together' (*una substantia in tribus cohaerentibus*; §12). One substance means one God, one monarchy, one power; but existing thrice over. This is the divine Trinity.

At this point, Tertullian has invented the vocabulary that would become enshrined in the Western tradition, and has stated the orthodox doctrine of the Trinity; however, the magnitude of this achievement should not be overstated. Tertullian is not here inventing a new doctrine, but stating with some clarity what must be said if the church's confession about Jesus is to be true, and if the patterns of devotion common to the life of the church are justified.[47] He has not, however, given any account of how to think about God – how is it meaningful to say 'one substance, three persons'; can this assertion even be coherent? He has, in my view, succeeded – brilliantly – in clarifying the terms of the problem, but he has done no more than that. To succeed in being faithful to the faith and worship of the tradition, any account of God's life must be able to say with some exactness what Tertullian says; he himself, however, offers us (almost) no account of the divine life. After Tertullian, we still do not know how to speak

---

[45] *Prax.* 7.

[46] Evans, *Tertullian's Treatise*, p. 47 for the quotation; see the discussion on pp. 46–50, also Braun, *Deus Christianorum*, pp. 207–42.

[47] See my comments on this in the introduction to this chapter above.

rightly about God; we do, however, know much better what speaking rightly about God will look like, and so how to judge any proposals that might come.

Tertullian also moved the problem from Christology to Trinity. The question is no longer how the Logos relates to God, but how Son and Spirit relate to the Father. Irenaeus had already made this move in the economy, but Tertullian shifts it to thinking about the eternal life of God; it is striking how little interest there is in the Holy Spirit in the Hippolytan corpus. Arguably, the key reason for this is his interest in Montanism, or 'the New Prophecy', a charismatic movement led by the female prophets Prisca and Maximilla, who were helped and supported by Montanus.[48] The three uttered prophecies claiming to come from God himself, and so to be as authoritative as Scripture; the message was the first of many historical instances of a classically apocalyptic Christian spirituality: the return of Christ and the end of all things was near; the poor and humble were receiving the word of God to encourage them to remain faithful; faithfulness demanded rigorous asceticism and uncompromising holiness.

In their native Asia the new prophets were excommunicated – although they gained extensive popular support. In the West, their influence was even more considerable. Tertullian is by some distance the most famous convert, but his sympathy is only representative of the wide hearing the New Prophecy gained in Africa. He suggests that the bishop of Rome was on the point of sending supportive letters to Asia before 'Praxeas' intervened;[49] there is reason to suppose that this is a somewhat inflated claim, but the movement was clearly popular and influential in the West,[50] and there is reason to believe that Tertullian's commitment to the cause decisively shaped his teaching in *Adversus Praxean*.[51]

Certainly, it was a central Montanist claim that the Holy Spirit still spoke authoritative revelations to the prophets; at one point – indeed, a central point – Tertullian appears to quote a prophecy to defend a doctrine in *Adversus Praxean*,[52] although the doctrine is defensible from Catholic Scripture, without recourse to the revelations of the

---

[48] See Anne Jensen, 'Prisca – Maximilla – Montanus: Who Was the Founder of "Montanism"?' *StPatr* 26 (1993): pp. 147–50 for this evaluation of Montanus's role.

[49] *Prax.* 1.

[50] Barnes, *Tertullian*, pp. 130–42 is still a helpful introduction to Montanism.

[51] See, e.g., Andrew McGowan, 'Tertullian and the "Heretical" Origins of the "Orthodox" Trinity', *JECS* 14 (2006), pp. 437–57.

[52] So McGowan, p. 445, citing *Prax.* 8.

New Prophecy. There seems little doubt, however, that it was a Montanist fascination with the work of the Spirit that led Tertullian to repeatedly stress the Trinitarian question, when theological debate to this point had generally considered only Father and Son.

Often histories of dogma have glossed over this point, suggesting that – in the fourth century as much as in the third – the real issue is a multiplicity of whatever sort in the divine being.[53] If God can be named as Father and Son, then there is no real problem in naming God as Father, Son, and Spirit, or so the argument has gone. There is some truth in this: multiplicity must be established before Trinity can be confessed, and it is much easier to work this out with the Father and the Son, given the nature of the biblical testimony. This, however, ignores the linked questions of justification and limit. As we have seen, albeit briefly, there was a Gnostic tradition of seemingly endlessly multiplying the entities in the divine fullness. If it is easy to confess three divine persons after confessing two, it is also easy to confess four after three, or twelve after eleven, or thirty after twenty-nine.

Of course, there was no appetite in Catholic faith for such endless multiplication; in practice, the question of limit was answered by justification. The Son had to be confessed as divine alongside the Father because Scripture and doxology demanded this; no other would be recognized as sharing the same rank without similarly adequate justification. There is good reason to believe that Tertullian's commitment to the New Prophecy focused his mind, and then the mind of the church as it borrowed its vocabulary from his *Adverus Praxean*, on the personhood and deity of the Holy Spirit.[54] Of course, triadic doxologies, a triadic baptismal formula, and a triadic rule of faith were all already in existence. The faith and worship of the church implicitly ranked the Spirit alongside the Father and the Son. But in exegetical and philosophical debate this point was never to the fore until Tertullian. It is a stretch, but perhaps not too much of one, to assert that the female prophets Prisca and Maximilla forced the church to adopt a Trinitarian confession.

---

[53] Pelikan makes this point helpfully in precisely this connection. Jaroslav Pelikan, 'Montanism and Its Trinitarian Significance', *CH* 25 (1956): pp. 99–109; see pp. 99–100.

[54] See McGowan and Pelikan, *arts cit.*

Origen of Alexandria

Origen's biography is better known than most of his predecessors or contemporaries, not least because the great ecclesiastical historian Eusebius of Caesarea had an enormous respect for Origen, was curator of his library, and had access to people who had known the earlier writer directly.[55] Origen was probably born AD 185–6, and died 254–5. Until either 231 or 233 he lived in his native Alexandria, where he saw his father martyred, learnt from the great philosophers of the day, and taught in the famous catechetical school; he latterly settled in Caesarea in Palestine, and continued teaching there. He is without question the greatest theologian of the pre-Nicene period, his voluminous corpus including such works as: the *Hexapla*, a major early experiment in Old Testament textual criticism; an astonishing amount of biblical commentary; controversial works; and theological treatises. Much is now lost, but what remains demonstrates one of the great minds of antiquity.

Biblical commentary was, without question, the heart of Origen's work; his great themes concern mystical experience, ascesis, and the living of the Christian life; his narrowly theological work is mostly controversial, aimed at combatting Gnostics and Marcion – and at defending the Christian faith from Celsus, arguably its last great pagan critic of antiquity. The one major text that does set out to offer constructive theological explorations is the famous treatise *De principiis*, or *On First Principles*.[56] Origen begins with the rule of faith, stressing his conformity to the apostolic tradition; there are, however, gaps in the rule of faith – nothing of vital importance is omitted, but some things are not discussed, and others are stated without explanation. Those who are intellectually able and zealous for an increase in their spiritual knowledge, then, might profitably explore both the gaps and the logical bases of the truths taught in the rule of faith. This, for Origen, is the work of dogmatic theology.

---

[55] See Eusebius, *Hist. eccl.* 6. We also have a celebratory speech delivered by St Gregory Thaumaturgus as he left Origen's school, and substantial fragments of Pamphilus's *Apology for Origen*. The accuracy of some of these sources has been extensively criticized by Pierre Nautin, *Origène, sa vie et son oeuvre* (Paris: Beauchesne, 1977); Nautin's criticisms have not generally found acceptance, however.

[56] See n. 9 in ch. 2 above for some discussion of the incomplete text that has come down to us, and a reference to the volumes of *SC* that together comprise the best critical edition.

Origen is very concerned to establish certain basic truths about God, truths which are not alien to the Christian, or earlier Jewish, tradition, but which are certainly coloured by his interest in, and interaction with, middle Platonic philosophy. So God is best defined as an absolutely simple intellectual nature. For Origen, only the Trinity is truly incorporeal; rational creatures (including angelic beings) are incorporeal as souls, but are always united to a body of some sort. As an intellectual nature, God is necessarily invisible, immutable, impassible, eternal, and omnipresent (at least in the sense that an intellectual nature cannot be confined to any defined place). It should be said, however, not only that these philosophical definitions are common to the earlier Christian tradition, but that, for Origen, they are established and controlled by exegesis. As for so many in the Christian tradition, God's ontological primacy and simplicity is established for Origen not by rational speculations about the necessary nature of the divine, but by a reading of Exodus 3:13–14; when it comes to impassibility, Origen will argue strongly in a famous homily on Ezekiel (*Hom. Eget.* 6.6) that the Father institutes the plan of redemption because he feels the passion of love, weeps over sinners, and rejoices in the salvation of human beings. The Bible, summed up in the rule of faith, is decisive for Origen's theology.[57]

The rule of faith is triadic, of course, and so the theological question of the Trinity is not whether to worship Father, Son, and Holy Spirit, but how to understand the triune life of God. Origen is familiar with monarchian concerns (perhaps because he had been in Rome as a young man while the debates were raging); he at one point acknowledges the offence of saying 'two Gods', and so the necessity of exploring the differing ways in which Father and Son are one and two.[58] In *De principiis*, and elsewhere (particularly in the *Commentary on John*),[59] Origen approaches this question through the Son's origin in the Father. He draws upon the, by now classic, images of Wisdom, Reason, Word, and makes the standard argument that the Father is

---

[57] R.P.C. Hanson, *Origen's Doctrine of Tradition* (London: SPCK, 1954) is still valuable in tracing Origen's strong commitment to biblical exegesis as the foundation of faith, and his relative distrust of appeals to tradition.

[58] *Dial.* 2.

[59] Again, the best edition is in SC: Origène, *Commentaire sur S. Jean: Text critique*, SC 120 bis; 157; 222; 290; et 385 (avant-propos, traduction et notes par Cécile Blanc; Paris, Les Éditions du Cerf, 1964–96). There is a modern English translation, by Ronald Heine, in the CUA Press series *Fathers of the Church* (vols 80 and 89); translations here are my own, however, unless noted.

never without his Wisdom, and so the Son is eternal alongside the Father. 'There was not [a time] when he was not,' claims Origen, at least three times.[60] To this he adds an argument from divine immutability: God does not change, and so the Father could not become the Father by begetting the Son; the Father must eternally be Father, and so the Son must eternally be.

Origen's images of the generation of the Son are dynamic, rather than static: this is something that is always happening (if such language has any purchase on eternity). The Father's unending contemplation of his own infinite depths is constantly productive of his infinite idea, which is the Logos;[61] God does not exist for a moment 'without begetting this Wisdom'.[62] Origen is concerned that language of 'Word' or 'Wisdom' might not adequately express the substantiality of the Logos, which must be asserted.[63] (Origen cites several times the opening of Psalm 44, 'My heart overflows with a good word', at one point [*Comm. Jo* 1.280–83] commenting that the verse is endlessly cited, but in demand of careful explanation.) That said, Origen sees the core Trinitarian problem acutely: an adequate assertion of the substantiality of the Logos seems inevitably to lead to an account in which the Logos is sufficiently separate from the Father that he must be understood either as a second God or as less than divine.[64] How is this to be negotiated?

Origen focuses in on the relationship implied in the language of 'Father' and 'Son', which implies both distinction and inseparability. The Father cannot be Father without a Son; nor can he be Father if the Son is merely an aspect of his own being.[65] Such language, however, implies bodily existence and a relationship mediated in materialistic terms. This has to be wrong. (Origen is extremely concerned, no doubt in part due to his study with the Platonic philosophers, to insist on the utter spirituality of God).[66] He transparently struggles to find the right language to speak of this relationship in ontological terms: he finds many inadequate expressions, but nothing that he can settle on as adequate. Gnostic language of emanation or coming out, which

---

[60] *Princ.* 1.2.9 and 4.4.1; *Comm. Rom.* 1.5.

[61] *Comm. Jo.* 2.18.

[62] *Princ.* 1.2.3, trans. from Peter Widdicombe, *The Fatherhood of God from Origen to Athanasius* (Oxford: Clarendon, 1994), p. 69.

[63] *Comm. Jo.* 1.125 and 1.151.

[64] See *Comm. Jo.* 1.151 and 2.16 for statements of this problem.

[65] See *Comm. Jo.* 10.246 for an argument to this effect.

[66] See, e.g., *Princ.* 1.1.

Origen knew especially through Valentinian texts, is inadequate not just because it sounds like a material or bodily event, but because it suggests that the act of generation causes a separation between Father and Son. Classic orthodox images, drawn from the Bible, such as 'light from light' or 'my heart exhales a good Word' fare better – Origen is basically committed to the orthodox inheritance – but require the careful theologian to explain the danger inherent in the image, of assuming a lack of differentiation. The casual hearer, Origen fears, might assume a modalistic interpretation of 'light from light', for instance, as it seemingly carries the implication that there is no distinction of essence. We should realize, however, that the light that the Father is is that 'in [which] there is no darkness at all' (1 John 1:5), whereas the light the Son is is that which 'shines in the darkness' (John 1:5); therefore there is a proper differentiation of essence – they 'are not the same'.[67]

That said, there is no doubt at all that Origen is committed to the unity of the Trinity, and the distinction of Father, Son, and Spirit from every creature. His most regular, and so we may presume most successful in his eyes, image for eternal generation is the Son as the perfect image of the Father. As perfect image, the Son is a second being, but every quality of which he is possessed is identical with that possessed by the Father. The perfect image of the Father's goodness must be identical with the Father's goodness, and so on. This even applies to mental faculties, if God may be spoken of in these terms. So against Celsus Origen insists that the Father and the Son share the same mind, speak with the same voice, and are one 'in the identity of their wills'.[68] In his biblical interpretation Origen will happily and regularly speak of the Father, Son, and Spirit sharing the same *ousia*;[69] this is sufficiently

---

[67] *Comm. Jo* 2.149. There is a degree of confusion over whether Origen will use the key Nicene term *homoousios* for the Son: a text is extant in which he apparently does, but it has been suggested, not implausibly given the state of the textual tradition for so many of Origen's works, that this is in fact a later interpolation by a copyist intent on establishing Origen's orthodoxy. For a strong recent argument that the term is in fact used by Origen, see M.J. Edwards, 'Did Origen Apply the Word homoousios to the Son?' *JTS NS* 49/2 (1998): pp. 658–70.

[68] *Cels.* 8.12.

[69] See I.L.E. Ramelli, 'Origen's Anti-Subordinationism and Its Heritage in the Nicene and Cappadocian Line', *VC* 65 (2011): pp. 21–49, pp. 27–30, for extensive examples of this. Ramelli's arguments that Origen's arguments were extensively and in detail borrowed by Athanasius and Nyssan seem to me convincing; her article, however, ignores the more subordinationist language that is also present in Origen, and perhaps overreaches itself in trying to find the entire fourth-century settlement expressed in terms in Origen's texts.

characteristic to suggest that Rufinus's Latin phrase 'unity of nature and being' is not, as has been argued, an interpolation into Origen's text but a faithful rendition of the (lost) Greek original.[70]

The language of 'light from light' raises perhaps the most interesting aspect of Origen's account, however: his extensive discussions of the names of the Son.[71] According to Crouzel, Origen treats about a hundred different names, fifty of them in the first book of the *Commentary on John*. The starting point might perhaps be apologetic or controversial: the Valentinian genealogies of spiritual beings began by hypostasizing the titles, assuming a one-one correspondence between words and things, and therefore that 'Logos' and 'Wisdom' and 'Son' must be different things. Origen's response is to describe the titles as *epinoiai*, a word which is difficult to translate, but which is of central importance during the fourth-century Trinitarian debates. For Origen, it refers to the difference, but also the connection, between our perception and God's reality. On the one hand, the fact that we give so many different titles to the one divine Son is an artefact of our inability to comprehend the fullness of who he is, and so we grasp at partial, perhaps sometimes metaphorical ('Bloom' or 'Branch' from Isa. 11),[72] descriptions to gesture towards the truth. On the other hand, in the context of God's gracious revelation, our grasping and gesturing is not false; it does not necessarily correspond to reality, in that we distinguish that which is in fact not separated, but it does, or at least can, succeed in communicating truth despite our inability.

The divine Son is Wisdom, Logos, Christ – *et cetera* – in our naming, not in his reality. To understand the fullness of his divine life, we need to distinguish roles and names, but this is a concession to the limits of our language and intellect, not any indication of a division of reality. Origen's Christological construction of this is actually rather strange: for instance, on the basis of Proverbs 8:22, he asserts that Wisdom, one of the *epinoiai* of the Son, is 'the beginning' in which the Logos, another *epinoia*, is found, according to John 1:1; this seeming ontological ordering of the names of the Son is difficult, theologically. Origen uses the *epinoiai* in the same way that the Valentinians had used the hierarchy of beings they believed the names represented, as a way of giving an account of

---

[70] Rufinus's phrase is *naturae ac substantiae unitatem*, found in *Princ.* 1.2.6.

[71] On this see H. Crouzel, 'Le contenu spirituel des dénominations du Christ selon le livre 1 du Commentaire sur Jean d'Origène', in *Origeniana Secunda* (ed. Crouzel and A. Quacquarelli; Rome: Editiona dell'Ateneo, 1980), pp. 131–50.

[72] *Comm. Jo.* 1.147; Origen follows LXX in having ἄνθος, 'bloom', where the Hebrew is better translated as 'bear fruit'.

the mediation between God and the creation. The Father's presence is mediated to the created order through the (to our perception manifold) offices of the Son. Two aspects of this construction are interesting for my story: the acknowledgement and development of a chastened theory of theological language, which recognizes our inability to speak precisely of divine realities; and the subordination of the Son to the Father that apparently results from this mediating role.

On the former point, Origen was hardly the first theologian to notice the difficulty of speaking adequately about divine reality, of course. His intimate acquaintance with philosophical schools that had long pondered the problem, and his commitment to making sense of the given text of Scripture, perhaps combined to give a peculiar urgency and precision to his construction, however. His basic strategy, of acknowledging a disconnect between our ability to name divine reality and that reality itself, and of solving this with an account of the use of *epinoiai* to speak partially but adequately of those realities, would be at the heart of the Cappadocian response to Eunomius, and so of the ecumenical settlement of the doctrine of the Trinity, as I shall discuss in the next chapter.

The second point raises the spectre of Origen's famous subordinationism. In matters of history, fame is no guarantee of truth, of course. I have already said that Origen struggled to find an adequate expression of the relationship of the Son to the Father; this becomes acute when the question of mediation is brought in, as here, in economic relations with the world, the Son clearly obeys and serves the Father. Origen maintains the Platonic hierarchy of being, in which there is an ontological gap between the perfect being of the Father and the partial or limited existence of the creatures; the Son in all his offices bridges this gap, but in so doing is located ontologically below the Father but above the creatures.[73] (The same may be said of the Spirit; tellingly, Origen fairly regularly takes biblical images of the agents of God's rule and applies them to the Son and the Spirit, as for instance the seraphim in Isaiah's temple vision.[74]) Irenaeus had answered the Gnostic accounts of ontological hierarchies by an insistence on God's

---

[73] J.A. Lyons, *The Cosmic Christ in Origen and Teilhard de Chardin: A Comparative Study* (Oxford: OUP, 1982) helpfully summarizes much of the evidence for subordinationism in Origen, and draws a similar conclusion concerning its connection with economic activity. See pp. 111–15; it should be noted, however, that Lyons reads assertions of origin and dependence as implying subordination, which is certainly not logically necessary and probably not intended by Origen. See p. 111.

[74] *Princ.* 1.3.4 and 4.3.14; see also *Hom. Isa.* 1:2.

personal presence in a good creation, but had offered no alternative ontological construction; Origen – not just a greater thinker, but a more instinctively philosophical one – seemingly finds it impossible to speak of God's activity in the creation without lapsing into subordinationist language.

Like Tertullian, Origen was able to name the Trinitarian problem with great exactness. He saw the dangers of various proposed solutions with unmatched clarity, and introduced crucial arguments and interpretative possibilities. He was considerably more explicit in his account of the divine life than either Irenaeus or Tertullian had been willing to be, and (perhaps as a result) left some crucial tensions in his work. Nonetheless, he set the scene for the arguments and discussions which were to follow.

Epilogue: The Logos and the Monarchy

One final dispute demands our notice, the condemnation of Paul of Samosata at the Council of Antioch in AD 268. It seems that the same problem, of reconciling Trinitarian devotion with a theological commitment to divine monarchy, continues to trouble the church. Callistus, Tertullian's 'Praxeas' (if he is indeed not Callistus), and Noetus had heard (we may presume) the language of 'two Gods' emanating from the Logos-theologians, and were (surely rightly) horrified enough to object. For these 'modalistic' Monarchians, the answer was to insist on the complete unity of Father and Son. There is one God, who presents himself to the world sometimes as Father, sometimes as Son. In Paul of Samosata, it seems that a different form of Monarchianism came to the fore, still however based on the crucial intuition that there can only be one being that is the *arche*, or ruler and origin, of all created things. For Callistus and Noetus, stressing the unity of the Godhead, and so the three 'persons' as mere modes of appearance, Trinity is squared with monarchy by collapsing the persons into one. Paul of Samosata apparently asserted the monarchy of the Father by diminishing the status of Son and Spirit and proposed that Jesus of Nazareth was a man who was eventually exalted to fellowship with God.[75]

---

[75] We have only fragmentary records of Paul's own teaching, together with some details of the decisions of the council of disputed authenticity, so any reconstruction must be extremely tentative. See Virginia Burrus, 'Rhetorical Stereotypes in

These approaches are united by a concern for monarchy, which is to say for practical monotheism. One God causes and rules all things. 'Second God' language must be excluded, and so the Logos theology, which tended in this direction, is profoundly dangerous. Speaking of the Logos alongside the Father is unacceptable; either the Logos must be collapsed into the Father, so there is one God unambiguously, or the Logos must be relegated to a subordinate position, so there is one God unambiguously. The solutions are diametrically opposed, but the problem being solved is the same.

Irenaeus, Hippolytus, Tertullian and Origen – and a great cloud of witnesses with them – informed in varying measure by liturgical practice, the rule of faith, their exegesis of the Scriptures, and their understanding of the tradition of the church, assumed that naming the Logos and the Spirit alongside the Father was not incompatible with asserting the monarchy. They clarified terminology, invented crucial lines of argument, and stated the problem with exactness. None of them could be said to have solved it, however. Origen's theology works, until the troubling question of the economy is brought into play. Irenaeus could give an adequate account of the economy, but had nothing to say about God's eternal life. When the debate next flared up, with Arius's complaints about the preaching of Bishop Alexander of Alexandria, two generations of argument would finally lead to an account which allowed the church to understand how it could pray as it always had in fact prayed.

---

the Portrait of Paul of Samosata', *VC* 43 (1989): pp. 215–25, and F.W. Norris, 'Paul of Samosata: *Procurator Ducenarius*', *JTS* NS 35 (1984): pp. 50–70, for some details of the textual and historical problems. Behr, *Way to Nicaea*, pp. 207–35, offers as plausible a reconstruction as we presently have.

4.

'From the *ousia* of the Father': The Fourth-Century Debates 1

The history of the Christian doctrine of the Trinity in the fourth century has been the focus of considerably more study than any other period, and is the one episode in the history of the debate that it is reasonably certain that someone who has completed an undergraduate programme in theology has encountered. It is thus, inevitably, the period that has been most often misunderstood and misrepresented. Thankfully, in the last generation a new wave of, quite excellent, scholarship has offered a much more convincing account of the debates than had previously been available.[1] This chapter draws gratefully on such scholarship to present an historical account which might, but should not, be rather different from that still routinely assumed in contemporary theology.

---

[1] Amongst works that treat the whole of the fourth century, pride of place must now go to Lewis Ayres, *Nicaea and Its Legacy: An Approach to Fourth-Century Trinitarian Theology* (Oxford: OUP, 2004). Ayres offers a complete reconsideration of the period with a constant eye to contemporary theological misrepresentations, which is always informed by close readings of primary texts and of the most recent scholarship, and is in large part simply compelling. R.P.C. Hanson, *The Search for the Christian Doctrine of God* (Edinburgh: T&T Clark, 1988) is also indispensable, as is Manlio Simonetti's *La Crisi Ariana nel IV Secolo* (Rome: Augustinianum, 1975) – the latter particularly for understanding the chronology of the debates and the relationships between the participants. John Behr, *The Nicene Faith (Formation of Christian Theology 2)* (2 vols; Crestwood, NY: SVS Press, 2004) is again excellent: the main body of the work is structured around extended readings of four key orthodox fathers: Athanasius, Basil, Nyssan, and Nazianzen; although the debates they are engaged in are traced in detail, and with sympathy to every side, this perhaps obscures a broader narrative. That said, Behr's single-chapter overview of the entire period (1:61–122) is simply masterful in its clarity and economy. There are also many vital works of more limited scope, which I shall reference as I treat particular figures or debates.

Arius and His Challenge

Two images of protest are iconic in theological history: Luther's nailing of his theses to the church door in Wittenberg, thus beginning the Protestant Reformation, and Arius's insistence that 'there was [a time] when He [the Logos] was not' in response to the preaching of Bishop Alexander in Alexandria, thus beginning the titanic struggle for orthodoxy in the fourth century. Luther probably never nailed anything to a church door, and certainly never intended to start a schism; Arius unquestionably did assert that 'there was when He was not', and this did in fact begin a controversy, but the fourth-century debates rapidly moved on to matters which had little or nothing to do with Arius.[2] The legacy of Origenistic theology, which was by some distance the majority tradition in the Greek-speaking churches, was unstable for reasons already noted in the previous chapter:[3] there was in Origen's own construction both a tendency to emphasize the unity of the Son and Father, and a tendency to emphasize the difference. The stable extreme points of each tendency – so emphasizing unity that all difference is excluded, as Noetus and Tertullian's Praxeas had done; and so emphasizing difference that all true unity is excluded as, at least by reputation, Paul of Samosata had done – had already been decisively rejected; equally, the commitment to monarchy, to belief in only one God, was not questioned. It is fair to say that, by the beginning of the fourth century, many or most theologians leaned to one or the other of Origen's tendencies: but an insistence on the sameness of Father and Son, with a repudiation of modalism, could easily sound as if it violated monarchy in asserting two eternal principles; and an insistence on the difference of Father and Son, locating monarchy solely in the Father, stood in tension with the liturgical tradition of the church. In this context, almost anyone's teaching could be heard by an unsympathetic listener to be questioning crucial doctrines of the faith.

---

[2] Rowan Williams offers an excellent account of the historical constructions of Arius as the heresiarch of the fourth century; *Arius: Heresy and Tradition* (London: SCM, 2nd edn, 2001), pp. 1–25, 247–67. See also Michael Slusser, 'Traditional Views of Late Arianism', in *Arianism after Arius* (ed. M. Barnes and D.H. Williams; Edinburgh: T&T Clark, 1993), pp. 3–30.

[3] Perhaps the most striking witness to this instability is Methodius of Olympus, who in the latter years of the third century directed a number of, sometimes vitriolic, works against (his understanding of) aspects of Origen's belief, whilst working with a broadly Origenist theology himself. See L.G. Patterson, *Methodius of Olympus: Divine Sovereignty, Human Freedom, and Life in Christ* (Washington, DC: CUA Press, 1997).

Arius was only one – of several – to query something he heard; there is no evidence at all that he founded a significant theological school: his major work, the *Thalia*, was probably virtually unknown (except when quoted by Athanasius) beyond Alexandria.[4] Athanasius worked hard from the 340s on to associate later anti-Nicene theologians with Arius, but the polemical purpose of such association is sufficiently obvious that there is no need to postulate an underlying historical influence.[5] Certainly, no later writer in the fourth century shows any desire to be associated with Arius; the evidence suggests rather the opposite, that even those who had no problems with regarding him as orthodox rather wished not to be associated with his name.[6] Why, then, has Arius's name become synonymous with the fourth-century debates?

One answer is certainly the success of Athanasius's polemic; later writers have taken him at his word, and read the fourth-century debate as an argument between followers of Arius and followers of the Council of Nicaea. This only pushes the question back, however: why did Athanasius light upon Arius (rather than, say, Lucian of Antioch, who taught, or at least influenced, Arius and a number of his prominent early supporters, or Secundus, or Theonas, both metropolitan bishops from Libya condemned along with Arius by Nicaea, and longer in exile as a result) as the heresiarch? The answer would seem to be that, in Athanasius's mind, Arius's criticisms of Alexander are the beginnings of the controversy that grows into the Council of Nicaea and the debates that follow. He is the root of the error, and all its branches and flowerings are, in the end, down to him.

What truth there is in this picture is strictly historical: the debate occasioned by Arius's criticisms of his bishop did in fact grow and mushroom to such an extent that it was the crucial issue on the table at Nicaea, and the language of Nicaea eventually became a central

---

[4] So Ayres, *Nicaea*, pp. 56–7; Williams has the text written in Palestine, and circulated to others associated with the memory of Lucian of Antioch (*Arius*, pp. 62–6), but rapidly and completely disappearing from view.

[5] Athanasius may have been completely sincere in his belief that Acacius, Eudoxius, and the rest were in fact re-presenting the theology of Arius, but he can offer no evidence of direct influence.

[6] The famous preface to the confession of Antioch in 341 is a case in point; the bishops note that they are not 'followers of Arius (for how could we as bishops follow a mere presbyter?) . . . being examiners and judges of his faith, we have accepted him [into communion], not followed him'. Athanasius, *Syn.* 22 (my trans.).

reference point for all further argument. Luther was not the first, and perhaps not the most able, to protest at abuses in the penitential system of the Roman Church; but his protest became a lasting mass-movement. Similarly, Arius happened to be the instigator of the argument that exploded. His ideas (unlike Luther's) were neither strikingly novel nor particularly influential, but they were the spark that fanned the flame into life.

(This reconstruction assumes that it is appropriate to see the events of the fourth century as one continuous, and discrete, debate, only concluding with the settlement at Constantinople in 381. This was certainly the understanding of those involved in the arguments – Constantinople quite deliberately reaffirms Nicaea, recognizing itself as offering a further response to the same questions, although it then addresses other ideas that had arisen in the meantime. It is also a picture that appears unquestioned, if also often unanalyzed, by contemporary historians. I will therefore assume it without further comment.)

It seems likely that the reasons Arius's criticisms became the decisive point of debate had as much or more to do with political and ecclesiastical contexts as with any particular theological acuity. The church in Alexandria was suffering a schism (for the then-usual reason of disputes over rigorist or liberal approaches to the readmission of those who had in some way surrendered or apostatized under persecution), and was also riven with political problems;[7] whereas in other dioceses a presbyter accusing his bishop of heresy might have been unthinkable, or at least swiftly dealt with, in Alexandria it seemingly provided a, welcome to some, focal point for opposition to the bishop.[8] Again, it seems that Arius was associated by birth with the province of Libya, and by education with Eusebius of Nicomedia, an influential bishop, and Asterius, an able theologian, both fellow pupils of Lucian. The two metropolitans of Libya were staunch supporters of Arius at Nicaea, and Eusebius and Asterius become crucial opponents of Alexander and his ally Marcellus of

---

[7] Williams, *Arius*, pp. 32–46, treats the context well; see also David Brakke, *Athanasius and the Politics of Asceticism* (Oxford: Clarendon, 1995), although Brakke's attempted rehabilitation of Arius on political grounds is somewhat eccentric.

[8] The lasting political alliance between supporters of Arius, and later opponents of Athanasius, and the local rigorist schismatics, the Melitians, is particularly striking. There is no evidence of any particular theological agreement; they both simply disliked the reigning bishop.

Ancyra[9] in the early years of the ensuing controversy (Arius finding a welcome from Eusebius after his deposition by Alexander). It is not difficult to suppose that existing political and/or theological tensions with Alexander encouraged such high-profile supporters to rally to Arius's cause, rapidly escalating a local case of church discipline into a significant ecclesiastical dispute. The fact, then, that the dispute happened to concern a major faultline in contemporary theology would have encouraged others to become interested, and perhaps involved. Finally, of course, the emperor, who had recently decided that Christianity would be a useful uniting tool for his empire, noticed the debate and became involved, summoning the council. In all of this, it will be noted, Arius's particular theological concerns are entirely incidental.

All that said, to what was Arius objecting, and what did he propose in response? The point of departure seems to have been Alexander's echoing of Origen's teaching on eternal generation: the Father can never be without the Son, or he would not be Father. For Arius, this raised the old spectre of the 'two Gods' language of the early Logos-theologians: if two principles exist eternally, the monarchy is compromised; therefore, one must believe that the Son is begotten in time. Alexander notes, but does not accept, Arius's dilemma: his way through this is to note that eternal existence is not the same thing as being unbegotten; the Son is properly honoured by asserting that his generation is 'without beginning'.[10] Alexander unquestionably emphasized divine transcendence, as Arius also wanted to. The Father is immutable and unchangeable, and creation is separated from him by an immense distance; the Son is the mid-point of this distance.[11] However, the Son is always there, and so for Arius, and for his early supporters, Alexander's formulations imply that there are two eternally existent beings.

There is no question that Arius's theology was profoundly apophatic. God is unknowable, spiritual, simple, and eternal, and in the beginning exists alone. Even the Son does not know the Father.

---

[9] On whom, in this connection, see Alistair H.B. Logan, 'Marcellus of Ancyra and the Councils of 325: Antioch, Ancyra, and Nicaea', *JTS* NS 43 (1992): pp. 428–46; also, for his later involvement, Sara Parvis, *Marcellus of Ancyra and the Lost Years of the Arian Controversy 325–345* (Oxford: OUP, 2006); and, for some theological analysis, Jon M. Robertson, *Christ as Mediator: A Study of the Theologies of Eusebius of Caesarea, Marcellus of Ancyra, and Athanasius of Alexandria* (Oxford: OUP, 2007).

[10] See *Ep. Alex.* 48–52, translated as 'Letter to Alexander of Thessalonica', in William G. Rusch, *The Trinitarian Controversy* (Philadelphia: Fortress, 1980), pp. 33–44.

[11] See *Ep. Alex.* 44–6.

This strong emphasis on the unknowability of God appears to have been distinctively Arius's, and not repeated even by his close supporters in the debate.[12] God wills to bring forth the Son, in time, but 'before all ages', and to pour out upon him all the gifts of the divine glory. The Son is properly, then, called divine (as is the Holy Spirit, who features little in Arius's theology, but the confession that there are three divine *hypostaseis* is clearly there). The monarchy is preserved by locating the Son in time, whereas the Father is eternal, and by the insistence that the Father alone is the unknowable God. That said, Son and Spirit may and should both be named as 'divine', because this is what the Catholic faith demands.

The precise chronology of the events before Nicaea is difficult to reconstruct:[13] Alexander sought to bring his presbyter under control by imposing a confession of faith; Arius refused to sign, and, by choice or compulsion, left Alexandria, travelling around the eastern Mediterranean and gathering support; at some point he returned in open opposition to Alexander. Emperor Constantine wanted the matter settled, and so a great council was summoned, to meet at Nicaea.

Nicaea and Athanasius

Nicaea took Alexander's part in the dispute, at least in the sense that Arius was condemned and exiled. That said, the Creed of Nicaea[14] stops short of affirming eternal generation – presumably because the idea was still too controversial – and instead uses philosophical language of *ousia*[15] to expound the relationship of the Son to the Father. The Son was confessed to be 'from the *ousia* of the Father'; the council lights upon an unusual word, *homoousios* (of the same *ousia*), to describe the relation of Son and Father, a word which appears to have been attractive because it was not owned by any of the competing

---

[12] So Williams, *Arius*, pp. 64–5; Ayres, *Nicaea*, p. 17.

[13] See variously Hanson, *Search*, pp. 134–5; Williams, *Arius*, pp. 48–61; and Simonetti, *La Crisi*, pp. 25–41.

[14] It is important to realize that the Creed of Nicaea (often referred to as 'N') is not the 'Nicene Creed' so often recited in Christian liturgy. The 'Nicene Creed', more properly the Niceano-Constantinopolitan Creed (a term not often used in liturgy for some reason . . .), is the creed which the Council of Chalcedon asserted was agreed by the Council of Constantinople.

[15] *Ousia* is usually translated 'substance' or 'essence' in English. I intend to simply transliterate it, in order to draw attention to changing and contested usages through the fourth century.

parties, but was known to be a term Arius refused to use; finally, in the anathemas attached to the creed, all who assert that the Son is from anything other than the *ousia* or *hypostasis* of the Father are condemned.

Alexander had charged Arius with claiming the Son to be 'from nothing', and Arius had earlier objected to the term *homoousios*, so the creed and anathemas served their key function of excluding Arius. The language chosen was not altogether happy, and certainly not easy to understand, however. *Homoousios* carried unfortunate baggage: it had been used to describe the unity of Gnostic emanations, and condemned in the context of Paul of Samosata's usage at the Council of Antioch in 268. To many, it would have carried an implication of materialism: two things fashioned out of the same material substance; its basic connotation, however, was as diffuse as shared class-membership.[16] Although *homoousios* was to be the decisive term later, there is reason to suppose that, for those present at Nicaea, it was understood as merely clarifying or reasserting 'from the *ousia* of the Father', which was the crucial dogmatic claim.[17] This claim, however, is inchoate: it implies, without actually insisting on, some shared ontology, but gives little content to what that might mean, and retains both the worrying implication of material existence, and the unacceptable potential implication that Father and Son are members of the same class, violating the monarchy.

This lack of theological precision opened the way to continuing disputes. Eusebius of Caesarea accused Eustathius of Antioch of modalism, and succeeded in having him deposed; a wider and more lasting controversy arose between some pupils of Arius's teacher Lucian – notably Asterius, Eusebius of Caesarea, and Eusebius of Nicomedia – and Marcellus of Ancyra. It is striking, however, that in this controversy Arius is never named or defended.

Marcellus had a distinctive theological position of his own,[18] although he had supported Alexander in the pre-Nicene controversies,

---

[16] See Ayres, *Nicaea*, pp. 93–7; the best text on possible meanings of *ousia* remains Christopher Stead, *Divine Substance* (Oxford: OUP, 1977).

[17] So Ayres, *Nicaea*, p. 96, with convincing evidence.

[18] On which see Robertson, *Christ as Mediator*, pp. 97–136 and Parvis, *Marcellus*, pp. 30–37. Undisputed works of Marcellus only survive in fragments, which are collected in Markus Vinzent, hrsg., *Markell von Ankyra: Die Fragmente der Brief an Julius von Rom*, Supplements to *VC* 39 (Leiden: Brill, 1997); Vinzent's account of Marcellus's theology is also helpful. Several other works that survived as presumed parts of the Athanasian corpus have been ascribed to Marcellus, but there is little agreement on these ascriptions.

and was to continue to support Eustathius and Athanasius through the troubled years to come. He used Logos and Wisdom language as the clue to understanding the relation of the Father to the Son. A person is never without their reason, so the Father is never without the Logos. This argument is of course reminiscent of earlier Logos-theologies (although Parvis offers good evidence to suppose that the key earlier influence on Marcellus was Irenaeus),[19] and Marcellus's theology, including its failings, can be understood by analogy with this tradition. It will be recalled that many of the second-century theologians had only a hazy idea of the immanent Trinity, narrating Trinitarian theology largely in terms of the economy. Marcellus wants to claim that much language that his opponents – Eusebius and Asterius – take to be proof of the Son as a second personal existence in eternity should be all read as concerning the incarnation. As Parvis puts it, Marcellus 'accepts, for purposes of argument, the proposition that there are two distinct acting subjects referred to in Scripture, of whom one is created and finite. But if there are, then the second is the Word made Flesh, not the Word qua Word.'[20]

The Father is not without his Word in eternity, but the eternal Word has no separate personal existence; there is an economic 'going forth', an expansion of the eternal undivided monad into an economic triad.[21] In eternity, God is one; one with his Word and his Spirit, but still, one. Marcellus maintains the monarchy by picturing the eternal Son and Spirit as aspects of the Father's being, rather than beings in their own right. Eusebius of Caesarea and Asterius attacked this doctrine for denying the reality of the divine Son. For them, the pre-incarnate Word had to have distinct personal existence. The Son is the image of the Father, begotten of the will of the Father, a separate and lesser being, through whom the transcendent Father could interact with the world. In terms of the Origenist heritage, Marcellus leant very far to the side of emphasizing the unity of Father and Son, whereas his opponents emphasized the difference extremely heavily.

Marcellus lost the argument, and was exiled to the West, where he found the general theological mood more receptive to his concerns.[22] He also encountered Athanasius, who had succeeded Alexander as bishop of Alexandria in 328, but had been deposed and exiled after

---

[19] Parvis, *Marcellus*, pp. 31–4.
[20] Parvis, *Marcellus*, p. 35.
[21] See Ayres, *Nicaea*, pp. 63–6.
[22] I will say more about developments in the West in the next chapter.

complaints that his governance had been violent. Recent historical scholarship has not been kind to Athanasius. Timothy Barnes's description is as
memorable as it is brutal: 'like a modern gangster, he evoked widespread
mistrust, proclaimed total innocence – and usually succeeded in evading
conviction on specific charges.'[23] There is little question that Athanasius
fought dirty in theological dispute; in this, however, he was hardly alone
in the fourth century; in any case, my concern is with his theology, not his
character, and his theological contribution is, without question, enormous.

In his early writings Athanasius, who was Alexander's deacon,
maintained his mentor's account of transcendence,[24] and his account of
eternal generation, whilst at least downplaying Alexander's account of
the Son's mediating ontological status; by the 350s, crucially, he would
refuse to consider any possibility of a mediating ontology. On meeting
Marcellus, they begin to make common cause against those who teach
that the Son is a different *hypostasis* to the Father, although they themselves were divided by a terminological difference that eventually
became crucial: Athanasius, following (however deliberately)[25] Nicaea,
takes his stand on the claim that Father and Son share the same *ousia*,
whereas Marcellus insists on one *hypostasis*. Probably when they met
in the 340s this seemed a trivial point; by the end of the debate it would
not be. It is at this point that Athanasius develops his rhetorical strategy of linking his opponents together as students and defenders of
Arius, who is presented as teaching a novel and heretical theology.[26] In
the *Orations against the Arians*, written around this time, Athanasius
begins by presenting this genealogy, but devotes most of his text to a
refutation of Asterius, whom he clearly perceives as the key theologian
amongst his opponents.[27]

---

[23] T.D. Barnes, *Constantine and Eusebius* (Cambridge, MA: Harvard UP, 1981), p. 230.
It should be noted that in a later work Barnes was rather more sympathetic: T.D.
Barnes, *Athanasius and Constantius: Theology and Politics in the Constantinian Empire*
(Cambridge, MA: Harvard UP, 1993).

[24] Khaled Anatolios, *Athanasius: The Coherence of His Thought* (London: Routledge,
2nd edn, 2005) stresses this theme.

[25] '. . . while many scholars rightly note the one appearance of *homoousios* in the
Orations as evidence of Athanasius' lack of commitment to Nicaea's terminology
at this stage of his career, we need also to note the character of his growing
engagement with Nicaea's creed.' Ayres, *Nicaea*, pp. 114–15.

[26] On this construction, and its imperfect reflection of reality, see David M. Gwynn,
*The Eusebians: The Polemic of Athanasius of Alexandria and the Construction of the
'Arian Controversy'* (Oxford: OUP, 2007).

[27] So Ayres, *Nicaea*, p. 111, although he there suggests that Asterius is first quoted in
1.32, whereas in fact there is a quotation in 1.30.

Asterius had (like Alexander, even) accepted the need for ontological mediation between the perfect and transcendent deity and the
passing and imperfect creation; one of Athanasius's key moves is to
cut through this assumption:[28] the Son is not a middle term between
the Father and the created order; the Son and the Father together
(with the Spirit) are divine and transcendent, and (as Irenaeus had
argued, although I am not aware of any good evidence for direct
dependence) this God is able to interact directly with the world he has
created, the Father acting through the Son and the Spirit. Texts which
speak clearly of a created mediator – Athanasius includes Proverbs
8:22 – are to be understood of the economy, the created human nature
of the incarnate Son (to use more technical language than the fourth
century knew).[29] Athanasius is withering in his mockery of the 'Arian'
position that the Father created only the Son, and that all other things
are created by the Son: first, if one mediator is necessary, why not the
myriads of the old Gnostic schemes?[30] Second, a creature cannot create, at least not *ex nihilo*.[31] Third, it is surely unworthy to suggest that
the Father's creative ability is exhausted with the creation of the Son
only.[32]

How, then, are we to understand the relation of Father to Son, if it
is not Creator to Mediator? Negatively, Athanasius is scathing about
his opponents' use of analogy. The 'Arians' are too ready to take scriptural analogies that compare the divine life to created things, and treat
them as if they are exact demonstrations of the nature of God's being
– or, worse, to treat, crassly, as woodenly literal those aspects which
would tend to support their theology whilst ignoring other aspects
that would lead them into truth. On Father-Son language, for example (Athanasius's own favoured image), he accuses them of taking the
analogy to demand that the Son has an origin in time, whilst ignoring
what it should in fact teach, that the Son's being is of the Father's
being.[33] The favourite 'Arian' question, for instance, concerning the
origin of the Son – was it from nothing, or from something already

---

[28] The oft-quoted judgement that Athanasius moves the debate from cosmology to
soteriology is, I think, best understood as a consequence of this insight concerning God not needing mediation in his dealings with the world.

[29] See, e.g., *C. Ar.* 2.45; this interpretation of the text remains eccentric, and perhaps
was borrowed from Marcellus.

[30] So, e.g., *C. Ar.* 2.29.

[31] *C. Ar.* 2.21.

[32] *C. Ar.* 2.24, e.g.

[33] *C. Ar.* 1.26.

existing? – is met with the charge that even asking the question assumes that God's creative activity is limited in the same way that ours is.[34]

Positively, we can begin to grasp the relationship between Father and Son if we pay attention to the Son's work. Simply put, the Father and the Son do the same thing – as befits two who are one *ousia*. So in the work of creation, it is not that the Father sends the Son to create, but that the Son, who is the Wisdom and Word and Will of the Father, is one with the Father in divine creative action.[35] How, then, are the Father and Son to be distinguished? This is the theme of the third *Oration*, which was probably written a little after the first two, and with the intention of rebutting the charge that Athanasius (and Marcellus) so emphasize the unity of Father and Son that they fall into the error of Sabellius.[36] Athanasius considers John 14:10, 'I am in the Father and the Father is in me', first rejecting Asterius's attempts to evade the plain meaning of the text, then insisting that it implies the identity (*idios*) of Father and Son, and the 'unity of *ousia*'. Father and Son are distinct in the ineffable life of God because they are named twice over: 'the Father is Father and is not also Son, and the Son is Son and not also Father.'[38] (This in direct repudiation of Sabellianism.) That, however, is about as far as Athanasius will go in distinguishing Father and Son in the *Orations*.

The Rise and Splintering of Homoian Theology

The tangled history of the middle of the fourth century, with abortive councils and imperial interference, need not concern us here;[39]

---

[34] *C. Ar.* 1.22–6.

[35] *C. Ar.* 2.31.

[36] For dating see Hanson, *Search*, pp. 418–19; Ayres, *Nicaea*, p. 110, and particularly n. 16 there. The crucial argument for a later dating is Charles Kannengiesser, *Athanase d'Alexandrie évêque et écrivain: Une lecture des traités contre les Ariens* (Paris: Beauchesne, 1983); I am, however, in agreement with the general view that Kannengiesser's case for the pseudonymity of the third Oration is unconvincing. For a counter-proposal, locating all three Orations in 338, but not responding to Kannengiesser's arguments, see E. Moutsoulas, 'Le problème de la date des "Trois Discours" contre les Ariens d'Athanase d'Alexandrie', *StPatr* 16 (1985), pp. 324–41.

[37] *C. Ar.* 3.4.

[38] *C. Ar.* 3.4.

[39] Hanson, *Search*, pp. 181–636 is exhaustive and careful; Ayres, *Nicaea*, pp. 85–186 is equally convincing, and rather more manageable; Behr, *Nicene Faith*, pp. 75–103, is astonishingly concise and informative.

theologically, the most important developments were: the rise of the 'Homoian' theology; the development of the *homoiousian* position; and the appearance of the radical theology of Aetius and Eunomius, the last-named being, far more than Arius, the crucial heresiarch of the fourth century.[40] Homoian theologians were united by their distaste for the Nicene language of *homoousios*; indeed, they rejected any discussion of divine *ousia* at all; finding the term, with its materialistic overtones, inevitably misleading and unhelpful. They would confess that Father and the Son were 'like' each other, a choice of language that would seem to be a political compromise more than a developed theological position.[41] The party was united more by its opposition to the perceived Sabellian tendencies of Marcellus and his school, particularly Photinus of Sirmium, than by any shared theological commitments.

Photinus was repeatedly condemned for denying the deity of Christ, which he almost certainly did not.[42] He has been largely written out of standard histories of the period (even Ayres passes over him quite quickly), but his ideas are being widely condemned right through the fourth century, by imperial edicts, in theological treatises, and even at the Council of Constantinople. There is considerable evidence for the persistent and widespread adoption of his ideas,[43] and pro-Nicene unity was achieved in part by reaffirmations of his condemnation.[44] Unfortunately, none of his works has survived, so it is difficult to reconstruct his teaching with any clarity. He seems to have

---

[40] 'We have full-scale works, or references to full-scale works, *contra Eunomium* by Apollinarius, Basil, Didymus the Blind, Diodore of Tarsus, Gregory of Nyssa, Theodore of Mopsuestia, Theodoret of Cyrus and Sophronius.' R.P. Vaggione, *Eunomius: The Extant Works*, OECT (Oxford: Clarendon, 1987), p. xiii. See also Michel R. Barnes, 'The Fourth Century as Trinitarian Canon', in *Christian Origins: Theology, Rhetoric, and Community* (ed. Lewis Ayres and Gareth Jones; London: Routledge, 1998), pp. 47–67.

[41] 'One of the difficulties with tracing the rise and development of eastern Homoianism is that Homoianism was often as much a series of political alliances designed to secure some semblance of ecclesiastical order as a theological perspective.' Mark Weedman, 'Hilary and the Homoiousians: Using New Categories to Map the Trinitarian Controversy', *CH* 76 (2007): pp. 491–510, quotation from p. 496.

[42] See Parvis, *Marcellus*, p. 248 for both the condemnation and the judgement that it is unfair.

[43] See D.H. Williams, 'Monarchianism and Photinus of Sirmium as the Persistent Heretical Face of the Fourth Century', *HTR* 99 (2006): pp. 187–206, pp. 191–2.

[44] See Martin Tetz, 'Markellianer und Athanasios von Alexandrien: Die markellianische Expositio fidei ad Athanasium des Diakons Eugenios von Ankyra', *ZNW* 64 (1973): pp. 75–121.

taught a form of adoptionistic monarchianism, denying the Son's eternal existence with the Father, but affirming the true deity of the Son from his appearance in the Virgin's womb on.[45]

It seems that Photinus becomes a cipher in the debates of the 340s and 350s for an unacceptable *homoousian* theology, which so stresses the unity of the Godhead as to deny the real and eternal existence of the Son (and Spirit). As such, he can be used as one pole, opposite Arius, of a *via media* style construction of orthodoxy (Williams suggests that Pseudo-Athanasius, Hilary of Poitiers, Phoebadius of Agen, Eusebius of Vercelli, and Ambrose all adopt such a device[46]). He also provided a way of attacking the line, fairly standard in the West in the 340s, that there was only one divine *hypostasis*. The Homoian alliance was an attempt to root out such ideas. It rapidly fractured, with divisions over the extent to which 'likeness' or 'similarity' implied difference and subordination.[47] Aetius and Eunomius developed a trajectory of theology out of the Homoian tradition which so stressed the subordination and difference of the Son to the Father that any sense of likeness was in danger of being obscured. Eunomius and the response to his theology will occupy much of my next chapter.

A second, initially minority, position that developed through the 340s and early 350s was the *homoiousian* party, who would accept the term *homoiousios*, 'of like/similar *ousia*', as an appropriate form of language to speak of Father and Son. The key leader here was Basil of Ancyra. There are many fascinating figures in this period, who proposed interesting and distinctive theologies that were not, however, significant to the overall trajectory of the debate, when it is considered with the benefit of hindsight; equally, we should be very wary of assuming that our later reconstructions of the theological developments reflect the participants' perceptions of what was important.[48]

---

[45] Williams, 'Monarchianism', pp. 193–204 offers a plausible reconstruction.

[46] Williams, 'Monarchianism', p. 188.

[47] On Homoian theology, see Hanson, *Search*, pp. 557–97; Hanns C. Brennecke, *Studien zur Geschichte der Homöer: Der Osten bis zum Ende der homöischen Reichskirche* (Tübingen: JCB Mohr, 1988).

[48] Weedman notes the modern tendency to discount the strong evidence of friendship and even alliance between Hilary of Poitiers and Basil of Ancyra, because in retrospect we place them in different parties in the debate; however, there is evidence to suggest that they were not at that stage constructing the debate in the way we now do, although Hilary was to later. Weedman, 'Hilary and the Homoiousians'.

The prevailing mood, particularly in the East, was initially strongly Homoian, with a broad alliance gathered to resist any use of *ousia*-language (an important confession, which Hilary was to term 'the Blasphemy', coming out of a small gathering of bishops at Sirmium in 357 demanded that the language of *ousia* not be used or preached). In 360, the Homoians won a crucial victory over the homoiousians, leading to many bishops being deposed and replaced. The variety of theologies in the early Homoian alliance is striking, however: some perhaps sought to resist using any language to speak of the eternal life of God; more wanted some moderate form of subordinationism, which protected the monarchy of the Father by excluding the Son from it; at the extreme end of the alliance, a sophisticated radical subordinationism was already being developed by Aetius.

At the same time, there were moves towards a return to the language of Nicaea. The 357 Sirmium confession so alarmed some in the West – including Hilary of Poitiers – that they began writing texts calling for a return to the old confession. Athanasius had already begun his new argumentative strategy of appealing to, defining, and defending the authority of Nicaea in *De decretis* before 357.[49] This text introduces two arguments which will become crucial in the later discussion, concerning simplicity and ontological dualism. On simplicity, Athanasius brings language of the divine essence to the fore of his discussions – so the importance of the *homoousion*. God's essence is of course ineffable and inexpressible; even Arius and Alexander had been united on this point. However, Athanasius thinks that we may know certain things to be true of the divine essence, one being its ontological simplicity. This means that the manifold qualities which we ascribe to God are not parts of his being, but different ways of referring to the one simple, uncompounded essence. If, however, the divine Son is indeed *homoousios*, of the same essence, then the divine Son is simply God, equally identical with all the divine properties. How do we maintain simplicity whilst holding that both Father and Son are divine? Athanasius says little, but seems to rely on an appeal to the ineffability of the divine essence: this is the way it is, on the basis of scriptural testimony; how it can be like this we cannot hope to know.

---

[49] There is little doubt that *De decretis* is Athanasius's earliest work to defend at length the characteristic Nicene language of *homoousios*; it can be dated 350–56, but no more accurate dating is possible. Gwynn, *Eusebians*, pp. 29–33, surveys several possible positions, and confesses his inability to decide between them. On the use of the term in the work, see Lewis Ayres, 'Athanasius' Initial Defence of the term ὁμοούσιος: Rereading the *De decretis*', *JECS* 12 (2004): pp. 337–53.

Athanasius also introduces, or better assumes,[50] a strong ontological dualism. There are two ways of being: eternal, necessary, divine being; and contingent, created, temporal being. Beside this vast gulf fixed, any gradations in created ontology pale into insignificance: the archangel may look vastly superior to the worm from where we stand, but in the light of divine existence they are so close in being as to be indistinguishable. With such an account in play, and the assumed lack of any middle ground (a decisive move beyond the theology of Alexander), Athanasius is able to press the question, 'On which side is the Son?' Of course, his opponents should respond by denying the assumed premise, but the repeated appeal is rhetorically powerful, and becomes a staple of pro-Nicene theology in the 360s.

Conclusion

Basil of Caesarea paints a famous picture of the situation of the churches in his *De Spiritu Sancto*. He asks us to imagine a naval battle, with the fleets fully engaged; a huge storm erupts, and darkness falls. The fight is desperate and utterly confused; no-one can tell friend from foe, let alone who is winning the battle.[51] The picture is intended to describe the state of the churches in 375, when the book was written, but if anything the situation had been even more confused fifteen years before. The Homoian consensus had perhaps seemed able at one point, around 355, to impose its doctrines on the churches, but it was already becoming clear that it had no shared doctrines, only shared enemies. Clarity would begin to emerge, however, with Eunomius, by some distance the best mind amongst the Homoians, and the attempts to refute his theology. This is the subject of my next chapter.

---

[50] 'Athanasius' arguments here rest on some unexpressed assumptions. Most importantly, his assumption of a complete break between the created and the uncreated . . .' Ayres, *Nicaea*, p. 143.

[51] *De Spir.* 76.

5.

'The Godhead is by nature simple': The Fourth-Century Debates 2

Eunomius

I have noted already the instability of the Homoian position, based as it was on a shared rejection of Marcellus and Photinus, and those holding similar theologies, rather than any positive position. The most radical version of Homoian theology was the 'Heterousian'[1] theology of Aetius and Eunomius; it was in their attempts to oppose Eunomius that the Cappadocian Fathers developed most of the arguments that formed the basis of the final Trinitarian settlement. Aetius came to prominence in the late 350s; Eunomius was his secretary at this time, but rapidly became the central figure in the swirling debates. Aetius and Eunomius were united in a strong doctrine of divine simplicity which, however, lacked the element of ineffability so central to Athanasius's constructions.

Hanson pictures Eunomius and Aetius as enamoured of a rationalistic methodology, and therefore completely out of step with other theologians, let alone church members, of their day.[2] It is true that they prized clarity of argument but, as I have argued in connection with accusations of 'rationalism' in theology elsewhere, clarity can never be a defect in theological work.[3] Aetius is fairly described as rational-

---

[1] The term is Ayres's; others use 'neo-Arian' or 'Anomoian'. For reasons to prefer his novel coinage, see Ayres, *Nicaea*, p. 145.

[2] See Hanson, *Search*, pp. 862–3 for a general comment; Eunomius is accused of 'all-prevailing rationalism' on p. 632, and 'rationalist Unitarianism' on p. 636; on p. 611 we read that 'Rationalism is in fact Aetius' outstanding characteristic.'

[3] See my *Listening to the Past: On the Place of Tradition in Theology* (Carlisle: Paternoster, 2002), pp. 73–6.

istic, in the technical sense that he seemingly felt able to derive a complete account of God's existence from first principles;[4] Eunomius had a high view of what might be known of God by human reason, as will become clear later, but his fundamental authorities for theological claims were appeals to Scripture and tradition.[5] Dismissing Eunomius as 'rationalistic' is lazy, and indeed may not even be correct, as Maurice Wiles has argued;[6] we need to explore his arguments to find out why he was judged to be wrong.[7]

According to Eunomius, God, the one whom Jesus addressed as Father, is properly named as 'the Ingenerate' (or 'unbegotten');[8] from this point, Hanson claims, all else flowed.[9] This is God's nature. The Son, however, is essentially generate, or begotten; therefore, the essence of the Son is not the same, or even like (*homoiousios*), that of the Father; the Son is of a different substance to the Father. The One Ingenerate, being immortal, simple and indivisible, cannot establish by will another that is ingenerate,[10] because the one who is so established is by definition generate; nor can the One Ingenerate beget out of his own *ousia*, because that would be to divide that which is necessarily indivisible. Impassibly, God 'begets' the Son, alike in every way as the Scriptures insist, but alike in will and action, not in *ousia*. The Son is therefore begotten of the will of God, not of the essence/*ousia*.[11]

---

[4] See the reconstruction by Lionel Wickham: L.R. Wickham, 'The *Syntagmation* of Aetius the Anomean', *JTS* NS 19 (1968), pp. 532–69.

[5] See Eunomius, *Lib. Apol.* §§2–7. For a critical text and translation, see R.P. Vaggione, *Eunomius*, pp. 34–75.

[6] Maurice Wiles, 'Eunomius: Hair-splitting Dialectician or Defender of the Accessibility of Salvation?' in *The Making of Orthodoxy* (ed. R.D. Williams; Cambridge: CUP, 1989), pp. 157–72. See also Ayres's interesting suggestion that Eunomius is in fact recovering themes from third-century theology: *Nicaea*, pp. 148–9.

[7] As the writers who responded to him recognized. Whilst they were not averse to rhetorical flourishes accusing him of thinking he could reason his way to knowledge of the divine, these stood in the context of detailed engagements with the arguments.

[8] Eunomius, *Lib. Apol.* §7; see also the confession of faith probably by Eunomius himself, in §28. As Vaggione notes, Eunomius does not distinguish conceptually between ἀγένητος and ἀγέννητος, and the MS tradition shows much variation; *Extant Works*, p. 29. For a claim that the confession of §28 is authentic, see Hanson, *Search*, p. 619; Vaggione is less sure, but in no doubt that it represents authentic Eunomian teaching; *Extant Works*, p. 16.

[9] Hanson, *Search*, p. 621.

[10] *Lib. Apol.* §28.

[11] *Lib. Apol.* §§23–4.

How, then, should we describe Eunomius's account of the life of God? The Father, alone ingenerate, chooses to beget another, the Son, who is generate, and so of a different *ousia*, and who does not share the Father's honour or glory, but is nonetheless given glory by the Father and glorified by every creature. The Spirit is brought forth by God through the Son,[12] a third, ranked below the Father and below the Son, but infinitely above every creature. The unity of Father, Son and Spirit is a unity of act: the Son 'resembles his begetter with a most exact likeness . . .'[13] as 'the image and seal of the whole activity and power of the Almighty, the seal of the Father's deeds, words and counsels.'[14] The Spirit 'brings every activity and teaching to completion according to the Son's will.'[15] If we were to sum it up in a slogan: 'unlike in essence, but united in activity'.

Such arguments seem cogent at first sight, which is perhaps why Eunomius was perceived as such a threat, and repudiated with such energy, by pro-Nicene theologians of his day. Indeed, historically it would seem that horror at the implications of the radical theology of Aetius and Eunomius was a significant factor in a hardening of the position of certain *homoiousian* theologians – notably the significant leader Basil of Ancyra – into conscious attempts to oppose subordinationism. This trajectory perhaps provided the context for the early theology of Basil of Caesarea, and certainly provided a relevant background for his attempts to build a pro-Nicene consensus in the 370s. Perhaps the obvious response to such views would be to deny the premises: if the essence of God is not simple, or ingenerate, then Eunomius's conclusions are clearly false. It may have been possible theologically, if not culturally, to deny divine simplicity, but divine ingenerateness is rather more difficult, so the pro-Nicene response turned on different lines. Essentially, the successful response pressed Eunomius on his theory of language.

Eunomius claims that the term 'ingenerate' adequately names, indeed properly defines, the essence of God; early in his *Liber Apologeticus*, he contrasts this with a position that, anachronistically, we may describe as nominalist, contrasting 'honour[ing] God only in name'[16] with 'honour[ing] God . . . in conformity to reality'. God really

---

[12] . . . γενόνενον ὑπὸ τοῦ μόνου θεοῦ διὰ τοῦ μονογενοῦς . . . *Exp. Fid.* 4 (Vaggione, p. 156).

[13] . . . τοῦτον ὅμοιον τῷ γεννήσαντι μόνον κατ ἐξαίρετον ὁμοιότητ κατὰ τὴν ἰδιάζουσαν ἐννοιαν . . . *Exp. Fid.* 3 (Vaggione, p. 154).

[14] Vaggione, p. 155.

[15] Vaggione, p. 157.

[16] *Lib. Apol.* §8.

is ingenerate; and would be so whether a created human mouth had ever breathed the word or not. On this point, the pro-Nicenes would agree with him.[17] However, Eunomius develops his position later in the book: it is not just that human language can adequately refer to the divine essence, but it can exhaustively and definitively refer. Names, properly used, correspond on a one-one mapping to entities; if God is called both 'Ingenerate' and 'Light', then either there are two things, or one of these usages is figurative, and the other precise. Denying, of course, complexity or multiplicity in the divine, and so the possibility that more than one name might adequately refer, Eunomius asserts that the proper name for God is 'the Ingenerate', and that all other names and titles are 'equivalent in force of meaning to' this one.[18]

Jean Daniélou has argued that this theory of language, although finally derived from the *Cratylus*, of course, comes more immediately from a contemporary Neoplatonism that owes much to Iamblichus.[19] Whether this is right or wrong, the results of the theory are startling. Eunomius is, by it, committed not just to the claim that we can know exactly and exhaustively what God's being is, i.e. 'ingenerateness', but that 'God does not know anything more about his own essence than we do . . .'![20] The pro-Nicene theologians, by contrast, are working with

---

[17] So Zachhuber, but the point seems reasonably clear. Johannes Zachhuber, 'Christological Titles – Conceptually Applied?' in *Gregory of Nyssa: Contra Eunomium II: An English Version with Supporting Studies* (ed. L. Karfíková, S. Douglass and J. Zachhuber; Leiden: Brill, 2007), pp. 257–78, p. 258.

[18] *Lib. Apol.* §19.

[19] Jean Daniélou, 'Eunome l'Arien et l'exégèse platonicienne du Cratyle', *Revue D'Études Grecques* 69 (1956): pp. 412–32. See also, more recently, Lenka Karfíková, 'Der Ursprung der Sprache nach Eunomius und Gregor vor dem Hintergrund der Antiken Sprachtheorien', Karfíková, et al., eds, *Gregory of Nyssa*, pp. 279–305, especially pp. 279–85.

[20] So Socrates, *Hist. eccl.* 4.7, claiming to quote Eunomius, although the passage is not in any extant work. The full quotation from Socrates is as follows:

Ὁ Θεὸς περὶ τῆς ἑαυτοῦ οὐσίας οὐδὲν πλέον ἡμῶν ἐπίσταται, οὐδε ἐστιν αὔτῃμᾶλλον μὲν ἐκείνῳ ἧττον δεἡμῖν γινωσκομένη, ἀλλ᾽ ὅπερ ἂν εἰδείημεν ἡμεῖς περὶαὐτῆς, τοῦτο πάντως κἀκεῖνος οἶδεν, ὃ δ᾽ αὖ πάλιν ἐκεῖνος, τοῦτο εὑπήσεις ἀπαραλλάκτως ἐν ἡμῖν.

(Text from SC 505.) Vaggione, *Extant Works*, cites the fragment (from Migne, but the text appears identical) and gives reasons for assuming it to be genuine. See pp. 178–9 for the citation, and pp. 167–70 for some discussion. Hanson, *Search*, also claims the fragment is genuine, on the basis of similarities to other quotations from Eunomius. See pp. 629–30. Ayres regards it as spurious, although the only evidence he offers is the fact that a similar statement was ascribed to Aetius, and a reconstruction of Eunomius's theology that downplays this theme concerning

what we may, again anachronistically, term a strong doctrine of analogy, stressing the ineffability of the divine, and the necessary imprecision in human language in naming God. O'Leary suggests, not without reason, that Gregory of Nyssa and Basil alike err in having too strong a doctrine of analogy: 'the attributes do not name the essence, but represent our human conceptions concerning it';[21] I think that this is perhaps an over-systematization of the evidence, in that it is not clear to me that the two Cappadocians had made precisely that distinction, and decided on which side of it they fell, but the point is basically correct. As we shall see, pro-Nicene theology operated with a strong doctrine of divine incomprehensibility, which made Eunomius's confident syllogisms about the divine essence seem not just the height of blasphemy, but extremely uncertain as logical claims.

Basil of Casarea and Gregory of Nyssa *contra Eunomium*

This account of divine incomprehensibility, and particularly its dogmatic use in Trinitarian debates, was largely the achievement of Basil. In his earliest writings, it seems that he felt the force of Eunomius's strictures. Writing to Apollinaris about the difficulties with *homoousian* language, he comments: 'if anyone should speak of the substance of the Father as intelligible light, eternal, unbegotten, he would also call the substance of the Only-begotten intelligible light, eternal, unbegotten . . .'[22] – Eunomius's point precisely. Two or three years later, however, in his major treatise Contra Eunomium, Basil has developed his theology of the divine names.[23]

---

the divine names. Finding Vaggione's reconstruction of the theology more convincing, I take it that the fragment is genuine. Ayres, *Nicaea*, p. 149.

[21] Joseph S. O'Leary, 'Divine Simplicity and the Plurality of Attributes', in *Gregory of Nyssa* (ed. Karfíková, et al.), pp. 307–37, quotation from p. 316.

[22] Basil, *Ep.* 361, translation from Ayres, *Nicaea*, p. 190; the Greek reads: ὥστε εἰ φῶς ἀίδιον ἀγέννητον καὶ τὴν τοῦ Πατρὸς οὐσίαν τις λέγοι φῶς ϛοητόν ἀίδιον ἀγέννητον καὶ τὴν τοῦ Μονογενοῦς ἐρεῖ. For a survey of doubts concerning the authenticity of this letter, and compelling reasons for rejecting them, see G.L. Prestige, *St Basil the Great and Apollinaris of Laodicea* (London: SPCK, 1956).

[23] The text can be found in Bernard Sesboüé, ed., *Basil de Césarée Contre Eunome*, SC 299 et 305 (Paris: Les Éditions du Cerf, 1982-3); there is no English translation of which I am aware. Milton V. Anastos, 'Basil's Κατα Εὐνομιου, A Critical Analysis', in *Basil of Caesarea: Christian, Humanist, Ascetic: A Sixteen-Hundredth Anniversary Symposium* (2 vols; ed. Paul J. Fedwick; Toronto: PIMS, 1981), 1:67–136 is an extremely useful guide to the text.

The first volume of the *Contra Eunomium* addresses the question of how names are applied to God. Eunomius had contrasted 'expressions based on invention' (*epinoia*) with reality (*Lib. Apol.* 8); Basil seizes on this word and launches into an exposition of how human language refers to God. Jesus calls himself variously the door, the way, the bread, the vine, the shepherd . . . but all these refer to one substance.[24] Just so, different divine names can refer to the same substance, each the product of *epinoia*, understood by Basil as 'ratiocination' rather than 'invention'. We look backwards and see that God is without beginning, so we own him to be uncreated; we look forwards and see that God will never end, and so we confess him as incorruptible.[25]

Basil's argument against Eunomius turns on the impropriety of selecting merely one of the divine names and claiming priority for it;[26] his positive argument concerning the divine names is an insistence, first, that no single divine name is adequate to define God's nature, and, second, that all the divine names refer in a partial but real way to the divine nature. Hence, difference of name does not imply difference of *ousia*. What it does imply, Basil goes on to argue in Book 2, is difference of *idiomata*, or individual characteristics. Peter and Paul share the same *ousia* but have different names, different personal or particular characteristics. So it is with Father and Son.[27]

Ayres has argued that Basil's genius in his response to Eunomius was to treat the problem of the unity and differentiation of the divine persons at the same time as treating the problem of the knowability of the divine essence. 'Basil articulates a distinction between natures and individuated realities that enables him to assert that Father and Son are, indeed, the same in essence, but distinct at another level . . .'[28] Father and Son language, for Basil, is not a description of what God is – the divine essence is necessarily simple and so ineffable – but of *how* God is.[29]

Eunomius's response to Basil in the *Apologia Apologiae* probably appeared after Basil's death;[30] Gregory of Nyssa took up the defence of

---

[24] *C.E.* 1.7; Sesboüé 1:188.
[25] *C.E.* 1.7; Sesboüé 1:192.
[26] See Mark DelCogliano, *Basil of Caesarea's Anti-Eunomian Theology of Names* (Leiden: Brill, 2010) for a full discussion of this aspect of Basil's argument.
[27] See *C.E.* 1.19 (Sesboüé 1:240–42) for the clearest statement of this theme.
[28] Ayres, *Nicaea*, p. 195.
[29] See Ayres, *Nicaea*, pp. 198-202 for some explication and defence of this claim.
[30] The alternative account, offered by Philostorgius (*Hist. eccl.* 8.12; PG 65:565), that Basil was so overcome by the power of Eunomius's refutation that he fell down dead on reading it, may safely be discarded as polemical legend.

his brother's work, and also left other significant works on the Trinity, notably the little book to Ablabius, and Pseudo-Basil's *Epistula* 38, assuming it is by Gregory, which are less focused on the Eunomian controversy, and so provide an interesting counterpoint to the more controversial work. Gregory responded to Eunomius in two main works, the *Contra Eunomium* and the *Refutatio Confessionis Eunomii*.[31] Gregory's response has much rhetorical invective – one gets the sense that he was really annoyed at Eunomius's attack on his brother – and a whole series of interesting arguments. The two of most relevance to my argument are Gregory's repeated rejection of any account of onto-logical gradation – Athanasius's ontological dualism, although any direct dependence on Athanasius is hard to demonstrate – and his engagement on the divine names.

Gregory argues repeatedly that Eunomius's account of three divine beings at differing levels of divinity is incoherent: as Basil had claimed, and as the second-century doctrine of *creatio ex nihilo* had already logically demanded, there are only two possible onto-logical states: divine, eternal, self-originate, necessary being; and created, time-bound, contingent being.[32] Mühlenberg has argued that Gregory's invention of the idea of divine infinity is his key to establishing this absolute binary distinction;[33] as Meredith notes, however, whether Gregory invented divine infinity might be doub-ted; it is, however, clear that he deploys it repeatedly to reject any notion of ontological hierarchy.[34] Meredith further suggests that

---

[31] It is necessary to use Jaeger's edition: *Contra Eunomium Libri*, Gregorii Nysseni Opera 1 and 2 (ed. Wernerus Jaeger; Leiden: E.J. Brill, 1960) to get the works in the intended order. Older editions (and the NPNF translation) have the *Refutatio* as Book 2 of the *C.E.*, and *C.E.* Book 2 as either a separate work or Book 12B of the *C.E.*

[32] Ayres makes this point: 'On Not Three People', pp. 19–20. See also my own 'Triune Creativity: Trinity, Creation, Art, and Science', in *Trinitarian Soundings in Systematic Theology* (ed. Paul Metzger; London: T&T Clark, 2005), pp. 73–85, or Colin Gunton's *The Triune Creator: A Historical and Systematic Study* (Edinburgh: EUP, 1998). For a lapidary statement of the point in the patristic tradition, see Basil of Caesarea, *De Spir.* 20: Τὰ γὰρ σύμπαντα, φησὶ, δοῦλα σά· εἰ δεύπὲρ τὴν κτίσιν ἐστὶ, τῆς βασιλείας ἐστὶ κοινωνόν.

[33] Ekkehard Mühlenberg, *Die Unendlichkeit Gottes bei Gregor von Nyssa: Gregors Kritik am Gottesbegriff der klassischen Metaphysik* (Göttingen: Vandenhöck & Ruprecht, 1966).

[34] Anthony Meredith, 'The Idea of God in Gregory of Nyssa', in *Studien zu Gregor von Nyssa und der Christlichen Spätantike* (ed. H.R. Drobner and Christoph Klock; Leiden: Brill, 1990), pp. 127–47. See especially pp. 133–4 for the point, and refer-ences to Gregory's works.

alongside infinity, Gregory uses eternity and creation to establish this point.[35]

On the divine names, Gregory is scathing about Eunomius's assumption that the divine essence can be adequately named. His arguments on this point are often unsatisfactory, turning regularly on an assumption that the same divine names apply to the Son as to the Father, which is rather the point to be proved, but within it all he is offering a distinctively different account of how God is named from that of Eunomius. In contrast to Eunomius's insistence that we can accurately speak of the divine essence, it will be recalled that Basil had suggested that all our names for God are the result of *epinoia*. In Basil's usage, this term was an acknowledgement of the fact that we have no unmediated perception of the divine, and so that all our language about God derives from reflection on the divine works – Athanasius's theme of divine ineffability. We call God 'immutable' because we see that his works do not change, and so we infer that his essence does not change.

Eunomius apparently chose to interpret Basil's use of *epinoia* as meaning something very like 'imagination',[36] and so castigates him for thinking that we can only know God by invented names, rather than speaking truthfully of him. Gregory's response is to point out that assuming our names for God accurately refer leads to all sorts of logical confusions. Consider the following passage:

> They say that God is declared to be without generation, that the Godhead is by nature simple, and that which is simple admits of no composition. If, then, God Who is declared to be without generation is by His nature without composition, His title of Ungenerate must belong to His very nature, and that nature is identical with ungeneracy. To whom we reply that the terms incomposite and ungenerate are not the same thing, for the former represents the simplicity of the subject, the other its being without origin, and these expressions are not convertible in meaning, though both are predicated of one subject. But from the appellation of Ungenerate we have been taught that He Who is so named is without origin, and from the appellation of simple that He is free from all admixture (or composition), and these terms cannot be substituted for each other.[37]

---

[35] Meredith, 'Idea of God', pp. 133–5.
[36] See, e.g., the lines quoted in Gregory's *C.E.* 2: τὴν μακαριωτάτην τοῦ θεοῦ ζωὴν τοῖς παρὰ τῆς ἐπινοίας ἀγάλλει ὀνόμασι (Jaeger 1:270).
[37] *NPNF* trans., p. 252; for original, see Jaeger 1:233.

Gregory's argument is that 'simplicity' and 'ingeneracy' are different properties, and therefore that if Eunomius argues that God is both simple and ingenerate, and that these terms are held to adequately define God's essence, then Eunomius has already descended into absurdity, since he is postulating two realities in God's confessedly simple essence. This is no more than a particularly elegant version of what became the standard argument against divine simplicity in the twentieth century, that the doctrine makes God's properties identical with each other.

How will Gregory avoid a similar trap, however? He refuses to deny that God is simple. Instead, he insists that the words we use to refer to God do not name God's essence, which is ineffable and beyond any of our language. If God's essence could be named, there would be one name; however, none of the names we have can achieve this. Can they, then, refer with any meaning to God? Gregory's response turns on his refutation of Eunomius's dismissal of *epinoia*. What we can see and know are the divine works, and we reflect on those works to discover names of God. But each name is the result of our reflection on the ways in which we have experienced God's effects, and so stands at several removes from being a straightforward property of God.

What, then, of the hypostatic names, Father, Son and Spirit? These are clearly different, in that they do not refer to the operations of God. Gregory follows the standard Cappadocian line in distinguishing first between universal nature and particular existence. In *Contra Eunomium* Gregory uses the image of three men,[38] of the composition of a work of art,[39] and a slightly curious image concerning the circles around the sun.[40] Importantly, particular existence, with its very particularities, is necessary for the existence of the universal nature.[41] All of which invites the question that Gregory turns to in the much-anthologized short treatise addressed *Ad ablabium*, usually known as *Quod non sint tres dei*, or 'On Not Three Gods'.[42]

---

[38] Jaeger 1:93.

[39] Jaeger 2:74.

[40] Jaeger 2:190.

[41] Jaeger 1:80.

[42] The best text is to be found in Jaeger's edition: *Gregorii Nysseni Opera Dogmatica Minora, Gregorii Nysseni Opera* 3.1; ed. Friderick Mueller; Leiden: E.J. Brill, 1958); the text is on pp. 37–57, and there are useful text-critical notes on pp. xxxi–xliii. Many translations are available; I am following 'An Answer to Ablabius: That We Should Not Think of Saying There Are Three Gods', trans. Cyril C. Richardson, in *Christology of the Later Fathers*, LCC 3 (ed. E.R. Hardy; London: SCM, 1954), pp. 256–67.

Ablabius, a younger bishop, has referred to Gregory anti-Nicene questions that he has found himself unable to answer. It seems that the questions attack the Cappadocian distinction between *ousia* and *hypostasis*: as Gregory expresses it, presumably quoting Ablabius's charge, if we say that Peter, James and John share a common nature – *ousia* – that we call humanity, we cheerfully call them three men. Why not then call Father, Son and Spirit three Gods? The charge is intended as a *reductio*: all agree, including Gregory,[43] that it is absurd to speak of three Gods, so this argument is intended to prove that one should deny the Nicene *homoousion*.

Ayres has demonstrated that the charge originates with a group who accept, broadly, Nicene orthodoxy concerning the deity of the Son, but balk at extending the same recognition to the Holy Spirit.[44] This makes the charge odd: why accept an account of two divine persons as compatible with the divine monarchy, whilst refusing three? To grasp this, we need to remember the context: both pre-Nicaea and in the Homoian tradition, a basically Origenist theology had found ways of combining an insistence on the simplicity and indivisibility of deity with Christological themes by a complex account of degrees of subordinate divinity. As we have seen, the fourth-century battle was fought on several fronts, which included exegetical claims that the Son must be spoken of alongside the Father, and metaphysical claims that any account of intermediaries between God and creation must be done away with.

If, then, the Macedonians (those who, accepting the Nicene claims concerning the deity of the Son, nonetheless refused the same recognition to the Holy Spirit) accepted the exegetical arguments without considering the metaphysical arguments,[45] it is possible to see how the situation indicated faced by Gregory could obtain. Gregory's great need, then, was to defend simultaneously three things: the core conception of

---

[43] '. . . τρεῖς λέγειν θεούς, ὅπερ ἀθέμιτον.'

[44] Lewis Ayres, 'On Not Three People: The Fundamental Themes of Gregory of Nyssa's Trinitarian Theology as Seen in Ablabius: On Not Three Gods', in *Rethinking Gregory of Nyssa* (ed. Sarah Coakley; Oxford: Blackwell, 2003), pp. 15–44. On pp. 18–19, Ayres points to Nyssan's own *Contra Eunomius*, and Gregory of Nazianzus's *Oration* 31, as repeating the same charge and giving evidence for this origin.

[45] Of course, it is possible that someone might accept both the exegetical and metaphysical arguments, but not accept that there is good exegetical reason to believe in the deity of the Spirit. In such a case, however, the argument which Gregory is seeking to answer, the charge that believing in the Spirit's deity leads to tritheism, would not be posed.

deity as one, simple, and undivided; the basic binary metaphysical distinction between Creator and creation which therefore does not admit any degrees of deity; and the exegetical and liturgical imperative to confess that Father, Son and Holy Spirit are each real and distinguishable, and each properly named God.

Gregory offers two main lines of argument as to why his theology does not lead to saying that there are three Gods.[46] The first concerns the nature of 'natures', which, he insists, are in fact indivisible, although we often speak lazily as if they could be divided. The second suggests that unity of operation implies unity of potency, and that unity of potency implies unity of nature; Father, Son and Spirit do one thing, and so their potency, and hence their nature, is one.

Ayres claims that this second argument is the heart of the treatise;[47] whether it is or not, it is the most interesting aspect of it for my purposes. Gregory argues a series of points. The first, and perhaps most interesting, is that we cannot know, or name, the ineffable divine nature. This is an echo, in less polemical language, of the point made repeatedly against Eunomius. Gregory addresses himself to the hardest case: 'Godhead' (Gk, θεότης) is not a proper name for the divine nature, but, like every other name we give to that nature, an account of the divine perfections. θεότης, opines Gregory, probably wrongly, is derived from θέα, 'seeing'. God is the one who sees us; the name is no different from any other divine name, be it 'the just', 'the good', 'the loving', 'omnipotent', or whatever.

Father, Son and Spirit are alike all-seeing, as Gregory demonstrates from Scripture; but an obvious objection presents itself: a lamb chop served to me in a restaurant has been cooked by several cooks and prior to that was farmed by several farmhands; we do not speak of 'one cook' or 'one farmer'. Gregory's response is that the cooks and farmers are engaged in several similar actions directed to the same end, whereas God's actions are one and undivided. Recalling a distinction made by Basil,[48] Gregory argues that all divine actions are single, having their

---

[46] This analysis follows Ayres in broad outline at least.

[47] Contrast G. Christopher Stead, 'Why Not Three Gods?' in *Studien* (ed. Drobner and Klock), pp. 149–63. Stead assumes that the argument about natures is the heart of the piece, completely ignoring, as far as I can see, the argument about action. Bizarrely, though, he concludes with a reflection of his own on a 'unity' derived through shared action ('An actual conversation is a concrete reality, though it is not a thing but a shared action . . .'), although this unity has more to do with Gregory's analogues of cooks or farmers than with his strict argument about God.

[48] *De Spir.* 38.

origin in the Father, proceeding through the Son, and finding completion in the Holy Spirit.

Why, then, do we not speak of three Gods, as Peter, James and John are three men? Because, argues Gregory, the divine nature is indivisible. We know this not because we have any grasp on the divine nature, but because we know the operations of the divine nature, and we know that they are indivisible. Throughout this treatise, Gregory assumes, without naming, the concept of divine simplicity.[49] Gregory's debates with the Macedonians suggest that in this discussion (unlike that with Eunomius), it is precisely his belief in divine simplicity that enables him to defend Trinitarian theology.

What does all this tell us? According to Gregory, and he is representative of the mainstream of pro-Nicene theology on this point, if more sophisticated than most, the deployment of divine simplicity, ingenerateness, and the rest, then, looks something like this: The divine essence is fundamentally beyond our conceptions; all our language and thought, limited as it is by created categories, is inadequate to speak of what God is.[50] Through God's gracious revelation of himself, we have been given names to name God, and actions by which we might perceive God at work. However, our names suffer from the same limitations as our language and thought: they point towards the ineffable; they do not define or grasp it. The core illustration of this is their multiplicity: we know that the simple essence of God cannot be subject to composition, because composition is one of those created realities we can grasp.

Given all this, what can we say of the mystery of divine triunity? We observe that the Son and Spirit are named with the same divine names as the Father, and perform the same divine actions; we therefore discern that Father, Son and Spirit are not three dissimilar, or even similar, essences but one essence – the one, simple, ingenerate, divine essence. The task of theology is to find a grammar that will speak of this adequately, a task completed by the Cappadocian fathers in Greek and St Augustine in Latin, at least in the judgement of the majority witness of the Christian tradition. The question both had to answer, of course, was how to speak of the threeness of God without compromising the prior confession of simplicity.

---

[49] On which see Joseph S. O'Leary, 'Divine Simplicity and the Plurality of Attributes', in *Gregory of Nyssa: Contra Eunomium II: An English Version with Supporting Studies*, Supplements to *VC* 82 (ed. Lenka Larfíkoá, Scot Douglass and Johannes Zachhuber; Leiden: Brill, 2007), pp. 307–37.

[50] The classical illustration, of course, is the refusal to speak of the 'oneness' of the divine essence, as God is beyond number as well as beyond all other things.

What is being sought, however, is emphatically grammar, not logic. It is a coherent way of speaking, not a set of convincing arguments. *Contra* Aetius, we cannot reason our way to knowledge of the divine essence, or even, except in a very limited way, to knowledge of the divine actions: God is ineffable, and his actions are freely chosen, not necessary or inevitable, and so not even potentially discoverable by human argument. We have claims about God made by Scripture and tradition, and so known to be true; the necessary task of theology is not to determine what is true, but to determine how language works so that these claims can all be true without any appearance of contradiction or incoherence.

Eunomius's error was to imagine that language referred in some straightforward way to the ineffable, and therefore that he could construct positive arguments using it. The divine names, for him, were not warnings about the extent of our ignorance, but invitations to construct speculative arguments. The truth, such as it is, in claims that Eunomius was overly rationalistic is here: he claims that the divine names, which are in fact fundamentally trophic, accurately refer, thus the clarity of his thought is spurious; he is pretending to, and arguing from, exact knowledge about things we cannot be exact about. Like the traveller who mistakes her sketch map for a satellite photograph, and so trusts rough approximations as if they are precise details, he errs not in seeking clarity of thought, but in lacking clarity about the nature of the signs he is using.

One methodological result of Eunomius's manner of proceeding is the claim that the names of God refer to the *hypostaseis*, not to the common *ousia* – obviously, in that he denies the existence of any common ousia. Gregory, by contrast, builds a significant part of his argument on the repeated assertion that one and the same divine name indifferently refers to Father, Son and Holy Spirit. Turning to the doctrine of the Trinity, Eunomius and his pro-Nicene opponents both acknowledge the real existence of three *hypostaseis*, and are both prepared to describe all three as divine. The division is over what such description might mean. For Eunomius, 'divine' is a class based essentially on operation; his repetitive slogan is 'alike in operation, unlike in essence'. For Gregory, identity – not likeness – of operation implies identity of essence. Eunomius's Trinity consists of three divine persons, united by commonality of action and intention; Gregory's of one divine being who wills one intention with one will and performs one action with one operation, and who exists three times over.

I have focused at some length on the theology of this debate, because it is the decisive argument for the settlement of Trinitarian orthodoxy. Historically, Basil was politically very active in seeking to create an alliance of pro-Nicene theologians through the 370s, with some degree of success, at least. The multiplicity of positions of the 350s gradually coalesced into a basic division: was the Son to be named alongside the Father, or not? Insisting that this distinction was the basic question to be answered had been Athanasius's strategy as far back as *De decretis*, and perhaps earlier; Basil had similarly pressed the point (see, for example, his comments in defending the deity of the Spirit against the 'Macedonians').[51] It may be that Basil's undoubted political brilliance enabled him to shape the debate into the lines along which he wanted to argue; I suspect, however, that as clarity of thought prevailed, it became clear on every side that this simply was the real issue: was the monarchy the Father's alone, in which case the Son was of an infinitely lower rank, whatever language was used of him, and whatever might be said about his glory vis-à-vis the (other) creatures; or was the monarchy the shared glory of Father and Son (and Holy Spirit), in which case the Son was of the same rank as the Father, and the choice of whether to say *homoousios* or *homoiousios* was of comparably little moment.

The events of the mid-370s are again decisively affected by imperial policy, as the co-emperors Valentinian and Valens died within a couple of years of each other, to be replaced by Gratian in the West (in 375) and Theodosius in the East, whom Gratian elevated to co-imperial status in 379. Exiled bishops, including Gregory of Nyssa, were allowed to return; freedom of worship was allowed to all except Photinians and Eunomians.[52] An extremely important but rather shadowy council was called by Meletius of Antioch, which composed a pro-Nicene confession (or perhaps agreed to one sent to them by Pope Damasus), petitioned the emperor, and sent Gregory of Nazianzus to seek to resurrect pro-Nicene theology in the imperial capital, Constantinople.

---

[51] See the quotation above in n. 32, p. 103.

[52] The order of events is somewhat confused; for a plausible reconstruction, see Timothy Barnes, 'The Collapse of the Homoeans in the East', *StPatr* 29 (1997): pp. 3–16.

Gregory of Nazianzus and the Council of Constantinople

The five 'theological orations' of Gregory of Nazianzus,[53] preached in Constaninople, the imperial capital, in 380, were seemingly intended from the first as a summary statement of the pro-Nicene position. They have been justly celebrated, and I will offer an extended reading here in an attempt to demonstrate what a formal statement of (one version of) pro-Nicene theology looked like just before the Council of Constantinople. The first two deal with theology as a study. It is a fundamentally ascetic discipline, which demands holiness more than cleverness. The impious or uneducated will twist or misunderstand certain words and concepts, and so we should be reticent of introducing them into discourse. Gregory here differentiates 'theology' from 'economy' (*Or.* 27.10): many people can speak well of the salvation won by Christ, of the creation of the world, the Christian virtues, and so on, and this will always be useful for their hearers. We should, however, be hesitant of discussing the eternal divine life.

Gregory's point would seem to be polemical: he is suggesting or implying that the Eunomian majority in Constantinople have been neglecting instruction on the core matters of the gospel to promote their own partisan views. In so doing, they show themselves careless of the people, who need practical instruction in Christian spirituality, not polemic speculations about the eternal life of God. Anyone so careless of the proper charge of a Christian teacher should not be believed when he speaks about matters of theology, since he has already demonstrated that he lacks the necessary virtue and holiness.

The second theological oration begins with a robust, if playful, assertion of God's unknowability. Gregory teases his audience with an account of the ascent of Mt Sinai, with himself in the role of Moses, seemingly promising reports of visions of God, which at the end collapses instead into a confession of the complete ineffability of the divine. We know that God is, but not what God is; the words we reach for most readily are words which express only our ignorance: God is incorporeal, ingenerate, unoriginate, immutable, and immortal: no-one will deny such points, but nor are they particularly interesting. (The anti-Eunomian jibe is clear, if unstated.) Much better to speak in

---

[53] P. Gallay and M. Jourjon, *Grégoire de Nazianze, Discours 27–31*, Discours Théologiques, SC 250 (Paris: Cerf, 1978). The English translation in St Gregory of Nazianzus, *On God and Christ* (trans. Frederick Williams and Lionel Wickham; Crestwood, NY: SVS Press, 2002), pp. 25–148 is easy to read and alive to the nuances of the arguments. I will be quoting this translation below.

positive, not privative, terms. God is incorporeal, but we are not. This is not the reason we cannot know God, nor is it to be mourned: Abraham saw God in the form of three men; Jacob wrestled God in the form of a man; Elijah felt a light breeze; Paul heard a voice. God can, and graciously does, reveal himself to his children through, not despite, our physical senses. On this basis, Gregory turns to a lengthy discussion of the created order, inviting us to marvel at God's power and profundity.

The third theological oration turns to the Son. Gregory begins by staking a claim about the monarchy (*Or.* 29.2). Monarchy is not fundamentally about number, because even a single being can descend into plurality if someone is double-minded. Rather, a perfect equality of nature, harmony of will, and identity of action, establishes monarchy, even if there is a plurality (Gregory adds 'convergence towards their source', a conception I will return to). Of course, such perfect harmony and equality is unknown and unimaginable in created nature, but this is the life of God, numerically distinct but undivided in essence. Gregory also here introduces a curious image which he uses elsewhere, stating that 'a one eternally changes to a two and stops at three'.[54] This is perhaps reminiscent of Plotinus, and foreshadows a strand of speculative Trinitarian theology we shall meet again, which finds a fundamental instability in duality, and sees the Spirit as the necessary completion of the divine life.[55] The Father begets the Son and spirates the Spirit, impassibly, timelessly and incorporeally. The Son is simply the one begotten, and the Spirit the one who emanates. This language is already too material; however, nothing better is available. The act of begetting and spirating is personal and volitional, not some sort of involuntary overflowing.

Gregory then turns to rehearsing the standard pro-Nicene responses to Eunomian challenges. Many of them turn on the notion of eternal generation; in different ways, Gregory addresses objections which assume that an account of causing or begetting must imply a temporal change. Origination does not, however, argues Gregory, imply temporal separation; Son and Spirit are 'from' the Father, but not 'after' him, as 'the sun is not prior to its light' (*Or.* 29.3). Nor does origination imply change; the Father did not become Father; the Father is Father, because the Son is (*Or.* 29.5). The nature of the begotten is identical, necessarily,

---

[54] *Or.* 29.2; for similar arguments, see Ayres, *Nicaea*, pp. 245–6.

[55] Augustine's view of the Spirit as the *vinculum caritas* is perhaps another mainstream expression of this theme.

with the nature of the begetter: to claim that the names 'unbegotten' and 'begotten' must apply to different natures is mere sophistry (*Or.* 29.10). The reverse of the argument also holds: it does not follow that, because the Son is of the same substance as the Father, and the Father is unbegotten, then the Son must be unbegotten too; this would only be true if unbegottenness were the divine substance (*Or.* 29.12). Unbegottenness is what makes the Father the Father, not what makes the Father divine. Finally in this section, Gregory repeats Basil's 'no middle rank' argument: whatever is called God is God 'in the full and proper sense' (*Or.* 29.13).

Gregory then goes on the offensive, refuting positive Eunomian theology. If, in response to this last point, it is maintained that we use words by transference all the time, using 'dog' of both an animal and a fish for instance, he claims that we cannot transfer the divine name without being guilty of blasphemy (*Or.* 29.14); the claim that the Father must be greater than the Son because he is cause of the Son is a confusion of natural and personal property: the Father is the personal cause of the Son, but they share the same nature (*Or.* 29.15). Finally, he addresses the question of the whatness of Father and Son, facing up to the Eunomian claim that 'Father' must either name the nature (in which case the Son is not of the same nature) or an activity (in which case the Son is created, not begotten). Gregory responds that 'Father' designates 'the relationship, the manner of being, which holds good between the Father and the Son' (*Or.* 29.16).

The remaining sections of the Oration deal with exegetical arguments. Gregory starts with the favoured texts of pro-Nicene theology: the Son is God, Word, in the beginning, Lord, King, Almighty. Other texts, of course, seem to support the subordinationist cause: 'the Father is greater than I'; the Son is 'obedient', 'wills nothing of himself', and so on. Gregory's response is to throw a series of other texts into the mix: the Son 'was hungry', 'was tired', 'wept', 'was in agony'. 'Maybe you reproach him for his cross and death,' comments Gregory, waspishly (*Or.* 29.18), and then suggests that the proper procedure with all these texts is to realize that some things in Scripture must be predicated of the Godhead which the Son shares; other things of the incarnate Son who emptied himself and was made man. This exegetical rule will of course become central in the Christological debates of the next century, but Gregory's deployment of it to cut through the subordinationist debates is powerful.

The fourth theological oration continues the same theme, and deploys his new exegetical rule on a series of texts advanced by the

Eunomians. The texts are in general particularly difficult for Gregory because they seem to speak of the Son neither as divine, nor as incarnate, but as an exalted being who is nonetheless ranked lower than the Father. So he begins with Proverbs 8:22, perhaps the most exegeted text in the fourth century: 'the LORD created me at the beginning of his work' (NRSV). It is hard to read this as applying to the incarnation, which happened 'late in time'; nonetheless, this is the approach Gregory takes, applying the creation of verse 22 to the human nature of the incarnate Son, whilst noting that Wisdom also speaks of herself being 'begotten' before all things in verse 25. The text thus teaches (what would come to be called) two natures Christology. This is not his unvarying procedure, however: faced, for example, with texts that seem to speak of an eschatological subordination of Son to Father, he offers a different argument. He lists a series of texts of the form 'he will reign until . . .' and argues that the 'until' does not imply an ending, only the promise of a continuation to that point. Christ's promise, 'I will be with you always, until the end of the age', does not, he suggests, imply that Christ will not be with us in the eschaton, only that he has promised to be with us until that point. This might seem somewhat sophistical, but Gregory offers a plausible defence: the eschatological moment decisively changes the nature of Christ's rule, or of Christ's presence with his people, and so the language of 'until' is appropriate (as a politician might say, 'We will maintain careful watch on the economy until the end of this present crisis', not implying a lack of watchfulness afterwards, but implying a particular quality of carefulness in the meantime).

Gregory deals with many texts that might be cited against pro-Nicene theology, but closes the Oration with some positive theology defending his position in a discussion of the titles of the Son. Of course, God cannot be named, but the most exalted titles we have are 'He who is' and 'God' (*Or*. 30.18). On the basis of (dubious, although perhaps then-convincing) etymology, Gregory argues that 'God', like 'Lord', is a relational term, and so that 'He who is' stands as the best description of God's own life, rather than his economic relation to creation. Many other names of God can be found in the Scriptures, which can be divided into two groups: some which refer to his power ('Almighty'), others which refer to his providence ('God of Abraham'). These names, however, are all shared; the hypostatic names are Father, Son, and Spirit. The Son is named variously as 'only-begotten', 'Word', 'Truth', 'Wisdom', and so on: these allow Gregory to rehearse in compact form some standard points of pro-Nicene theology. These titles apply both to the pre-incarnate Son and to the incarnate Son – he does not cease to be Lord, Word, and Wisdom in his incarnate state. He does, however, have other titles, which apply only to his incarnate state: Son of Man; Lamb of God; High Priest; and so on.

The fifth theological oration turns to the Holy Spirit. Gregory is aware of the Macedonian position, accepting a pro-Nicene account of the Son's nature, but denying it of the Spirit. Gregory begins by asserting that the same things are said of Father, Son, and Spirit: all three are light; all three are eternal; to deny one is to be left with 'incomplete deity' (*Or.* 31:4). His first argument concerns the identity of God's holiness with the Holy Spirit, and of course God cannot ever have been without his holiness (this is presumably deliberate mirror to the Son-as-wisdom argument used regularly by pro-Nicene theologians). He appeals again to the 'no middle rank' principle: 'if he did not exist from the beginning, he has the same rank as I have, though with a slight priority – we are both separated from God by time . . .' (*Or.* 31.4) Gregory then defends the hypostatic existence of the Spirit: he is not merely an activity of the Father, but is active himself, speaking, being grieved, and sanctifying (*Or.* 31.6).

After this, Gregory turns to Trinitarian arguments: is the Spirit ingenerate or begotten? Neither; according to the biblical testimony, he 'proceeds'. Gregory states, curiously, that 'procession is the mean between ingeneracy and generacy', but refuses further definition: '[y]ou explain the ingeneracy of the Father and I will give you a biological account of the Son's begetting and the Spirit's proceeding . . .' (*Or.* 31.8) So, finally, we reach the question of triunity: 'If, it is asserted, we use the word "God" three times, must there not be three Gods?' (*Or.* 31.13) Against the Macedonians, Gregory makes the obvious point that, having once accepted plurality in the Godhead in the person of the Son, it is hardly a stretch to admit the Spirit; however, he accepts the need for explanation. His summary statement is this:

> We have one God, because there is a single Godhead. Though there are three objects of belief, they derive from the single whole and have reference to it . . . They are not sundered in will or divided in power. You cannot find there any of the properties inherent in things divisible . . . the Godhead exists undivided in things divided. It is as if there were a single intermingling of light, which existed in three mutually connected Suns . . . (*Or.* 31.14)

Is this just a 'genus-species' argument? No, says Gregory: in created things, genera are mental constructs ('the universal is only a unity for speculative thought' [*Or.* 31.15]) this is because of our instability and changeableness. In God, 'each of the Trinity is in entire unity as much with himself as with the partnership, by identity of being and power' (*Or.* 31.16). Although he will search for analogies at the end of the oration, offering the standard pictures of source-spring-river and sunbeam-light, he expresses himself dissatisfied with any analogy he has found. God's nature is just not susceptible to created analogy. The Godhead is simple, and exists thrice-over, in *hypostases* distinguished by relations of origin, and not otherwise. This is Cappadocian Trinitarianism.

In 380, Emperor Theodosius issued an edict naming as standards of orthodoxy Pope Damasus, and Peter of Alexandria (Athanasius's successor), and insisting on a Nicene faith. He called a council for the imperial capital, Constantinople, in 381. The evidence seems to suggest that the intention was more to settle the problems in the city than to hold a general council after the manner of Nicaea. The history of the council is rather obscure – even the creed it promulgated is known to us from its re-publication at Chalcedon in 451.[56] Gregory of Nazianzus was made patriarch of Constantinople after the Homoian incumbent, Demophilus, was deposed for refusing the emperor's instruction to accept the Nicene faith; when Meletius died, Gregory assumed the presidency of the council. He was temperamentally unsuited for the role, however, and, when he offered his resignation, it was accepted gladly. He is on record as believing that the council failed to affirm an adequate orthodoxy.[57] The Council of Constantinople was not the end of Trinitarian debate in the East; it did not intend its creed to supplant that of Nicaea as the key standard of orthodoxy, nor did it reunite the warring factions – even those who, theologically, were on the same side (the open hostility shown to Gregory by the Egyptian bishops is a case in point). It deserves its place in history, however, because the Trinitarian question was now settled for the church, if not for individual bishops and believers.

---

[56] There seems good reason to believe that the creed does originate from Constantinople, however. See J.N.D. Kelly, *Early Christian Creeds* (Harlow: Longman, 3rd edn, 1972), pp. 296–331, for a case that has neither been bettered nor answered.

[57] See, variously, *Or.* 42; *Ep.* 130; and the relevant passages in *De vita sua.*

The Later Reception of Trinitarianism in the East: John of Damascus

The debate in the Greek church rapidly shifted to Christological questions (subordinationist theology remained a live problem far longer in the West); by the time of Chalcedon, at least, partisan debates and questions over the breadth of acceptable orthodoxy had been forgotten, and Cappadocian Trinitarianism as mediated by the Council of Constantinople was received as the authentic and single voice of the tradition. Christological debates continued, focusing now on numbering the volitional centres in Christ, now on the propriety of the use of iconography in worship. This last debate was solved, brilliantly, by John of Damascus, who saw with clarity that it was, simply and precisely, a Christological question, in that it turned on the relation of created things to the divine, and on the potential visibility of God – a question the incarnation necessarily answered.[58]

My interest in John is not here, though. His writings, particularly the third volume of his *magnum opus, The Fountainhead of Knowledge,* usually known as *On the Orthodox Faith,* or *De fide orthodoxa,*[59] act as a filter, or perhaps a funnel, through which the received doctrines of the Eastern Fathers are transmitted. John's methodology is in one sense closely akin to that of the *florilegia,* the collections of patristic sayings that circulated widely in Byzantine theology; his account of this or that doctrine is often no more than a catena of judiciously chosen patristic quotations. This is not to decry his ability: he lived in an age that had a horror of originality, and there is little doubt that he had 'a genius for selection',[60] a profound ability to construct a new and beautiful mosaic out of the fragments of earlier writings which he had gathered. In John, then, we find the harvest of Greek theology gathered up and presented to us, with discrimination and intelligence.

Perhaps because of this, John was also an immensely important transmitter of the earlier tradition to the medieval theologians. He is one of Thomas Aquinas's key sources; his eleventh-century Greek *Life* portrays him as one supremely gifted by the Mother of God to write

---

[58] Andrew Louth, *St John Damascene: Tradition and Originality in Byzantine Theology* (Oxford: OUP, 2002) remains the best introduction to John's thought.

[59] There is a fine critical edition of John's works: Bonifatius Kotter, OSB, ed., *Die Schriften des Johannes von Damaskos* (5 vols; Berlin: Walter de Gruyter, 1969–88); the *De fid. orth.* can be found in 2:7–239. As far as I am aware, there is no more recent English translation that the *NPNF.*

[60] Louth, *St John Damascene,* p. 15.

and compose.[61] The harvest of Greek theology was, through John, received by the later tradition – and even when they knew the original texts, John's consolidated presentations of collected highlights were revered. As Louth puts it, 'the theological tradition to which he belonged . . . may be said to have culminated in John, and it is John who represents this tradition in later theology.'[62] In this spirit, I invoke John as one who knows intimately the tradition of Trinitarian thought that has come before, and seeks to present a harmony of it.

How does John present Trinitarian theology? There is in fact a prior question: John's presentation is remarkably close to another text, Pseudo-Cyril's *De Sancta Trinitate*;[63] if, has been often argued, this text predates John, then his work is essentially a large-scale repetition of the earlier work. There is an older tradition of scholarship, still acknowledged, that dates the Cyriline text quite exactly to a few decades before John's time;[64] however, the suggestion has recently been powerfully made that the dependence is the other way around: the Cyriline text borrows from John, not vice versa.[65] The arguments seem to me to be powerful, and I am going to assume the latter position in what follows.

This is important, not because of the content of the teaching (doctrine is doctrine, after all, whatever the dependence), but because it allows us to make assumptions about John's intentionality in his architectonic construction. In *De fide orthodoxa*, John places his positive doctrine of the Trinity in-between two chunks of material asserting and affirming the unknowability of God;[66] if this is not accidental, or an artefact of John's borrowings, it is profoundly suggestive of his basic theological commitments. God is unknown and unknowable; John's account of divine ineffability owes much to the anti-Eunomian works of the Cappadocians and John Chrysostom, and something to the extreme apophaticism of Pseudo-Dionysius.

Can we know anything about the divine? True proof comes from

---

[61] *On the Life*, and a similar text, see Louth, *St John Damascene*, pp. 16–22.
[62] Louth, *St John Damascene*, p. 16.
[63] For the text, see *PG* 77:1120–73.
[64] B. Fraigneau-Julien, 'Un traité anonyme de la Sainte Trinité attribué à s. Cyrille d'Alexandrie', *Recherches de Science Religieuse* 49 (1961): pp. 188–211 and 386–405, with a dating between 657–81 asserted on p. 402; this is followed by, e.g., Daniel F. Stramara, 'Gregory of Nyssa's Terminology for Trinitarian Perichoresis', *VC* 52 (1998): pp. 257–63, p. 258.
[65] See Vassa L. Conticello, 'Pseudo-Cyril's "De SS. Trinitate": A Compilation of Joseph the Philosopher', *OCP* 61 (1995): pp. 117–29.
[66] *De fid. orth.* chs 5 – 8 are placed between chs 1 – 4 and 9 – 14.

the performing of miracles, according to John, but he lacks this charisma, so offers logic instead. In chapter 3, John asserts the 'no middle rank' argument, and then suggests that all created being stands in need of explanation, which is provided only by the existence of God, so the divine must be. The divine names – goodness, power, omniscience, eternity, etc. – demonstrate the unknowability of God, because we can only speak of God's nature partially and severally, and yet God's nature is one, simple, and uncompounded. This point is reaffirmed in chapter 9, where John returns to the question of divine ineffability. Even the word 'God' refers only to an operation, he thinks, following the suggestions of Gregory of Nyssa and Gregory of Nazianzus. On this basis, he turns to the developed teaching of Pseudo-Dionysius, that God's simple essence is never named by our language, which always points to God's activity or perfection or something less than his essence.

Between these assertions of ineffability, John offers a doctrine of the Trinity. Initially, he borrows freely from Gregory of Nyssa's *Great Catechetical Oration*, although emphasizing the oneness of God far more than Gregory did (perhaps a reflection of his context, with the nascent threat of Islam looming): God is never *alogos* – 'irrational' or 'without a word'; the semantic confusion in Greek suggests that rational exteriority demands the possession of a principle of rationality, a *logos*. But God is perfect, and will not eternally be possessed of an unreal *logos*, so the existence of the *logos* must be actual – hypostatic – existence. Following Gregory, John argues that Word demands Breath, and so we should believe in the eternal, consubstantial, existence of God, his Word, and his Spirit.

This argument starts from the oneness of God, and it is reasonable to presuppose that John adopted it in conscious awareness of Islamic positions, given his geographical context. These Trinitarian arguments are at best inchoate, however, and their development in chapter 8 is one of the crucial moves in the *De fide orthodoxa*. Chapter 8 discusses how one might continue to believe in the Trinity in the face of 'strict monotheistic' objections from Jew or Muslim. John asserts that Christians do in fact believe in one God, albeit one God ineffable in nature and purpose. John rehearses traditional Trinitarian arguments concerning the difference between begetting (and procession) and creation. The Son is begotten, not created; the Spirit proceeds, and so is not created. Many traditional analogies are explored, but in the end John acknowledges the inadequacy of all of them. God is one, although existing in three *hypostases*. The summation of this is a rhetorical exordium that, in John's mind (and no serious scholar has disputed this to my knowledge) sums up the received doctrine of the Trinity in the mid-eighth century:

> For there the community and unity are observed in fact, through the co-eternity of the subsistences, and through their having the same essence and energy and will and concord of mind, and then being identical in authority and power and goodness – I do not say similar but identical – and then movement by one impulse. For there is one essence, one goodness, one power, one will, one energy, one authority, one and the same, I repeat, not three resembling each other. But the three subsistences have one and the same movement. For each one of them is related as closely to the other as to itself: that is to say that the Father, the Son, and the Holy Spirit are one in all respects, save those of not being begotten, of birth and of procession.[67]

God is, and is ineffable. God is triune: Father, Son, and Holy Spirit. The church believes, adores, and worships the one simple divine essence, which exists three times over, as Father, Son, and Holy Spirit, inseparably united in life and in action, one in everything save in their relations of origin.

---

[67] John Damascene, *De fid. orth.* ch. 8; the original reads in part: μία ψὰρ οὐσία μία ἀγαθότης μία δύναμις μία θέλησις μία ἐνέργεια μία ἐξουσία μία καὶ ἡ αὐτὴοὐ τρεῖς ὅμοιαι ἀλλήλαις ἀλλὰμία καὶ ἡ αὐτὴκίνησις τῶν τριῶν ὑποστάσεων.

6

'Understood by a few saints and holy persons': The West and Augustine

Introduction: The Latin West in the Fourth Century

It is easy to tell the story of the fourth-century Trinitarian debates as if they were conducted entirely in Greek, and amongst theologians located between the Adriatic Sea and the Eastern Mediterranean seaboard. The reality is, of course, that the debates went wider: Ephrem the Syrian's liturgical texts in Syriac, for instance, made a contribution to the anti-Eunomian cause, and there are many examples of Western writers involving themselves in the disputes. The fact that the West was generally less open to subordinationist theology (notwithstanding the existence of a significant Western Homoian party) became increasingly politically important in various ways from the 357 Council of Sirmium onwards, although Basil of Caesarea seemingly became somewhat exasperated by the West's, specifically the Pope's, apparent inability to understand the subtleties of the theological arguments in play.

That said, considered theologically, the achievement of Cappadocian theology was a Greek achievement solving a Greek argument. The West may have been politically important at times, but it is difficult to point to a theological argument of importance to the ongoing debate that was developed or solved by a Latin theologian. It is perhaps ironic, then, that the greatest single account of the settled theology of the church was written in Latin, but St Augustine of Hippo was a figure of rare genius, who found a native Latin terminology to express the faith defined at Constantinople, and advanced many of the unresolved exegetical arguments. Of course, in the context of contemporary theology, describing Augustine as the greatest interpreter of the Cappadocian theology is sufficiently controversial as to border on the eccentric; for this reason, the majority of this chapter will be taken up with describing Augustine's doctrine, and locating its continuities and discontinuities with the Greek tradition of the previous generation. Before turning to this, however, the earlier Western development will be sketched, and one figure in particular of the fourth century demands attention, as offering the most well-articulated Latin Trinitarian theology prior to Augustine.

Hilary of Poitiers

Hilary's contributions to the Trinitarian debates are concentrated in the late 350s, whilst he was in exile in the East. Given that the last Latin theologians treated in my history were Tertullian and the school around Hippolytus, in the first few decades of the third century, the long silence deserves explanation. The simple fact is that there is little evidence of developments in Latin Trinitarian theology in this period, and what we do have is potentially idiosyncratic. Novatian wrote a treatise *On the Trinity* circa 250, which clearly owes much to Tertullian, but Novatian (like Tertullian) left the church, in his case to found a rigorist movement that refused the readmission to the church of those who had lapsed under persecution. Of course, that he held to a rigorist ethics does not imply that his Trinitarian theology was in any way unusual, but it does potentially place him outside of the mainstream.

Like so many texts prior to the fourth century, Novatian's *On the Trinity* is very clear about the ideas it is attempting to exclude or refute, rather less so about what it is arguing for.[1] Novatian knows the modalistic monarchian tradition of Noetius and Tertullian's Praxeas, and is determined to refute that; he is also aware of an adoptionistic monarchian tradition, which holds that the Father alone is the monarchy, who assumes or adopts the Jewish man Jesus Christ into his own life for soteriological purposes. Novatian's response is primarily to insist on

---

[1] Novatian's *De Trinitate* can be found in CCSL vol. 4; the most recent English translation is that of R.J. Desimone: Novatian, *On the Trinity; the Spectables; Jewish Foods; in Praise of Purity; Letters*, FC 67 (Washington, DC: CUA Press, 1974). For a recent analysis of the text and its context, see G.D. Dunn, 'The Diversity and Unity of God in Novatian's De Trinitate', *ETL* 78 (2002): pp. 385–409. An older, full-length, discussion may be found in R.J. Simone, *The Treatise of Novatian the Presbyter on the Trinity: A Study of the Text and the Doctrine* (Rome: Institutum Patristicum Augustinianum, 1970).

the true deity of the Son;[2] the Trinitarian question, of how then to speak of the relationship of the Father and the Son, is not to the fore in his reasoning. His general argument seems to be that the Son is the visibility of God, the one who is seen in all divine theophanies, and of course in the incarnation. Father and Son are different 'persons';[3] the Son is 'of the Father' (*ex Patre*), and this is sufficient to establish the unity of Father and Son.[4] Novatian holds still to the old idea of the Logos, eternally present within the Father, becoming external in the work of creation.[5]

Lactantius wrote *The Divine Institutes* c.310; the fourth book discusses the Son's generation at some length.[6] The text pre-empts some central fourth-century themes in interesting ways, arguing for the reciprocality of Father-Son language, for instance. Lactantius again teaches a 'becoming external' of the Logos, which is again connected with the work of creation, although he holds the Son, like the Father, to be invisible. Recent scholarship has tended to treat Lactantius as disconnected from the theological tradition – he appears ignorant of other writers on topics that are more generally treated, offering idiosyncratic, if often brilliant, musings of his own. (Lactantius was not a bishop, but a rhetor-turned-civil servant; it is not difficult to imagine that he was simply an outsider to many contemporary conversations.) The fact that he maintains the older theology, then, might simply be witness to his failure to catch up with more recent developments, or it might be witness to the fact that the older theology in fact remained current; in the absence of other evidence, we cannot know.

That said, most recent scholarship on Hilary's earliest work has suggested that, before becoming aware of the Trinitarian controversy raging in the East, he wrote to oppose adoptionism,[7] and that a two-stage generation of the Son is at least implied in his words.[8] This

---

[2] So Dunn, 'Diversity', pp. 394–9.

[3] *De Trin.* 27.3.

[4] *De Trin.* 27.5.

[5] *De Trin.* 31.12–31.

[6] There is an excellent recent edition of the text: Lactantius, *Divinarum institutionum libri septum* (ed. Eberhard Heck et Antonie Wlosok; Monachii et Lisiae: Saur, 2005); Book 4 is in fasc. 3; and also a recent translation: Lactantius, *Divine Institutes* (trans. Anthony Bowen and Peter Garnsey; Liverpool: Liverpool UP, 2003).

[7] See now Mark Weedman, *The Trinitarian Theology of Hilary of Poitiers*, Supplements to *VC* 89 (Leiden: Brill, 2007), pp. 25–43. The anti-adoptionism argument is made throughout this chapter.

[8] See, e.g., the *regula fidei* in In *Matt.* 4.14; '. . . he is God from God, Son from the substance of the Father, existing within the substance of the Father, first made human, next subjected to death . . .'

would suggest, if not demonstrate, that Lactantius is a credible witness, and that anti-modalism was the basic concern of Latin
Trinitarian theology from 200 to 350. There is, further, evidence of a
bishop being deposed for adoptionism by a council in Cologne in 346,
although there is some doubt over the authenticity of the record.[9]
These hints taken together might imply that the live debates in the
West remained those around forms of modalism, right down until the
350s.

In the 350s two Eastern bishops, Valens and Ursacius, travelled
around the West, convening a series of councils (Arles [353]; Milan
[355]; and Béziers [356]). The stated agenda was the upholding of
canon law, with regard to the person of Athanasius: he had been formally condemned, and this condemnation needed repeating, and his
supporters needed to be exposed and deposed themselves.[10] Behind
this lay a Homoian agenda, supported by the emperor, which some
apparently began to suspect, but which became clear after the Council
of Sirmium in 357. This council, a small gathering of like-minded bishops, published a document which has been described as more nearly
a 'position paper' than a formal creed.[11] Whatever the significance, or
lack thereof, of the council, and whatever the deficiencies of the creed,
however, the full force of the Homoian theology was seen here for the
first time. The Son is subordinate to the Father in every way; *ousia* language is to be avoided as misleading and unhelpful – after all, citing
Isaiah 53:8, 'who can declare his generation?'

No doubt the blast against *ousia* language is aimed at the *homoiousians*, particularly Basil of Ancyra, and secondarily at anyone who,
despite the comprehensive condemnation of Athanasius, was hoping
to revive the memory of Nicea. It had the side effect, however, when

---

[9] See Carl Beckwith, 'Photinian Opponents in Hilary of Poitiers' Commentarium in Matthaeum', *JEH* 58 (2007): pp. 611–27; on the council, see pp. 615–6. Beckwith links, convincingly, the deposed bishop, Eufrata, to Photinus, thus locating the event within the larger narrative of the fourth-century Trinitarian debates, even if Hilary was not aware of that context at the time.

[10] So Liberius of Rome was exiled for refusing to endorse the synod of Milan (355); Hilary himself was exiled following Béziers; there is in fact no direct evidence that Athanasius was under discussion at Béziers, but the supposition seems reason-able given what we know of Arles and Milan; equally, it is at best supposition that Hilary's exile was a result of support for Athanasius. See P. Smulders, *Hilary of Poitiers' Preface to His Opus Historicum* (Leiden: Brill, 1995), pp. 126–31.

[11] The term is coined by D.H. Williams, *Ambrose of Milan and the End of the Arian-Nicene Conflicts* (Oxford: Clarendon, 1995), p. 19; it is borrowed by Weedman, *Trinitarian Theology*, p. 49.

translated into Latin, of excluding language of *substantia*, as a way of discussing the relationship of Son and Father, thus excluding Tertullian and with him seemingly the entire Western tradition (including, *inter alia*, Novatian). Unsurprisingly, significant numbers in the West objected, and several responses were offered. Phoebadius of Agen offered a considered response in writing the same year, 357, drawing heavily on the heritage of Tertullian to refute the Homoians; Marius Victorinus provides an eccentrically brilliant response which draws mainly on contemporary Neoplatonic philosophy, and seeks to respond not just to Sirmium, but also to Basil of Ancyra's response to Sirmium. Indeed, Victorinus's *Adversus Arium* 1A, marks the first point at which an extant Western writer is forced to move beyond the heritage of Tertullian and engage more deeply in the debates of the East. Hilary did so far more convincingly, but he seemingly knew Victorinus's work, and drew on some of his exegetical moves.

As noted above, Hilary was exiled in 356. He travelled to the East, learnt Greek, and somewhere gained access to an extensive library of contemporary theological and polemical works. His polemic develops, of course, and the development can be traced through a pair of works in particular, the *Liber adversus Valentem et Ursacium* and the *De fide*.[12] The polemical aspect of his work reaches its fullest flower in his own rapid response to the Blasphemy, *De synodis*.[13] Here, Hilary constructs a polemical genealogy of the various creeds which have been promulgated since Nicaea, locating the Blasphemy as an explicit refusal to accept the crucial points demanded by earlier councils. As Weedman notes, he is also developing a theological vocabulary and toolkit to respond to Homoian theology.[14] The response is not there, yet, but the terms are being defined, the distinctions are being made, and the arguments are being gathered, the whole in conversation with a series of public doctrinal positions in the various councils. The second section of the work is focused entirely on Nicaea, and discusses the relationship between *homoousios* and *homoiousios*; on the one hand encouraging Western bishops to understand that the term *homoousios* names their crucial Trinitarian concerns, and so to accept

---

[12] I will not treat these works in any detail; the interested reader may find a full and convincing account in Weedman, *Trinitarian Theology*, pp. 74–91.

[13] For the time being, we are forced to rely on nineteenth-century editions and translations; the best text is *PL* 10:479–546; the most recent English translation is in *NPNF* 9.

[14] Weedman, *Trinitarian Theology*, p. 92, calls it 'an attempt to establish what theological categories will be necessary to refute Homoian theology.'

Nicaea as their defining document, on the other hand encouraging Eastern *homoiousians* to accept a *rapprochement* with Hilary and others who confess the Son to be *homoousios*, since the term is patient of an orthodox meaning, untainted by the errors of Marcellus and Photinus. In a manner reminiscent of Athanasius, Hilary is re-narrating history, redefining technical language, and reasserting his core theological insights in an attempt to provide a convincing narrative of the ongoing debate that will favour his preferred position.

If his polemic reaches its height in *De synodis*, his theology comes to fullest flower in *De Trinitate* – or rather, in the latest sections of *De Trinitate*.[15] The book is clearly written over several years, and Hilary's thought is developing over that time. Books 1–3 represent an earlier 'old Latin' theology, beginning with an assertion of Trinitarian unity, making much use of traditional 'X from X' arguments, and representing the debate as a need to steer a middle course between the 'Sabellians' (i.e. modalists), who deny any real distinction of persons, and some 'in the present time' who separate the Son from the Father by insisting on a creation in time. Books 4–12, by contrast, are much more concerned with details of the present Eastern debates. The 'middle course' rhetoric is still there, but the 'X from X' arguments are largely dropped (as they could be deployed on all sides of the current debates), and a set of exegetical discussions over currently popular proof texts offered by either side come to a new prominence.[16] His strategy, in simple terms, is repeatedly to compare scripture with scripture. So, in Book 4, accepting the Homoian citation of Deuteronomy 6:4 ('Hear, O Israel, the Lord your God is one'), Hilary's strategy is to press the question of who Moses (he of course assumes Mosaic authorship of the Pentateuch) meant when he said 'the Lord your God'. Hilary cites the famous plural in Genesis 1:26 ('God said, "Let *us* make humanity . . ."'); he also follows Novatian in seeing the

---

[15] There is a choice of editions; I have used G. Pelland, ed., *La Trinité*, SC 462 (Paris: Éditions du Cerf, 1999), but CCSL 62–62a is also a modern edition. The best recent English translation is Stephen McKenna, trans., *The Trinity*, FC 25 (Washington, DC: CUA Press, 1954).

[16] On Hilary's exegesis, see Jean Doignon, *Hilaire de Poitiers: Disciple et témoin de la vérité* (Paris: Études Augustiniennes, 2005), which gives a convincing account of his method, whilst however focusing almost entirely for its examples on his Psalms commentary, written late in his life. Charles Kannengiesser, 'L'exégèse d'Hilaire', in *Hilaire et son Temps* (Paris: Études Augustiniennes, 1969), pp. 127–42 offers a bit more direct engagement with exegesis in *De Trin*. Very specifically, Weedman, *Trinitarian Theology*, pp. 119–35 addresses Hilary's exegetical strategies in *De Trin*.

Son as the one who appears in the theophanies in Genesis. With the theophanies in view, he can focus in on the biblical ambiguity between the 'angel of the Lord' and 'the Lord', noting an ambiguity between apparently separated mediatorial figures, and the divine life itself; as a result he finds that the Lord God who is one, is the triune God who is Father, Son and Spirit. In Book 9, he gathers a whole series of texts and suggests that the Christ-hymn of Philippians 2:6–11 will be a useful guide for interpreting those texts which appear to suggest the subordination of Son to Father. According to the Philippian hymn, the Son who takes the form of a slave does not in so doing lose the divine form; therefore we must always recall that we are discussing 'a person of two natures' (9.14). Given this, he is prepared to claim that the Homoians make the same error with all their favourite texts, taking language that speaks of the Logos in slave form as applying to the Logos in divine form.

A second rupture and new departure occurs at the beginning of Book 7, where Hilary suddenly and unexpectedly announces that, without repudiating everything that has come before, he wants it to be understood that this book is his closest approach to the mystery of faith. In it, he pauses to consider concepts of the divine name, and divine birth, before returning to his exegetical discussions. These conceptual asides represent Hilary's creative appropriation of natively Eastern theology;[17] there is nothing like them in his Western heritage (at least that we know of), and his expression of them is an original development when compared to the Eastern originals. Names, he thinks, can be divided into the merely arbitrary, and those which express the nature of a thing. The biblical names of the divine Son are of the latter sort, because given by the Father and revealed in Scripture. The Son truly is Word, Wisdom, and Power. Equally, when Thomas confesses before Jesus, 'My Lord and my God!' (John 20:28), he is using a proper name, which corresponds to who Jesus is. Thomas knew this because, seeing the risen Son, he understood that Jesus had been doing things that only God could do.[18]

Hilary analyzes the concept of birth in classically pro-Nicene ways. 'Birth' implies transmission of properties and nature; the Son did not come from nothing, or from something foreign to the Father, therefore the Son must share the Father's nature and properties. If

---

[17] See Weedman, *Trinitarian Theology*, pp. 144–56 for an account of the early Greek use of these concepts, and the claim that there is nothing comparable in the West.

[18] For the material in this paragraph, see *De Trin.* 7.10–13.

the Son did not come from nothing, his birth must be eternal. This picture of a birth, further, allows Hilary to give an account of the divine life which avoids both modalism and subordinationism. A birth means there must be two – the begetter and the one begotten; but it also means the two must share the same nature, and so there can be no subordination.[19] These two themes, name and generation, give Hilary his conceptual tools for the exegesis that follows: he will repeatedly argue of this or that act of the Son that it is an act possible only for God, and therefore that the Son must be God. The power required to perform such a divine act is given to the Son by the Father in the generation of the Son, which makes the Son's nature truly divine.

Hilary's final development in *De Trinitate* comes in Book 12. The context is probably a Homoian appropriation of Hilary's theology of names, turning his own arguments against him: the term 'Son' names a generated nature, which therefore necessarily has a beginning. Hilary's response is first to withdraw somewhat from his claim concerning names and natures: Father–Son language is an analogy, and the limits of an analogy must always be respected.[20] He then nuances his argument from Book 7 slightly: instead of a straightforward claim that something born shares the nature of its parent, he focuses in on the negative perfections of God, particularly infinity and eternity. That which is born in eternity is necessarily eternal, and so with infinity. These categories provide him with the material for an extended exegetical treatment of Proverbs 8, which faces up to such language as 'created' and 'the first of his works' and nevertheless maintains a robust account of eternal generation.

Hilary is interesting both as a fairly typical representative of the developing pro-Nicene theology of the mid-fourth century, and as an illustrative figure, albeit a brilliant one, of the ways in which the old concerns of the West began to be transformed by encounter with the Eastern debates. It is difficult to pinpoint much that Hilary contributed to the developing argument in the East – difficult, indeed, to know how much he was known in the East, given that he wrote in Latin. What is perhaps most interesting about Hilary's *De Trinitate*

---

[19] For the points made so far, see *De Trin.* 7.14–16.

[20] There are earlier references to the limits of analogy in *De Trin.*, notably in 6.9; Weedman indicates that there is some reason to suppose these to be later amendments, inserting the doctrine of Book 12 back into the earlier books, however. Weedman, *Trinitarian Theology*, p. 186, citing an unpublished PhD dissertation by Beckwith.

when compared to other works addressing the controversy in the period is the sheer preponderance of exegesis, as opposed to any other sort of material. Hilary's theological concepts and distinctions are introduced quickly in order to allow him to interpret texts of Scripture; if we are in search of a genuine contribution to the debates from him, it is likely to be found in his answering a particularly difficult exegetical problem in a more satisfying way than it had been answered before. The same may be said of his most illustrious successor in the work of developing Latin Trinitarianism, Augustine of Hippo.

Augustine

St Augustine, by any estimation, towers like a colossus over Western theology; his influence may be perceived as positive, baleful, or profoundly ambiguous, but it can never be denied. He defined the Western doctrine of the church in argument with the Donatists (yet another rigorist schismatic group who objected to the forgiveness offered to those who had lapsed during a persecution), and the Western doctrine of salvation in argument with Pelagius and his followers; his *Confessions* defined Western spirituality, in part at least; his sermons were similarly influential on Western hermeneutics and homiletics; his greatest works, however, were the *City of God*, more wide-ranging than any of these, and his massive treatise on *The Trinity*.

At present, the theological reading of Augustine's *De Trinitate* is seriously contested. A text which was received as a classic of Trinitarian theology, virtually without a single dissenting voice has, for half a century or more, been found profoundly wanting by its theological interpreters. At the same time, patristics scholars have criticized these theological readings extensively, suggesting that whatever the dogmatic wrongness of what is being attacked, it is unrecognizable as an interpretation of Augustine. A genealogy of the debate has been proposed, and also criticized. The proposal is that a paradigm for interpreting patristic Trinitarianism was offered by Theodore de Régnon over a century ago; this paradigm suggested that Latin Trinitarianism, supremely represented by Augustine, started with the one God, and asked how he could be triune; by contrast Greek Trinitarianism began with the three hypostases, and asked how they could be one God.[21] The criticism that has come forward so far has not particularly attacked the notion that such a paradigm is in place (which reader of contemporary Trinitarian theology could doubt it?), or that it is inappropriate or unhelpful, but has queried whether blame for it can fairly be laid at de Régnon's door.[22] Bracketing its historical origins, then, for my purposes the reality, and the sharp criticism, of such an interpretative paradigm may be assumed.

Ironically, it seems that the original deployment of the paradigm was an attempt to criticize the Cappadocian theology and laud Augustine as the true crown of the patristic development; its current deployment is almost precisely the opposite: Augustine is held not to have understood the Cappadocian achievement, and to have stumbled through some metaphysical arguments which are, at best, sub-Trinitarian when compared to the glories of the two Gregories.[23] In this reversal, however, the notion that Augustine's theology is simply different from that of the Cappadocians and Constantinople remains unquestioned and determinative. What evidence might there be for this assumption?

It is perhaps best to start with the inherent unlikeliness of the assumption. Clearly, Augustine is not attempting to do anything different than was done at the Council of Constantinople;[24] if his theology is somehow radically different, it is a mistake. We are, that is, being asked to believe that, in attempting to expound a theological tradition, Augustine developed a radically different theology from that tradition and did not realize it. This seems an unlikely error for any well-trained theologian; for someone of Augustine's (unquestioned) knowledge and ability, it seems almost incredible. If any explanation is offered to account for this extraordinarily unlikely state of affairs, it usually turns on a suggestion that Augustine's grasp of Greek was at best partial, and therefore that he did not understand the texts that led to the Constantinopolitan settlement. Against this, we might note: that Augustine's grasp of Greek was actually rather good,

---

[21] The text accused of introducing this paradigm is Theodore de Régnon, *Études de théologie positive sur la Sainte Trinité* (4 vols; Paris: Victor Retaux, 1892–8); for a classic statement of the accusation, see Michel René Barnes, 'Augustine in Contemporary Theology', *TS* 56 (1995): pp. 237–50.

[22] See especially Kristin Hennessy, 'An Answer to de Régnon's Accusers: Why We Should Not Speak of "His" Paradigm', *HTR* 100 (2007): pp. 179–97.

[23] This is endemic in the twentieth-century Trinitarian theology with which I began, as even the most casual reader will be aware. For a striking statement by a serious scholar of a previous generation, however, see Prestige, *God*, pp. 235–7.

[24] *Haec et mea fides est, quando haec est catholica fides. De Trin.* 1.7.

at least by the time he wrote *De Trinitate*;[25] that there are several earlier Latin interpreters of Nicene theology whom he could have read, some of whom we know he stood in close relationship to (e.g. Ambrose of Milan);[26] and that no writer of the day accuses Augustine of misunderstanding Constantinopolitan Trinitarianism. Further, my discussion of Hilary, above, has indicated just how dependent on Eastern categories his developed Trinitarian theology was; and the increasing involvement of Western pro-Nicenes, who built significantly on Hilary's accounts, was politically important in the run-up to Constantinople; therefore, for Augustine to be presenting a theology radically different from that of the Greeks, we are required to postulate a basic methodological rupture that occurred, apparently completely unnoticed by anyone, either in Augustine's work, or in the two decades immediately preceding.[27]

All of this is not disproof of the claim, of course, but it is powerful reason to ask for very clear proofs before we accept it. If there is incontrovertible textual evidence, it must be believed – but is there? The general shape of the arguments is not promising, relying as they do on assertions of different analogical constructions, or on vague accusations of Neoplatonic influence.[28] Nonetheless, it is time to look closely at Augustine's theology of the Trinity[29]

---

[25] Gerald Bonner, *St Augustine of Hippo: Life and Controversies* (Norwich: The Canterbury Press, 1986), pp. 394–5.

[26] On whom, in this regard, see Daniel H. Williams, *Ambrose of Milan and the End of the Arian-Nicene Conflicts* (Oxford: OUP, 1995).

[27] One of the striking features of many of the accounts which postulate a fundamental rupture between Augustine and the Greek tradition is their simple lack of awareness of the hinterland of Latin pro-Nicene theology. One can be left with the odd impression that no-one in the West thought about, let alone wrote about, Trinitarian doctrine between Hilary and Augustine. Ambrose, Optatus, Gregory of Elvira, Jerome, Ambrosiaster, even Pope Damasus, might all never have existed, not to mention some more minor figures. Daniel Williams has demonstrated that catechetical formation in the period typically combined instruction in the basic faith with particular attention to the current theological disputes; given this, it is reasonable to assume that Augustine was well schooled from his conversion in the basic contours of Latin pro-Nicene, and anti-Homoian, theology. See D.H. Williams, 'Constantine and the "Fall" of the Church', in *Christian Origins: Theology, Rhetoric, and Community* (ed. L. Ayres and G. Jones; London: Routledge, 1998), pp. 117–36, pp. 127–30.

[28] There is at least one serious attempt to demonstrate this thesis on the basis of close readings of the texts, Olivier du Roy, *L'Intelligence de la Foi en la Trinité selon Saint Augustin. Genèse de sa Théologie Trinitaire jusqu'en 391* (Paris: Études Augustiniennes, 1966). For a comprehensive consideration of, and response to, du Roy, see Ayres, *Augustine*, pp. 19–41.

[29] The text is available in *CCSL* 50/50A; there are several modern translations – I like Augustine, *The Trinity* (trans. Edmund Hill; New York: New City, 1991), but see

De Trinitate is not, of course, either Augustine's first comment on the doctrine of the Trinity or his last, and to read it outside of the context of his other works is to invite misunderstanding. We might start with a letter, *Epistula* 11, dated to 389, just three years after Augustine's conversion, and written in response to a puzzled request from a friend, Nebridius, who had asked why it is the Son, not the Father or the Spirit, who becomes incarnate. The question itself is revealing: Nebridius assumes (and assumes Augustine assumes) a basic equality of status amongst the persons of the Godhead, and so some sort of Nicene Trinitarianism, however inchoate;[30] the question simply makes no sense within a Homoian theology, or any theology that taught a subordination of Son to Father. Augustine's response is to stress the inseparability of divine operations as a basic principle of faith: 'For according to the Catholic faith, the Trinity is proposed to our belief and believed – and even understood by a few saints and holy persons – as so inseparable that whatever action is performed by it must be thought to be performed at the same time by the Father and by the Son and by the Holy Spirit . . .'[31]

This easy assumption of inseparable operations stands firmly in the Latin pro-Nicene tradition,[32] and repeats a central theme developed by Basil and Gregory of Nyssa.[33] It is also, as he will go on to note in the

---

also FC 45 (trans. Stephen McKenna: Washington, DC: CUA Press, 1963). In terms of secondary literature, it is voluminous, and I will refer to several works in what follows. It is safe to say, however, that Lewis Ayres, *Augustine and the Trinity* (Cambridge: CUP, 2011) is so comprehensive and compelling that it will be the point of departure for English-language scholarship, at least, for years to come. It is not, however, a book that invites the general reader; one needs to know more than a little of the debates before being able to understand Ayres's position and contribution.

[30] I assume that Nebridius was in fact fairly well versed in the Constantinopolitan settlement, but the letter gives no evidence of this, except perhaps Augustine's expressed surprise that his friend had not already allowed for the inseparability of divine operations.

[31] *Ep.* 11.2; trans. from Lewis Ayres, '"Remember That You Are Catholic" (Serm. 52.2): Augustine on the Unity of the Triune God', *JECS* 8 (2000): pp. 39–82, p. 46. Ayres reproduces the Latin in a footnote there.

[32] See, e.g., Hilary, *De Trin.* 7.17–18; Ambrose, *Comm. in Luc.* prol. 5. See also Ayres, *Augustine*, pp. 72–92, for an argument that the *De fide* of 393 represents a conscious turn to an engagement with the Latin anti-modalist tradition, as developed by Hilary, Damasus, and other Latin pro-Nicenes. Prior to this point – including *Ep.* 11 – Ayres has previously argued that Augustine's language and thought has drawn on the pro-Nicene tradition, but his core target has been Manichaeism.

[33] On which, see ch. 5 above; Michel Barnes has argued at length that, for Gregory, that argument from unity of operation to divine unity is central. See M.R. Barnes,

letter, a theme that only makes Nebridius's problem harder, and so its invocation here must be out of concern for a commitment to received orthodoxy. From the beginning, then, Augustine is firmly within a recognizably pro-Nicene tradition that spans East and West.

There is not space here to trace the full development of Augustine's Trinitarianism; a full-orbed treatment would need to range very widely across the corpus. Nor should *De Trinitate* be taken as the crowning summary. After *De Trinitate* was finished, Augustine continued to explore Trinitarian ideas, sometimes in passing in other works, sometimes as exegetical need arose in sermons, sometimes in explicitly controversial mode, as in his debates with Maximinus, a Homoian bishop. In these texts he makes some things explicit which are either implicit or simply undeveloped in the longer work, in particular some further reflections on the inseparability of divine operations, the theme that he was already assuming three years after his conversion, but which lies largely unexplored in *De Trinitate* itself.

Tractate 23 on John's gospel is particularly interesting in this regard; Augustine picks up another text that has been a focus of controversy, John 5:19. The text reads (NRSV, but there is little at stake in translation decisions), 'Jesus said to them, "Very truly, I tell you, the Son can do nothing on his own, but only what he sees the Father doing; for whatever the Father does, the Son does likewise."' Clearly, it offered ammunition to both sides in the debate over the subordination of the Son, the former part of the saying suggesting a subordination, and the latter part implying equality of action between Father and Son. The text was thus very regularly invoked in the later fourth-century debates, with each side emphasizing the part that supported their own position, and seeking to find a reading that would weaken the apparent support for the alternative position.[34]

Augustine's own interpretation aligns the Father's showing (which he takes to be implied in the verse) and the Son's seeing with the eternal relation of origin: 'the Father's showing begets the Son's seeing in the same

---

'The Power of God': Dunamis Theology in Gregory of Nyssa's Trinitarian Theology (Washington, DC: CUA Press, 2000). See also his argument that this point unites various strands of the pro-Nicene tradition in '"One Nature, One Power": Consensus Doctrine in Pro-Nicene Polemic', *StPatr* 29 (1997): pp. 205–23.

[34] Ayres, *Augustine* offers a succinct history of the debate, pp. 233–40; for a more extensive treatment, see Basil Studer, 'Johannes 5, 19f. in der Trinitätslehre der Kirchenväter', in *Imaginer la théologie catholique. Permanence et transformations de la foi en attendant Jésus-Christ* (ed. J. Driscoll; Rome: Centro Studi S. Anselmo, 2000), pp. 515–41.

way as the Father begets the Son.'[35] Given, however, Augustine's constant commitment to simplicity (on which more later), the Father is necessarily identical with his act of showing, and the Son simply identical with his act of seeing. This movement of showing and seeing, then, is identical with the Father's begetting of the Son. Note that there is an order, a *taxis*, here: showing begets seeing, not seeing showing; the Father begets the Son, not vice versa. There is also, however, a reciprocity: the Father's showing requires the Son's seeing just as being the Father requires the being of the Son. In the text from John's gospel, this showing and seeing is referring to divine works; Augustine has thus argued for an inseparability of divine works, but also for a proper ordering of the persons in the inseparable work, both of which are based in the eternal relations of origin within the Trinity. This, of course, was identified as a core theme of Cappadocian Trinitarianism in the previous chapter.

Taken in sum, Augustine's Trinitarian theology is remarkably restrained in its expression. As a result of reflection on the inseparable unity of divine action, he is committed to an account of divine simplicity, which, however, is less interested in numerical oneness (although he would not deny that) than with the more philosophical claim that there is nothing accidental in God. Everything God is, God is fully, eternally, immutably, necessarily, and substantially.[36] Because of this, each divine person is himself the fullness of deity, and the three together are no more than the fullness of deity. Finally, the Father is the dynamic eternal origin of the Son and the Spirit, whose origin is from the Father's essence, and who are therefore eternally co-equal with the Father. The Father, however, is thus (to recall the older language) himself the monarchy. The point of all this reflection is to provide a set of theological definitions and distinctions with which one might more adequately read Scripture.[37]

What, however, of *De Trinitate* itself? Lewis Ayres and Michel Barnes have argued, simply convincingly in my view, and over two decades now, that Augustine's concern in the book is largely polemical, and that at the heart of the polemic is an ongoing engagement with the Homoian tradition.[38] Much of the first half of the book is a

---

[35] *Tract. Ev. Jo.* 23.11, ref. and trans. from Ayres, *Augustine*, p. 244.

[36] Ayres suggests that Augustine found this, perhaps more philosophical, account of simplicity in Ambrose and Marius Victorinus. *Augustine*, p. 211.

[37] This paragraph is essentially a summary of Ayres, *Augustine*, pp. 177–272.

[38] M.R. Barnes, 'Exegesis and Polemic in Augustine's *De Trinitate* I', *AugStud* 30 (1999): pp. 43–59 is an excellent example, showing how the exegetical engagements are shaped by polemical concerns. Ayres offers a helpful summary of the interwoven polemics that he finds in the text in *Augustine*, pp. 171–3.

treatment of a series of biblical texts, arranged thematically, and covering such things as the Old Testament theophanies, the relation of the divine missions to the divine processions, and the relation of Creator to creation. Similarly to Hilary's work, Augustine is in fact engaging deeply in an ongoing argument which is largely exegetical: certain texts seem to support the Homoian position, and Augustine thinks that, with the aid of some theological distinctions, he can offer a more convincing pro-Nicene reading than has previously been offered.[39]

This is already to intrude on one of the most significant questions concerning the book, that of how its – apparently rather strange – arrangement relates to its meaning. These scriptural engagements are found in Books 1–4, with Book 1 taking up Hilary's 'form of God/ form of a slave' distinction to deal with apparently subordinationist texts that refer to the incarnation, Books 2 and 3 considering missions and theophanies, and Book 4 considering the incarnation itself. Books 5–7 switch gear to a discussion of appropriate forms of language to be used when talking about God: substance; essence; person; relation . . . Books 8–10 offer an account of pure human self-knowledge as an image of the Trinity, or at least as a necessary lens through which we might begin to glimpse the ineffable life of God. Books 11–13 are further glosses on this theme, expanding it to consider other areas of theology. Book 14 is a return to the argument of Book 10 in particular, summing up the relationship between self-knowledge and contemplation of the divine. How do these disparate themes relate to each other?

Older readings tended to search for some careful structure in the book that would unify the whole. Perhaps it moved from biblical data, through theological construction, to analogical illustration? Or perhaps there is some elaborate chiastic structure, mirroring each theological point in the first half with a spiritual practice in the second half?[40] The problem with such readings is that they tend to ignore what we know about the construction of ancient books, which were not often built to such well thought-through patterns. I have already noted that Hilary's own *De Trinitate* seemingly grew and changed as new ideas occurred to him; there seems little doubt that Augustine's work developed similarly, over the twenty years or so it was in composition.[41] Segments – Books 8, 9 and 10, for example – have an inner coherence, and

---

[39] On the essentially exegetical nature of Trin. 1–6, see Ayres, *Augustine*, pp. 142–98.

[40] So Edmund Hill, in his introduction to *Augustine, The Trinity* (trans. Hill; ed. John Rotelle; New York: New City Press, 1991).

[41] See Ayres, *Augustine*, pp. 118–20 for some discussion of the dating of various parts, and of the redactional layers.

seemingly are composed together, but the whole lacks any such logic. In modern terms, to risk an inexact analogy that probably emphasizes the negative in an attempt to restore balance, it is perhaps better considered as a collection of papers on the Trinity than a monograph. There is a general coherence of thought – although also potentially some development – but themes are treated in various ways in various parts, without necessarily very much attention to the whole.[42]

The first point of my summary above, the definition of simplicity, is simply assumed in the early sections of *De Trinitate* 5 where, again, Augustine invokes it because it is necessarily orthodox, even though it makes his immediate argument harder. He is addressing an argument to the effect that everything said of God is said of God's substance,[43] which if true, it was argued, means that if God is properly called 'Father' then the Son cannot properly be God. In response, Augustine appeals to the concept of 'relation', which, he argues, in the context of a simple substance is necessarily not accidental. The Father–Son relation, that is, is eternal and necessary to God's being God.

(In this context comes a very famous passage concerning Augustine's inability to understand what the Greeks meant by the *ousia-hypostasis* distinction;[44] this has been taken as evidence that Augustine did not understand the Greek theology, but this is to misread the passage; Augustine understands what the language is being used to do, but believes that it is just not very useful in technical Trinitarian discourse.[45] His reasons for this have to do with some philosophical beliefs about the inevitable failure of any attempt to locate God in a genus. God can never be merely one example of a broader kind of thing [because if he were, the genus of which he was a member would be greater than him, as being God plus other things, and nothing can be greater than God];[46] 'substance' [along with, *inter alia*, 'essence' and 'person'] is the name of a genus, and so Augustine

---

[42] Augustine's declaration that the book was hastily and imperfectly finished fuels this point.

[43] Older scholarship tended to assume that this was a specifically Eunomian argument, but Barnes has argued cogently that Latin Homoians are more likely in view. Michel R. Barnes, 'The Arians of Book V, and the Genre of De trinitate', *JTS* NS 44 (1993): pp. 185–95.

[44] *Trin.* 5.8–9.

[45] So Richard Cross, '*Quid tres?* On What Precisely Augustine Professes Not to Understand in *De Trinitate* V and VII', *HTR* 100 (2007): pp. 215–32. See especially on this passage p. 218.

[46] This argument may not be convincing; in particular, it might seem to rely on an assumption that $\infty+1>\infty$, which, despite its evident plausibility, is a claim disproved

is profoundly doubtful about language which defines God as substance, or as anything else. The Greek response would no doubt to have been to point to their sustained witness to the fundamental gulf between divine *ousia* and all created *ousia*, and to the ineffability of the divine *ousia*, both suggesting that 'divine *ousia*' is not a member of the more general class *ousia*; thus, pushing beyond terminological preferences, there is in fact no distinction in doctrine here – Augustine accepts and offers the formulation 'there is nothing of this essence other than the Trinity' at one point.)[47]

In Books 6 and 7, Augustine's interest is in the classical 'X from X' formulations, long of significance in the tradition, and enshrined in the Creed. The Son is God from God, Light from Light, and so on; this, however, raises theological and exegetical problems in Augustine's view. The problems boil down to a single issue: if it is appropriate, as the tradition has, to call the Son 'Wisdom', then biblical language of 'God's wisdom', or classical theological defences of orthodoxy such as 'God is never without his wisdom', seemingly simultaneously deny that the Son is God, and that the Father is Wisdom. Augustine introduces the Holy Spirit into the discussion, and then appeals to the second principle I noted above, that the Spirit, like the Son, and no less than the Father, simply is the fullness of deity. This is a necessary deduction from divine simplicity. His argument for this proposition runs that each divine person is necessarily perfect, but perfection cannot be improved on, so it must be the case that each divine person is no less than the fullness of the Godhead.[48] 'X from X' language, then, must be understood in the strictest possible sense when applied to the divine. The Son is 'God from God' because the Son is no less the irreducibly perfect fullness of deity than the Father is (and the Spirit is also). The Father is perfect Wisdom, just as the Son is – and the Spirit is also.

Several troublesome or helpful texts are dealt with through the discussion, but the exegetical question which frames the two books is a consideration of 1 Corinthians 1:24, 'Christ the power of God and the wisdom of God'. This has been a classic pro-Nicene proof-text: God cannot be God without his power and his wisdom, so the Son must be

---

by nineteenth-century mathematicians. I suspect that the claim is not so narrowly mathematical, and so is retrievable, but make no attempt to prove that here. In any case, that Augustine and the whole of antiquity with him assumed the claim is beyond doubt.

[47] *Trin.* 7.6; *non enim aliquid aliud eius essentiae est praeter istam trinitatem* (my trans.).
[48] *Trin.* 6.8.

eternally with the Father. Augustine's theological reasoning has given reason to doubt the adequacy of this interpretation; what alternative reading may be offered? Augustine suggests that Scripture is in the habit of ascribing certain titles, properly belonging inseparably to the Trinity, to the Son, or to the Spirit, in order to emphasize the oneness of the Son and the Spirit with the Father, and to indicate that the saving economic acts of the Son and the Spirit are dependent on their full deity. In 1 Corinthians, the Son is called 'the power of God and the wisdom of God' in the context of a soteriological claim to highlight the fact that the Son is only able to save us because of his possession of the fullness of deity.

What is the point, then, of the psychological (and other) analogies for the Trinity in Books 8–15 of *De Trinitate*? What is the purpose of these famous passages, comparing the divine life to the interaction of memory, will, and intellect (or similar triads) in the isolated human mind? The fundamental answer lies in the mature account of the ordered inseparability of divine operations: each indivisible divine work is initiated by the Father, carried through intelligibly by the Son, and perfected in goodness by the Spirit.[49] If this is true of the work of creation, and indeed of the work of redemption, then we should expect to find that the application of this threefold order as an analytic principle for understanding what God has done in creation and redemption is generative. (I deliberately put the matter this way around; Augustine does not believe that the world is full of obvious nature-intellect-goodness triads which anyone can see; rather, I think, he believes that when we realize for theological reasons that this is the inherent shape of the world, and start using this as a tool to analyze aspects of our existence, we discover that in fact it does illuminate much.)[50]

If the possibilities of recognizing *vestigia trinitatis* in creation are so wide and varied, once we know to look for them, why does Augustine focus so narrowly on human psychology in *De Trinitate*? The answer is to do with the nature of true knowledge of the divine, which necessarily involves devotion and contemplation. Augustine's first illustration/

---

[49] At the risk of belabouring the point, let me note once more that this codification, here presented as the basis for the psychological analogies so often held up to be the most characteristically and idiosyncratically Western aspect of Augustine's Trinitarianism, is virtually indistinguishable from central statements made by Basil of Caesarea or Gregory of Nyssa.

[50] *Civ.* 11 offers a lengthy list of such helpful analyses, which go far beyond the psychological focus of *Trin.*

analogy concerns love; he imagines a person who believes the scriptural testimony that God is love, but is puzzled how this relates to the Trinity. Augustine analyzes the act of loving into the lover, the beloved, and the love they share. Because God is love, this is not just analogy; it is something not very far from description, allowing for the impossibility of adequately describing the triune life.

This turn to the divine life leads Augustine to move from a generic account of an act of love to think about self-love; the love that is God's own life, after all, must have this peculiar character. It will appear, however that the triad has been reduced to a diad by identifying the lover with the beloved. This cannot be right, since now we are talking most directly about God's love. Augustine invites us to examine the analogy more closely. The mind can only love itself if it knows itself, he suggests, and so offers a triad of self-love that includes the mind, its self-knowledge, and its self-love. Further, he argues that, to be perfect, these must be equal: it would be sinful for the mind to love itself more than it in fact should be loved, or less than it in fact should be loved; so the mind's love of itself must correspond with some exactness to the mind, and it can only so correspond if the mind has exact knowledge of itself, which determines the appropriate measure of love. Perfect self-love, then, is a telling image of the life of God.

The end of Augustine's reflections on the picture of the Trinity that may be derived from thinking about the human mind is added somewhat later,[51] but brings a profound and appropriate conclusion to the whole. If we are to seek for images of the Trinity in the human mind, then we should not consider any and every act of thinking or loving indifferently. The human mind was made for contemplation of the one who made it, and so is most truly what it should be in contemplating God. We will never achieve perfect contemplation this side of the ultimate gift of the beatific vision in heaven, but this is what the mind is made for: directed wholly towards the ineffable mystery of the divine Trinity, our memory, understanding, and desire will be perfectly united and yet properly distinguished in the contemplation and adoration of God, who himself inseparably is, thrice over.

---

[51] Ayres suggests Book 14 is dated five years or more after books 9–10. *Augustine*, p. 305.

Towards a Scholastic Trinitarianism: Boethius

Augustine's other great long work, *De civitate Dei*, addresses head-on the question of why God allowed the sack of Rome, and so implicitly bears witness to the slow but inexorable decline of the Western empire. East of the Danube, a culture that permitted the sort of intellectual enquiry that promoted serious theological work would continue for some centuries after the fourth-century Trinitarian settlements; the same cannot really be said of the West. After Augustine, for five centuries or more the story is one of monastic foundations dedicated to preserving and transmitting the heritage, which only very rarely offer any intellectual advances, and occasionally one of isolated geniuses who receive something at least of the tradition and make individual contributions. The general tenor of education in the period can be judged by Charlemagne's General Admonition of AD 789, which demanded a mass programme of instruction so that every priest should know the Lord's Prayer and the Creed, and be able to recite the liturgy. Charlemagne also commissioned Alcuin of York to produce a textbook outlining and defending traditional Trinitarian doctrine. A school gathered at Corbie in the ninth century and produced some original theology, and some bitter controversy, including some debate over whether it was orthodox to sing of God as 'three and one', phraseology defended by Gottschalk and attacked by Hincmar, whose arguments prevailed at the Synod of Soissons in 853. The Celtic monasteries produced some flowerings of letters, and some fine Trinitarian devotional lyrics. The culture of learning, however, was one of preservation and transmission, not one of innovation.

The most interesting Trinitarian proposal of this period of Western thought was that of John Scotus Eriugena (c.800–c.877), a ninth-century Irish monk who read widely in the Greek fathers and produced an astonishingly ambitious and complete Neoplatonic system of thought that was uniquely his own, albeit owing quite a lot to Pseudo-Dionysius. Eriugena's works were not influential in his day, and, although read with appreciation in some contexts in the high Middle Ages (notably at Saint-Denise and amongst the Victorines), they were later caught up in the condemnations of Aristotelian theses in Paris in the late thirteenth century. His influence after that was largely confined to the mystical theologians – Meister Eckhart and Nicholas de Cusa, for example. Eriugena was not really recovered as a significant thinker until Hegel; he has attracted some degree of attention in the last two centuries. His Trinitarian constructions, therefore, though interesting, are not really a relevant aspect of the story I am telling.[52]

Early in the period, Boethius (c.475-c.526)[53] is a less innovative thinker than Eriugena, but still added something to the developing tradition: he attempts to represent Catholic orthodoxy in terms of a fairly narrow philosophical base which he has inherited, and does so with invention and brilliance. His writings became important as a lens through which later generations of Latin theologians would read the older tradition. The *Consolations of Philosophy* is one of the great texts of the Latin Christian West, on any estimation; his more directly theological works, the five *opuscula*,[54] are less brilliant, but are of some importance in the later medieval reception of patristic Trinitarianism. Boethius was a senator, not a bishop; he was widely read in philosophy, and clearly had excellent Greek, but his theological reading in this area (and others) appears to be almost confined to Augustine. His contribution to the development of the Western Trinitarian tradition is less in his original ideas, important though one or two would become for Thomas Aquinas in particular, than for the clarity, and self-awareness, of his method. He wants to apply Aristotelian logic to currently disputed theological questions, in order to demonstrate the incoherence of heresy and the coherence of orthodoxy; in so doing, however, he is acutely aware of the points at which logical relations which apply in the created order cease to apply to God.

Boethius's particular concern stems from the visit of John Maxentius and a group of Scythian monks to Rome in 519, proposing a new confessional formula that might bring resolution to simmering debates in the churches. The phrase they offered for unity appeared simple: 'one of the Trinity suffered in the flesh'. The phrase was finally accepted at the Second Council of Constantinople in 553, the

---

[52] That said, his notion that creation happens within God might have been found suggestive for some in the twentieth century; it appears not to have been noticed, however.

[53] On Boethius see Henry Chadwick, *Boethius: The Consolations of Music, Logic, Theology, and Philosophy* (Oxford: OUP, 1981); John Marenbon, *Boethius* (Oxford: OUP, 1993); John Marenbon, ed., *The Cambridge Companion to Boethius* (Cambridge: CUP, 2009).

[54] For the *Opuscula Sacra* (OS), I have used the Loeb edition, for want of anything better. Boethius, *The Theological Tractates* (trans. H.F. Stewart and E.K. Rand; London: Heinemann, 1962). The authenticity of *OS* 4 was for a while doubted, but Bark's article settled the matter conclusively in favour of authenticity. William Bark, 'Boethius' Fourth Tractate, the So-Called *De Fide Catholica*', HTR 39 (1946): pp. 55–69.

West's agreement owing at least something to Boethius's arguments. The objectionable part of the phrasing, of course, was not the whiff of theopaschism – that the incarnate Son suffered *in the flesh* was not doubted at Chalcedon, and the teaching does not imply in any way that the impassible divine nature suffered. Rather, it was the idea that the divine persons can be numbered, and their works separated; can we really speak of 'one of the Trinity' doing anything and remain orthodox?

In *OS* 1, Boethius considers how the classical ten Aristotelian categories apply to God. He suggests that the categories should be divided into three groups: three of them, substance, quality, and quantity, are intrinsic, defining what a thing is in itself; six more – place, time, condition, doing, posture, and suffering – are extrinsic, defining only the external context of the thing. Extrinsic categories are thus necessarily accidental, and so do not apply to God because there is nothing accidental in the simple being that God is. Intrinsic categories, by contrast, can apply to God, because they define substance. The mode of attribution, however, is fundamentally different to created attribution, again because of simplicity: 'a man is one thing, and a just man is another thing; but God is truly that which is justice itself.'[55] The final category, relation, is more complicated still: Boethius notes that relation appears to be an extrinsic attribute; however, it establishes something about the thing related – a relationship of ownership establishes one person as master and another as slave, to use Boethius's own example.[56] With created things, this is easy to understand: a relation establishes a new accidental property attached to a thing – a man can move from being slave to being free to being master; all are accidental properties which can, but need not, attach to a particular human being.

What of relation applied to the divine? There are no accidental qualities in God; a relation within God, or a reflexive relation of God to God, is necessary, but not substantial. Father and Son (and Spirit) are, in Augustine's terms, names of eternal and necessary relations, and so there is a proper multiplicity within God, of three relations, which are indeed countable. However, the divine substance – and the divine operation – is one, or beyond number, simple, and undivided. Anything predicated of God save the relations themselves is predicated substantially, and so refers to the one substance which is repeated three times over in the relations. There are not three immortals, but one

---

[55] *OS* 1.4: *homo alter alter iustus, deus vero idem ipsum est quod est iustum* (my trans.).
[56] *OS* 1.5.

immortal, not three who are just, but one who is justice itself, and so on.

Boethius's method is carefully rational, following Aristotelian logic, but profoundly aware of where language breaks down. This is a development of, not a departure from, Augustine's method, and one that would pave the way for the great flowering of Christian theological development in the medieval schools. To that flowering I will turn in a moment, but first I will pause to summarize the great themes of patristic Trinitarianism.

Interlude:

The Harvest of Patristic Trinitarianism

One of my themes in this book is the falsity of what is called, however fairly, the 'de Régnon thesis': the idea that, from Augustine on, Trinitarian theology in the Greek-speaking East and the Latin-speaking West took decisively different turns, leading to two distinct traditions. Of course, the medieval debate over the *filioque* is generally cited as proof of this, and that debate needs addressing. I treat it in my next chapter. For now, however, I want, briefly, to examine some of the more fundamental claims for this division and address them, in order to demonstrate that the patristic inheritance, East and West, essentially spoke with one voice. Further, I want to summarize what that one voice said, so that we can take a simple but convincing statement of the harvest of patristic Trinitarianism into the remaining debates.

The first claim, offered by Zizioulas, Gunton, and others, is that Augustine, and with him the Western tradition, failed to understand the basic reorientation of ontology in a personalist direction that was the chief achievement of the Cappadocian fathers. I have already offered good reasons for assuming that Augustine's doctrine was rather traditional, based on its context and reception; the plausibility of this claim, it seems to me, depends on our ability to demonstrate that, specifically in questions of personality, Augustine thought differently from the Cappadocians. By 'personality' in the modern sense, I assume that we mean the possession of self-determination, and so volition, and of self-awareness, and so cognition. (If not, and I have noted earlier Zizioulas's protests over a somewhat similar construction of his doctrine, I simply ask, what do we mean? As I will show later, not only was there a general assumption amongst earlier theologians – Photius alone excluded – that East and West spoke with one voice, but specifically Augustinian themes could be appropriated unapologetically and without any apparent concern by so quintessentially an Eastern theologian as Gregory Palamas. The one who claims an East-West division, on any issue other than the narrow one of the *filioque*, is claiming something that the tradition never saw, and it is incumbent on him or her to specify the precise division, to demonstrate that it did in fact divide, and to account for the failure of generations of acute and holy theologians to perceive it.)

Let us accept, then, on this construction, that Augustine locates all that is truly 'personal' (knowledge, volition, action . . .) in the ineffable divine nature, not severally in the *hypostases*; do the Cappadocians do differently? Gregory Nazianzen's summary of his great statement of Cappadocian orthodoxy is clear: 'They are not sundered in will or divided in power. You cannot find there any of the properties inherent in things divisible . . . the Godhead exists undivided in things divided' (*Or.* 31.14); Gregory Nyssan and Basil had based their refutations of Eunomius and the Macedonians on the claim that the external acts of the Trinity are undivided. The language of the Son as the Father's *logos* (knowledge) or wisdom, insisting on one cognition, one wisdom, and one perception within the Trinity, is so traditional in Eastern pro-Nicene theology as to be inviolable, but Augustine criticized it for not allowing sufficient hypostatic reality to the three 'persons', insisting that the one divine wisdom and knowledge was common to all. East and West alike are united in insisting on the unity of the divine will and knowledge; Augustine is slightly more ready to explore what it means for this will and knowledge to exist three times over than the earlier Greek tradition. On the criteria presented for the argument, it is Augustine, not the Cappadocians, who is more ready to accept a 'personalist' construction of the three *hypostases*.

A second argument might concern the monarchy of the Father. This is complex: as we have seen, Zizioulas makes the sole monarchy of the Father the cornerstone of his theological construction; Moltmann, by contrast, would see the very notion of monarchy as oppressive and unhappy. At this point my task is only to indicate what the fathers said, not to adjudicate such debates. Is it the case that, either, the Cappadocian fathers insist on the sole monarchy of the Father, or that developed Trinitarianism refuses the sole monarchy in a proto-democratic impulse? Neither is true. The monarchy is a profoundly important doctrine in the patristic period, simply because it links so closely to monolatry, to the question of who should be worshipped. The monarchy is therefore not to be simply linked to the Father – Arius, Eunomius, and Photinus alike tried to develop that argument, and in each case, it was found to be wanting in fundamental ways. Within the divine life, the Father is the sole cause, begetting the Son and spi-rating the Spirit, but with creation in view, the monarchy is the shared possession of the three *hypostases*. This is clear from the textual evidence.

I stated above that Augustine is the most capable interpreter of Cappadocian Trinitarianism; in the absence of convincing arguments to the contrary, I stand on this judgement. There is no fundamental difference between East and West. The doctrine of the Trinity received from the fourth century might be codified as follows:

1. The divine nature is simple, incomposite, and ineffable. It is also unrepeatable, and so, in crude and inexact terms, 'one'.
2. Language referring to the divine nature is always inexact and trophic; nonetheless, if formulated with much care and more prayer, it might adequately, if not fully, refer.
3. There are three divine *hypostases* that are instantiations of the divine nature: Father, Son, and Holy Spirit.
4. The three divine *hypostases* exist really, eternally, and necessarily, and there is nothing divine that exists beyond or outside their existence.
5. The three divine *hypostases* are distinguished by eternal relations of origin – begetting and proceeding – and not otherwise.
6. All that is spoken of God, with the single and very limited exception of that language which refers to the relations of origin of the three *hypostases*, is spoken of the one life the three share, and so is indivisibly spoken of all three.
7. The relationships of origin express/establish relational distinctions between the three existent *hypostases*; no other distinctions are permissible.

This summary is rather cold and analytic: a proper account of the harvest of patristic Trinitarianism would have far more to say about exegesis and worship. In theological terms, however, on the evidence heretofore presented in the book, I submit that this is an adequate, if incomplete, epitome of necessarily orthodox teaching concerning the eternal life of God. With this in mind, we move to the medieval period.

7.

'Distinction in the persons but unity in the nature': The Medieval Doctrine of the Trinity

The *Filioque* Debate

As is well known, the Great Schism between Eastern and Western Christendom occurred over a matter of Trinitarian definition. Is it proper to say that the Holy Spirit proceeds from the Father and the Son (*ex patre filioque*), or should we rest content with the creedal confession that the Holy Spirit proceeds from the Father (*ex patre*), and remain silent about the Son? In fact, the *filioque* had been a standard part of Western Trinitarianism from the sixth century; Boethius asserted it; Charlemagne promoted it aggressively; Pope Leo III believed the teaching, even if he refused Charlemagne's request to insert it into the ecumenically received creed. This last point is the important one; the schism is not so much over the teaching of the filioque as over the right of the pope to change a creed promulgated by an ecumenical council. The question of the primacy of Rome, more than the question of the procession of the Spirit, finally divided the church.

The Third Synod of Toledo, 587, is the first witness to the practice of including *filioque* in the Niceano-Constantinopolitan Creed. It was at the time a useful barrier to a then locally popular form of subordinationist heresy; it seems, however, that Toledo did not consciously alter the Creed; those gathered assumed that the correct form of the Creed included the *filioque*. Later, less parochial, champions were conscious that there was a debate to be had, at least: Charlemagne called synods to press the case for the liturgical confession of *filioque*, notably at Frankfurt (794) and Friuli (796), having himself been convinced of the appropriateness of the confession by Alcuin of York. Except in odd cases where we have convincing evidence, however, we cannot know whether such champions were conscious of pressing for innovation, or merely choosing between two variant creeds of uncertain antiquity.[1] By 1014, the term was inserted into the creed on papal authority, and schism was inevitable. Inevitably, defences of each position, and proposals for unity, followed.[2]

The hope of reunification remained live virtually until the Reformation. The Council of Florence claimed to have achieved unity in the mid-fifteenth century, as the Second Council of Lyons had in the later thirteenth century; in each case, the concessions granted by those delegates who attended the council from the Eastern churches were soon rescinded, and union remained elusive. The constant striving, however, meant that the *filioque* was a live theological issue through the high Middle Ages, in both East and West, and one the best thinkers could not avoid. It will be a constant thread running through this chapter, therefore.

Anselm of Canterbury

One of the earliest defenders of the *filioque* was the great theologian Anselm of Canterbury (c.1033–1109). His treatise on the subject, entitled 'On the Procession of the Holy Spirit',[3] records the arguments he presented in defence of the *filioque* at the Council of Bari in 1098, and builds on his, essentially Augustinian, reflections on the Trinity in the *Monologion* and *De incarnatione verbi Dei*.[4] The argument in *De process.*

---

[1] The fact that extant records of the Council of Constantinople have no record of the text of the creed, which instead comes down from the Acts of Chalcedon, makes the problem a genuine one: even with access to a library, one would need a fairly sophisticated knowledge of church history to discover the urtext.

[2] For general discussion on the filioque debate, see now A.E. Siecienski, *The Filioque: The History of a Doctrinal Controversy* (Oxford: OUP, 2010).

[3] The standard edition of Anselm's works remains F.S. Schmitt, *Anselmi Cantuariensis Archiepiscopi Opera Omnia* (6 vols; Edinburgh: Thomas Nelson and Sons, 1940–61); *De process.* is in vol. 4.

[4] Much recent work on Anselm's Trinitarian theology has come from analytic philosophers of religion, and so assumes a level of confidence in our ability to reason about the divine that Anselm would have found rather strange. Nonetheless, it is valuable in exposing the underlying logic of some of his arguments. See particularly William E. Mann, 'Anselm on the Trinity', in *The Cambridge Companion to Anselm* (ed. Brian Davies and Brian Leftow; Cambridge: CUP, 2004), pp. 257–78.

follows the method of many of his works, in arguing from a series of premises which he believes his opponents share with him, to prove the matter under dispute.[5] Anselm is convinced that the Greeks agree with the Latins on all points of technical Trinitarian theology, save only the confession of the Spirit's procession from the Son. He begins his book by enumerating a series of points of agreement between East and West: divine simplicity; the fullness of the Godhead in each of the persons; the identity of the persons in all things save the relations of origin . . . This witness to agreement is not surprising for the student of historical theology, but an important indication that the de Régnon thesis of a basic bifurcation between Western and Eastern approaches after the fourth century was at least not recognized by earlier theologians.

Anselm has several arguments for the necessity of the *filioque*, and also addresses the question of the appropriateness of inserting it into the creed.[6] Amongst his arguments are an appeal to exegesis; an interesting, but flawed, logical argument relying on divine simplicity; and an argument from the Father–Son relation. There are others, but these three are the most interesting, and most helpfully reveal the nature of the debate and the historical development of Trinitarian doctrine. The exegetical argument is fairly simple: in the economy, the Son sends the Spirit; this point can be proved by straightforward appeal to several biblical texts (John 20:22 might be the most obvious, and is discussed by Anselm in §5). Further, there is a reciprocity in the biblical description of the economic gift of the Spirit according to Anselm: drawing on John 14:26 and John 15:26, he notes that in both texts the Father and the Son are mentioned, but in one it is the Father who sends the Spirit 'in my [the Son's] name', whereas in the other the Son sends the Spirit 'from the Father'.[7] In the economy of salvation, therefore, Father and Son are united in sending the Spirit. Anselm assumes, however, that the economic relations of the three *hypostases* reveal their eternal relations;[8] therefore, the Spirit proceeds from the Father and the Son.

The first argument in the book operates at a fairly high level of abstraction, working with the concept of 'existing from', which is a

---

[5] See my *Listening to the Past*, pp. 38–9 for some discussion of Anselm's methodology.

[6] Particularly considered in *De process.* §13; I will not examine these arguments in detail, as the question of authority to alter the creed is not especially relevant to my argument.

[7] *De process.* §4.

[8] '. . . the breathing of the Lord upon his disciples . . . was done in order to signify that the Spirit whom he gave proceeded from the hiddenness of this person . . .' *De process.* §5.

generic term to describe the relationships of origin. The Father does not exist from any other, but is himself the monarchy; the Son exists from the Father; the Spirit exists from the Father. This is what is confessed in the Creed. Having stated these points, however, Anselm makes a surprising claim: 'either the Son exists from the Holy Spirit or the Holy Spirit exists from the Son' (*De process.* §1). Why so? Anselm's argument is complex, but the core of it would seem to be something like this: the divine *hypostases* are identical in every way save only their relations of origin. Therefore, it is necessary that the relations of origin be different. But, at the level of abstraction Anselm is working at, the creed appears to say that the Son and the Spirit have the same relation of origin – viz. existing from the Father.[9] If there is genuinely no other differentiation, the Son and the Spirit must be identical, and so the same *hypostasis* (on the basis of divine simplicity, and hypostatic distinction being maintained only by the relations of origin). Of course, the Son and the Spirit are not identical; God is triune; and so there must, necessarily, be a distinction in relations of origin between them. The only possible contenders are that the Son exists from the Spirit or that the Spirit exists from the Son.

The problem with this argument is the level of confidence assumed in reasoning about divine reality. Anselm has reduced the biblical/credal language of 'begotten' and 'proceeding' to the abstract concept 'existing from', and asserted their logical identity. If the Spirit exists from the Father in a different way from the way in which the Son exists from the Father, the logic fails, and it seems impossible for us to know whether this is the case. The simple answer to Anselm's construction here is Gregory of Nazianzus's famous dismissal of those who ask what 'procession' means, and how it differs from 'generation'.

The last of Anselm's arguments that I want to consider concerns the Father–Son relation, and takes us towards the heart of what is at stake theologically in the *filioque* debate. The argument turns on the question of whether the Spirit proceeds from the common divine *ousia* or from the particular *hypostasis*. Anselm is steadfast in insisting on the former, and uses this claim both to reject a proposed compromise solution, and to insist again on the *filioque*. In section 9 he notes that he has heard that the Greeks propose the formula, 'the Spirit proceeds from the Father through the Son (*per filium*)'; Anselm's response is

---

[9] Anselm is not, of course, suggesting that the Creed is wrong, merely that something further than what is explicitly stated in the Creed must also be true for the logic to be complete.

simple: the Spirit proceeds from the Father's deity, not from the Father's paternity, and the Son's deity is the same as the Father's deity, so to speak of the Spirit proceeding both from and through the one simple divine *ousia* is obviously nonsense. This principle also gives Anselm his response to the Greek claim that the *filioque* suggests that the Spirit has two causes (an objection he anticipates at the beginning of §10): there is one cause, the one Godhead of the Father and Son.

Of course, the Holy Spirit is also the one God. Anselm has consistently, however, worked with the principle that no person can exist from himself, which precludes the Spirit being the origin of his own procession. Anselm's phrasing of this principle is potentially unhappy (in that it seems to deny the possibility of the Father's monarchy), but it is a deduction from a more basic position, later enshrined as a dogmatic proposition of Western Trinitarianism at the Council of Florence, that 'everything is one where the difference of a relation does not prevent this', a careful and formal statement of the 'no distinction except in relations of origin' principle. Anselm uses this, together with a belief that eternal origination is substantial and not hypostatic (i.e. the Son is begotten of the Father's deity, and the Spirit proceeds from the shared deity of Father and Son).

There are two comments to be made about this. First, as Anselm acknowledges, the same logic would seem to require that the Son is begotten of the shared deity of Father and Spirit, and so the argument fails, or at least leads to a conclusion that appears unacceptable, even in its own terms. The second comment is that Anselm appears to be confusing the central Trinitarian distinction between *ousia* and *hypostasis*: in the classical Trinitarianism bequeathed by the fathers, the relations of origin are rather precisely hypostatic, not substantial: the Son is begotten of the Father, not of the divine essence which the Father is (and the Son is also). Anselm regards such a position as so obviously in error as to be capable of immediate dismissal, however: 'perhaps someone will claim that the Holy Spirit proceeds not from the Father's deity but from his Fatherhood . . . this view is silenced by its obvious foolishness.'[10]

The point that procession – and generation – are properties of the *hypostases* and not of the *ousia* was made by Peter Lombard in the *Sentences*, the great medieval theological textbook.[11] Joachim of Fiore

---

[10] *De process.* §9.
[11] *Sent.* 1. d. 5.

challenged Peter's view, and the matter came to the Fourth Lateran Council in 1215, where it was clearly taught that '[the divine nature] is not the one begetting or the one begotten or the one proceeding, but it is the Father who begets, the Son who is begotten, and the Holy Ghost proceeds, in order that there may be distinctions in the Persons and unity in the nature'.[12] As will be obvious to the attentive reader of this book, the council is doing no more than reasserting the shared faith of Christian antiquity.[13] In Anselm, then, we find a truly great mind apparently reasoning on the basis of an insecure grasp of the question.

Richard of St Victor

The abbey of St Victor in Paris was the home of an influential school of mystical theology through the twelfth century, which was begun by William of Champeaux, and carried forward by three influential priors, Hugh, Richard, and Walter. Richard of St Victor (d.1173) is of interest because of a genuinely original account of Trinitarian doctrine, which inevitably included his own contribution to the *filioque* debate. Richard's theological method, shaped by the Victorine school, focused on contemplative reflections on the created order, disciplined of course by Catholic dogma, which enabled the worshipping soul to grasp something of the ineffable truth of the divine. Self-knowledge, reflection on one's own experience and life, was particularly important to Richard.

Book 3 of his *De Trinitate*[14] explores his, somewhat idiosyncratic, account of God's life. For Richard, the highest good is love.[15] Love is

---

[12] Canon 2, trans. from H.J. Schroeder, *Disciplinary Decrees of the General Councils: Text, Translation and Commentary* (St Louis: B. Herder, 1937), *in loc.*

[13] The error the council attributes to Joachim and condemns is interesting, although it may not be a completely fair account of Joachim's position. We are told that he teaches that all that exists is the three hypostases, and that the unity spoken of is merely a collective noun, 'Godhead' being analogous to 'church'. The similarity of this view to certain twentieth-century Trinitarian proposals will be evident.

[14] Gaston Salet, ed. and trans., *Richard de Saint-Victor: La Trinité*, SC 68 (Paris: Cerf, 1959).

[15] Many discussions of Richard's work use 'charity'; this seems to me unhelpful; the intention may be to signify a non-erotic love, which is certainly what Richard had in mind, and the English word 'charity' used to carry that sense, but this meaning is now obsolete (so *OED*), and the word carries a somewhat different natural sense; as a result, the use of the word is almost inevitably misleading.

necessarily directed towards another, which, for Richard, is already proof that God is not a monad (God's love cannot find fulfilment in being directed towards the creation, for that would make God's perfection necessarily dependent on the creation, which is impossible). Richard further thinks that an analysis of the perfection of love is able to prove God's triunity. He argues that the highest moment of mutual love is when a lover wishes that another should love, and be loved by, the beloved as fervently as the first lover does. On this basis, the perfection of love demands at least three agents: a lover, a beloved, and a co-lover.

This might suggest an infinite series, with love endlessly increased the more who are involved. Why, then, a Trinity? Richard's argument seems to have three strands. The first, unstated but decisive, is the fact of revelation: the church believes in a divine Trinity, and so the series must reach three and then stop. The second strand concerns a sense of completeness: with three persons, each one may love the beloved and rejoice in the love of a third for the beloved; there is thus no need to extend the series further. The third strand is a return to an Anselmian argument concerning divine relations of origin: in the Trinity, there is one who only gives existence, one who both gives and receives, and one who only receives. The simplicity axiom demands that there can be no more, because there is no other relationship of origin logically possible. (Richard later makes a similar argument that the Father exists from himself, the Son immediately from the Father, and the Spirit mediately from the Father; again, no other mode of existence is possible, and so the fullness of deity must be three persons and three only.)

It is already obvious that Richard more nearly assumes the *filioque* as argues for it. That said, his logical constructions of Trinity do assume it, and would not work without it. To this extent, then, they propose an argument for the *filioque* of the form 'it is not possible to understand the divine Trinity unless we confess the *filioque*; but revelation demands that it is possible to understand the divine Trinity; therefore we must confess the *filioque*.' Of course, this construction depends on the first premise being valid, a condition which is at least not obvious. Richard's arguments are ingenious and suggestive; that no equally ingenious arguments which do not assume the *filioque* could be offered is a point that he has not attempted to prove, and that seems unlikely.

In recent theology, Richard has been feted as a Westerner who understood the Eastern, personalist, approach. Insofar as I have suggested that the idea of a contrast between a Western essentialism and an Eastern personalism is simply false, I cannot regard this characterization as anything but misguided. I would further note Richard's dependence on Augustine, *De Trinitate* 8 for his basic image, on Anselmian logic for his arguments limiting the number of divine persons to three only, and on his necessary assumption of the *filioque*. Richard stands squarely within the orthodox Trinitarian tradition which is shared by East and West; to the extent that there is a divided approach, his instincts are entirely Western.

Thomas Aquinas

In contemporary reception, Thomas Aquinas (1225–74) towers over the rest of medieval theology; he is likely to be the only example of the period encountered by undergraduate students of the subject, and is routinely assumed to be typical in method and doctrine. He was in fact a somewhat controversial figure in his own time, embroiled in university politics (the University of Paris had been founded by scholars outside the religious orders; the Franciscans and Dominicans had succeeded in getting chairs – Thomas occupied the Dominican chair – which were resented by the secular masters), and in sharp intellectual dispute (his second spell in Paris was at a time when there was growing tension between philosophers in the Arts faculty and at least some of the theologians). Thomas was deeply involved in a major intellectual movement in his day, occasioned by the recovery (via Islamic scholars in Spain) of the complete works of Aristotle in Latin, and the reception of an Islamic commentary tradition. This has been described as a 'philosophical revolution',[16] and prompted sharp disputes and a pressing need to reconcile seemingly necessary philosophical positions with received Christian orthodoxy (Thomas was particularly involved with a debate on Aristotle's belief that the world was necessarily eternal). In 1277, famously, 219 'Aristotelian' propositions thought to have been taught in the university were formally condemned as heretical. Whilst it seems likely that the thrust of these propositions was a view of the role of philosophy which in fact Thomas had opposed,[17] the condemnation took place on the anniversary of his death, and it was not difficult to read it as a repudiation of his influence.

---

[16] David Knowles, quoted in Jan A. Aertsen, 'Aquinas' Philosophy in Its Historical Setting' in *The Cambridge Companion to Thomas Aquinas* (ed. Norman Kretzman and Eleanor Stump; Cambridge: CUP, 1993), pp. 12–37, p. 20.

[17] See David Piché, *La Condemnation parisienne de 1277* (Paris: Vrin, 1999).

The later hagiographic reception of Thomas has led to a different problem: he has repeatedly been hailed as the inspiration behind this or that theological movement, many of them standing in straightforward opposition to each other. Accounts of Thomas's theology which are in fact attempts to recruit him to this or that school and which in consequence distort or misrepresent it have been and are still unfortunately common.[18] Thomas was blamed by many in the twentieth-century Trinitarian revival for subordinating the doctrine of the Trinity to a philosophically determined account of God's life.[19] This account is simply unfair, and has been shown to be so;[20] Thomas's doctrine of God is thoroughly biblical and Trinitarian, if carefully stated and properly reticent about speculating about the divine life. It stands in full continuity with the received tradition, acknowledging and demonstrating the fundamental agreement in most matters between East and West. He did write a controversial work on the *filioque* controversy (and other matters of dispute between Rome and the Greeks), which is largely a gathering of testimonies from the fathers in favour of the Roman positions.[21]

It is true that Thomas discusses 'what concerns the divine essence' before he discusses 'what concerns the distinction of persons' in the *Summa theologiae*;[22] but this is not a relegation of Trinitarian doctrine; rather a recognition that in discussing the doctrine of the Trinity there are two sorts of things to be said, things that are true of the *ousia* and so common to the three *hypostases*, and things that are true of each of the *hypostases*.[23] (The practice of recent English translations of enti-

---

[18] On which, see Fergus Kerr, *After Aquinas: Versions of Thomism* (Oxford: Blackwell, 2002).

[19] See, e.g., Moltmann, *Trinity*, pp. 16–17; Rahner, *The Trinity*, pp. 15–21.

[20] See, variously, Gilles Emery, *Trinity in Aquinas* (Ypsilanti, MI: Sapienta Press, 2003); idem, 'The Doctrine of the Trinity in St Thomas Aquinas', in *Aquinas on Doctrine: A Critical Introduction* (ed. Thomas Weinandy, et al.; London: T&T Clark, 2004), pp. 45–65; idem, *The Trinitarian Theology of St Thomas Aquinas* (trans. Francesca Murphy; Oxford: OUP, 2007); Jean-Pierre Torrell, *Saint Thomas Aquinas, vol. 2: Spiritual Master* (Washington, DC: CUA Press, 2003); Matthew Levering, *Scripture and Metaphysics: Aquinas and the Renewal of Trinitarian Theology* (Oxford: Blackwell, 2004); for some well-placed but minor cautions to the picture presented in these works, see Karen Kilby, 'Aquinas, the Trinity and the Limits of Understanding', *IJST* 7 (2005), pp. 414–27.

[21] *Contra errores Graecorum*. I have used the Leonine edition, tomus 40A. I am not aware of an English translation.

[22] The Leonine edition remains the best; *ST* is in toma 4–12; none of the published English translations are wholly satisfactory, so I have generally supplied my own.

[23] Consider the prologue to q. 2: *Consideratio autem de Deo tripartita erit. Primo namque considerabimus ea quae ad essentiam divinam pertinent; secundo, ea quae pertinent ad distinctionem personarum; tertio, ea quae pertinent ad processum creaturarum ab ipso.*

tling the treatises 'on the one God' and 'on the blessed Trinity' is unhelpful and misleading, it must be admitted.[24]) The extent to which Thomas simply assumes the doctrine of the Trinity in the discussion of the divine essence can be gauged by the biblical text he appeals to for proof that God is identical with his nature (i.e. simple) in the *sed contra* of 1a q. 3 art. 3: 'It is said of God that he is life, not only that he is living, as is clear from John 14: "I am the way, the truth, and the life" . . .'[25] Thomas simply assumes that when Jesus uses the personal pronoun, the triune God is speaking.

The triune God is simple, perfect, infinite, *a se*, and eternal (*ST* 1a qq. 3–10); words apply to the divine essence only analogically, but, analogically, they do adequately refer, and so we may name God, imperfectly but accurately (1a q. 13). Following John Damascene, the most appropriate name for God is 'He who is', the name revealed to Moses at the bush. John had also apparently taught that 'God' is the name of an activity, not a substance;[26] this is not right, but 'He who is' is glossed as 'pure existence' and 'pure act', and so Thomas repeatedly hovers close to the idea that 'God' is a verb – as Kerr has it, 'the risk for Thomas is not to reify God as a static and motionless entity, but rather, just the opposite, to make so much of the divine essence as activity . . . that God becomes sheer process . . . Thomas's God . . . is more like an event than an entity.'[27]

This simple, dynamic, eternal being is triune. In the *ST*, Thomas begins his discussion of what is proper to the persons with the concept of procession; this is different from his procedure elsewhere, where he begins with the biblical revelation of Father, Son, and Spirit, and then shows how Scripture may best be read if we understand it to be speaking of a Trinity of consubstantial *hypostases* differentiated only by their relations.[28] The *ST* presentation is no doubt an attempt to aid conceptual clarity, but

---

[24] So, e.g., the FEDP translation; these titles are not present in the edition in the Leonine *Opera Omnia*; I am not aware of the point at which it became normal to divide the *ST* into treatises, or whence the titles given in various translations derive.

[25] *Contra, de Deo dicitur quod est vita, et non solum quod est vivens, ut patet Ioan. XIV, ego sum via, veritas et vita. Sicut autem se habet vita ad viventem, ita deitas ad Deum. Ergo Deus est ipsa deitas.*

[26] *Dicit enim Damascenus, in I libro, quod Deus dicitur a theein, quod est currere, et fovere universa; vel ab aethein, idest ardere (Deus enim noster ignis consumens est omnem malitiam); vel a theasthai, quod est considerare, omnia. Haec autem omnia ad operationem pertinent. Ergo hoc nomen Deus operationem significat, et non naturam.* 1a q. 13 art. 8 arg. 1.

[27] Kerr, *After Aquinas*, p. 190.

[28] So *Summa Contra Gentiles* IV.2–26; see Gilles Emery, 'Le Traité de saint Thomas sur la Trinité dans la Somme contre les Gentils', *Revue Thomistique* 96 (1996): pp. 5–40;

it is in danger of obscuring the exegetical basis of Thomas's doctrine if it is read in abstraction from the other treatments. Even in the *ST*, however, the concept of procession is introduced with a further citation of the words of Jesus: there must be procession in the divine nature, since Jesus said 'from God I proceeded' (John 8:42).[29] What might processions in a simple spiritual being look like? Thomas suggests (the argument is based on Aristotelian anthropology, although drastically modified;[30] the inspiration is surely Augustine) that there are two candidates only: the object of knowledge and the object of love.

These processions must be understood as internal, and that which proceeds must, in each case, be understood as substantially identical with that from which it proceeds. Thomas uses the ancient image of God's perfect thought of himself: a perfect idea of something is identical to the original in every way. In the particular case of a simple thing, whose existence is identical with its essence, the perfect idea must have genuine existence, because it perfectly reflects the essence. God's perfect dynamic life is one simple act of knowing and loving himself so perfectly that he exists thrice over. Thus stated, the doctrine is highly formal and abstract; even in the *ST*, however, it is worked out with constant references to traditional biblical proofs of the deity: equality, inseparability, and differentiation of Father, Son, and Holy Spirit.[31]

Unlike Anselm, Thomas differentiates between the two processions: one is properly termed generation; the other not so (q. 27 art. 4). The processions give rise to relations, which again are not identical (q. 28 art. 3). In discussing the nature of relation, Thomas follows Boethius's account of the Aristotelian categories fairly closely. Relations – all relations – must be understood in two modes: according to their existence, and according to their nature. The nature of relation is not to change the thing related, but merely to position it according to another thing. Relations in the divine being, then, do not change what God is – and considered according to their existence, they simply are what God is, as

---

pp. 11–21. Emery elsewhere claims that 'Thomas' commentary on St John's Gospel reveals the same method of working', but offers no reference. Emery, 'Doctrine', p. 51.

[29] 1a q. 27 art. 1 sc. Thomas quotes the Vulgate, of course: *ego ex Deo processi*; the translation may introduce a technical term which is not evident in the original Greek, but Thomas's point is simply the Augustinian one that the economic missions reveal the order of the eternal relations.

[30] See Emery, 'Doctrine', pp. 52–3 for an account of the argument which is attentive to the Aristotelian background.

[31] See particularly the *responsio* of 1a q. 27 art. 1.

God is simple – but they do place the being of God in a series of self-dif-
ferentiating relational oppositions. There are, Thomas thinks, four relations in God: paternity (the Father's relation to the Son); filiation (the
Son's relation to the Father); spiration (the shared relation of the Father
and the Son to the Spirit); and procession (the Spirit's relationship to the
Father and the Son) (q. 28 art. 4). All these relations stem from action[32] –
again, Thomas views God as superabundantly dynamic.

These relations subsist necessarily in the divine essence, and are
traditionally named 'persons'. (Thomas is well aware of the problems
attached to the term – see q. 29 art. 4 resp.) The persons are nothing
other than the active relations subsisting in the eternal divine *ousia*.
The Father is the divine paternity; the Son the divine filiation; the
Spirit the divine procession. Spiration, as a shared property, does not
constitute the Father or the Son, states Thomas. He has a neat logical
argument for the *filioque* here: the divine spiration cannot be the
Father, since the Father is the divine paternity; the divine spiration
cannot be the Son, since the Son is the divine filiation; nor can the
divine spiration be a fourth divine person, since Scripture speaks only
of three (and the original psychological argument could find only two
processions from a common origin in the divine life); therefore, the
Father and Son together must be the opposite relation to proces-
sion/the Spirit.[33]

This is highly formal and abstract, and intentionally so. Thomas is
laying out with care and clarity that which must be said of God for
orthodoxy to be maintained; he does not think that there are any helpful created analogies for the Trinity, or he would have invoked them;
we know what we have to say; that we cannot picture the reality
about which all these things must be said is neither important nor
surprising. God is beyond our conceptual grasp, but there are ways in
which we can speak truly, if inadequately of him.[34] We might offer an
analogy, not to God's triune life, but to our ability to speak meaning-
fully of that which we do not know. According to quantum physics,
what we are pleased to call 'subatomic particles' are very strange
things. They sometimes behave like particles, and sometimes like
waves; they can exist in more than one place at a time or (perhaps better) as dispersed probability clouds, 51 per cent here and 17 per cent
there; they can be entangled with other particles in ways that seem to

---

[32] . . . *realis relatio in Deo esse non possit, nisi super actionem fundata.* 1a q. 28 art. 4 resp.
[33] Thomas does not draw out this argument in *ST*; but the implication is clear. His
      Trinitarian logic demands the *filioque,* or something very like it.
[34] In these reflections I am simply following Kilby, 'Aquinas'.

breach the fundamental laws of the universe. All of this is to say that we have no conceptual grasp of what they are – no non-quantum analogue which allows us to say, 'They are a bit like that.' We know much about how they behave, and can speak truly and extensively of what they do. Similarly, Trinitarian doctrine for Thomas is not an exercise in description of what God is, because we cannot know what God is, but a discussion of how we may speak truly about God.

The Medieval East: Photius to Gregory Palamas

Greek theology had little new to say about the eternal life of God until forced to by abortive attempts at reunion after the Council of Lyons. An earlier and temporary schism between East and West had concerned the patriarchate of Photius I of Constantinople. Photius was first elevated to the patriarchate (from the laity) in 858, after the deposition of the previous patriarch, Ignatius, who had offended the emperor. The deposition was uncanonical, and Photius's rapid promotion scandalous, and Pope Nicholas I excommunicated Photius and reinstalled Ignatius in 863. Photius's response was to accuse Nicholas of heresy for confessing the *filioque*, and to excommunicate him in turn. Photius was eventually deposed in another political power struggle, and the schism healed. Photius left behind, however, a treatise on the procession of the Holy Spirit, the *Mystagogy*,[35] which asserted that the Spirit proceeds from the Father alone. This position was simply accepted by later generations, and the question was no longer discussed.[36] Photius's *Mystagogy* contains more invective and mockery than theology, it is fair to say, but he accepts all the standard orthodox claims: divine simplicity (6); all things are common in the Godhead save only the hypostatic properties (19); the inadequacy of human language to refer to the divine (41); etc. He takes his stand on the teaching that the unique hypostatic principle of the Father is to be

---

[35] St Photius the Great, *Mystagogy* (New York: Studion, 1983) contains the text in Greek and an adequate translation.

[36] '. . . the eternal relationship of the Son to the Spirit became a dead issue at Byzantium in the centuries after Photius . . .' Andrew J. Sopko, '"Palamism before Palamas" and the Theology of Gregory of Cyprus', *SVTQ* 23 (1979): pp. 139–47, p. 143. Sopko's discussion of Blemmydes's misunderstanding of the relationship of the *charismata* and the *hypostasis* of the Spirit (p. 144) demonstrates just how foreign reflection on the eternal life of God was to even a significant Byzantine theologian of the thirteenth century.

the fount of deity, and so the Spirit must proceed from the Father alone (the point is repeated, but see, e.g., 42–3). He further argues that everything said of the deity must be said either of the *ousia* or of precisely one of the *hypostases*, and that the *filioque* breaks this rule (36).

Thomas Aquinas died in March 1274, whilst on his way to a council summoned to meet at Lyons. The council was the result of much earlier work – perhaps two decades of diplomatic preparation[37] – and resulted in the declaration of reunion between East and West, on the basis, essentially, of a complete capitulation on all disputed points by the Eastern delegates. The pro-union John Beccus was elected patriarch of Constantinople in 1275; however, when Michael VII, the emperor who had engineered the union, died in 1282, his son Andronicus immediately deposed Beccus and other pro-union bishops, and ceased any attempts to promote or impose the union formulae. Soon afterwards, Gregory II of Cyprus became patriarch. Gregory presided at the Council of Blachernae in 1285, an attempt, with Beccus and others present, to explore the question of the procession of the Holy Spirit, and to find an adequately Orthodox answer. Beccus, apparently, was genuinely convinced that, if not the *filioque*, then something similar ('through the Son'?) was theologically necessary; Gregory was far from agreeing, but did seemingly realize that the Photian 'from the Father alone' was not adequate, even if correct, and something needed to be said about the relationship of Son and Spirit.[38]

Beccus's key ammunition was a well-known series of proof-texts from authors of impeccable orthodoxy asserting that the Spirit proceeded from the Father 'through the Son' – the phrase had even been used by Patriarch Tarasius at the Seventh Ecumenical Council, Nicaea III in 787. With technical Trinitarian theology in view, however, it is very difficult to see what 'through the Son' might mean; in what way is this a relationship of origin? Does the Father spirate mediately? It seemed that the only options for making sense of the language were to accept, as Beccus did, that 'through the Son' means much the same as 'and the Son', or to follow Photius's claim that language of 'through

---

[37] Papadakis offers the figure; Aristeides Papadakis, *Crisis in Byzantium: The Filioque Controversy in the Patriarchate of Gregory II of Cyprus (1283–1289)* (Crestwood, NY: SVS Press, 1997), p. xi.

[38] Papadakis offers the most recent and extensive history of the council and its debates. *Crisis*, pp. 83–138. Unfortunately Papadakis, a historian, simply does not understand the history of Trinitarian dogma, and so his interpretations of the theological points are often poor. He does, however, offer an English translation of the key result of the council, Gregory's *Tomus* (pp. 212–29), which is valuable.

the Son' referred only to the temporal sending of the Spirit, not to his eternal origin; neither approach seemed especially happy to Gregory.

To solve the problem, Gregory proposed a new distinction, between 'existing' and 'having existence'. The Spirit *exists* from the Father through the Son, but *has his existence* from the Father alone; what might this mean? It first means that Beccus is wrong: 'the all-Holy Spirit's existence is not "through the Son" and "from the Son" as they who hasten towards their destruction . . . teach.'[39] Further, it means that Gregory proposes a distinction between the immanent life of the Trinity, which is unknowable, and in which the Spirit proceeds from the Father alone, and the manifestation of that life, which is revealed to the saints, and in which the Spirit is made manifest by the Father through the Son. God not only exists in his eternal perfection, but also manifests himself intelligibly outside that eternal perfection so that the creatures may behold his glory. This neatly addresses the most troublesome of Beccus's patristic proofs: John Damascene's description of the Father as the 'projector' of the Spirit through the Son; it also moves towards a distinction which would become central in Orthodox theology two generations later, the distinction between God's essence and God's energies.

Gregory had no developed doctrine of the divine energies, certainly, but his distinction between God's life *in se* and God's life manifested invites the Palamite theology. Gregory Palamas (1296–1359) was a controversial figure in his day, but became revered as one of the major interpreters of Orthodoxy amongst later generations. A recent writer goes so far as to say that 'Palamas is considered to be the apex and keystone of the dogmatic system of the Greek Fathers by most contemporary Orthodox theologians.'[40] The heart of Palamas's theology, and the motor of his distinctive and hugely influential spirituality, is this distinction between essence and energies; for at least some contemporary Orthodox theologians, this distinction is so fundamental that they locate the irrevocable split between East and West not in the *filioque* controversy, but in the West's rejection of the essence-energies distinction.[41]

Palamas argued that we must distinguish between the essence of God, which remains hidden in unapproachable light, and the

---

[39] *Tomus*, trans. from Papadakis, p. 215.

[40] Reinhard Flogaus, 'Palamas and Barlaam Revisited: A Reassessment of East and West in the Hesychiast Controversy of 14th Century Byzantium', *SVTQ* 42 (1998): pp. 1–32, p. 1.

[41] So Flogaus, citing Yannaras and Evdokimov. 'Palamas and Barlaam', p. 2.

uncreated energies, which are the outflowing of God's essential life towards creation, and are approachable, indeed available for contemplation by the saints. Palamas stresses the hypostatic nature of the divine energy: it has real existence, which is not the Father, or the Son, or the Holy Spirit; its real existence is however entirely dependent (Palamas borrows the old Christological language of *enhypostasis*) on the essential life of the three divine persons. *Enhypostasis* means existence within, and dependent upon, a particular *hypostasis*. The divine light – the uncreated energy – exists as the ecstatic communication of the three divine *hypostases* to our souls. This theology allows for a profound and nuanced account of *theosis*, the classical Orthodox account of salvation as becoming-divine. The communication of the divine energy to the saint enables a personal, but not natural, sharing in divinity. The saint is thus made divine by grace, but not by nature, preserving the distinctions between the Trinity and the saints whilst upholding the account of salvation as deification.

The West rejected this formulation as at once too immanent and too transcendent. Too immanent in the sense that an account of the saints as 'becoming divine', however nuanced, violated the basic ontological divide between Creator and creation, which had been essential to Trinitarian doctrine from at least the fourth century. Too transcendent in that an account in which Father, Son, and Spirit communicated their lives to the world only through intermediaries again apparently recalled basic theological mistakes of the patristic period, reintroducing the need for mediation which Irenaeus and Athanasius had both argued against.

That said, the debate over salvation as divinization is not a part of my story, whatever the right answer may be. What did Palamas have to say about the eternal life of the Trinity? First, it must be noted that, despite repeated reports to the contrary, for Palamas the external work of the Trinity remained undivided. He did not teach that there was a particular hypostatic relation in the divine energies. We meet God, who is Father, Son, and Holy Spirit.[42] Second, as may be expected, Palamas taught and maintained the basic Trinitarian grammar shared by the fathers – West and East. Third, it is striking to note that he apparently borrowed and deployed with some cheerfulness the quintessential Augustinian/Western psychological analogy. In the *Capita Physica*, chapters 34–8, Palamas explores at some length a

---

[42] On this see Flogaus, 'Palamas', p. 30, and references there.

Trinitarian analogy based on a triad of mind-knowledge-love.[43] Historically, this is no surprise at all: there was a recent Greek translation of Augustine's *De Trinitate* by Maximus Planudes, and Thomas Aquinas's *Summa Contra Gentiles* had been translated by Demetrius Cydones in 1354. Theologically, if one is committed to the de Régnon thesis that Latin and Greek Trinitarianisms are fundamentally different traditions, Palamas's unapologetic embracing of Latin models is an acute embarrassment; if, however, we accept the essential unity of patristic Trinitarian reflection, Palamas's embracing of Augustinian images is natural and normal.[44] My own views on this point are clear enough to the reader by now, and I take it as a confirmation of the broad historical reconstruction I am offering to find the Palamite employing classical Augustinian analogies. Patristic Trinitarianism was united, as was medieval Trinitarianism with the exception of a debate over the appropriateness of *filioque* language; Gregory Palamas could as well draw from Augustine as from Basil.[45]

Filoque? By Way of Summary

In the high medieval period the received patristic doctrine of the Trinity was generally simply believed and taught. There was a dispute between East and West over the propriety of confessing the Spirit's procession *filioque*, and the advances in Western theology assumed the rightness of the *filioque* clause so reflexively that it became a part of their development of accounts of the Trinity. It is fair to say that, even in Palamas, the East had no thinker of the quality of Anselm or Aquinas – Palamas's authority came as much through his mysticism and asceticism as through his intellectual ability. That said,

---

[43] See M. Edmund Hussey, 'The Palamite Trinitarian Models', *SVTQ* 16 (1972): pp. 83–9, which includes an English translation of the relevant texts, pp. 83–5; also Jeremy D. Wilkins, ' "The Image of This Highest Love": The Trinitarian Analogy in Gregory Palamas's *Capita* 150', *SVTQ* 47 (2003): pp. 383–412. Hussey references earlier surprised citations by Meyendorff and Jugie.

[44] Hussey assumes the de Régnon model, referencing him at the conclusion of his paper, and thus tries hard, if unconvincingly, to find a distinction between Palamas's invocation of a psychological analogy and Augustine's.

[45] There was, it should be said, a tradition of anti-Augustinian rhetoric stemming from Photius, who, in declaring the *filioque* heretical, had to explain away the testimony of a number of Fathers. This remained eccentric in the Orthodox tradition, however, and there is no evidence for the influence of Photius on the Palamite on this point.

Palamas codifies and enshrines some novel elements of Greek theology in his teaching on the uncreated energies. His doctrine of the Trinity, however, is classical and lacking in innovation.

Within the bounds of classical Trinitarianism, the *filioque* debate was, in retrospect, inevitable: two relations of origin are proposed, the generation of the Son and the spiration of the Spirit. There are thus four relational terms: generating; being generated; spirating; and being spirated. These four terms then need to be divided between three *hypostases*. Two options appear natural and obvious: to identify the One who generates with the One who spirates, thus teaching the Father as sole cause and denying the *filoque*; or, following Thomas Aquinas, to affirm the *filioque* by making spiration a joint action of Father and Son, and so a non-hypostatic causal principle. (Other solutions are logically possible – identifying the one generated with the one who spirates, or identifying the one spirated with the one who generates, for instance – but all seem sufficiently obviously foreign to the economic order revealed in Scripture to be immediately excluded.)

Thus stated, it is clear that neither position on the filioque does violence to the received orthodox and catholic tradition. Historically, there was full communion between those who believed in the dual procession of the Spirit and those who believed in the sole causality of the Father for many centuries, and in this the church displayed its sure grasp of the proper contours of Trinitarian doctrine, and of what was, and more pertinently was not, at stake in the argument. This does not of course mean that the issue is trivial, or in principle insoluble; but in the second half of the first millennium the church remained aware that it did not have a common mind on the question, and felt no need to seek one. Gradually, however, on both sides, the voices of those who believed that the question needed moving forward became dominant, and both West and East defined their own position as a necessary component of Trinitarian dogma. The schism was complete, and will remain so unless and until such sectarian dogmatic decisions can be unpicked.

8.

'By the testimonies of the Scriptures or by manifest reason': Anti-Trinitarianism from the Reformation to the Eighteenth Century

The Ferment of the Reformation

After the Great Schism between East and West, the second great breach in popular tellings of church history is the Reformation of the sixteenth century. It can be presented as a fairly neat and contained movement, beginning with Luther's protest against the selling of indulgences in 1517 and resulting within two generations in the founding of a number of national Protestant churches, which emphasized salvation by faith alone, disdained church tradition in favour of the sole authority of Scripture, and reorganized the liturgy and church government in far-reaching ways – whilst, however, holding firmly to most of the essentials of catholic doctrine, including the doctrine of the Trinity. Of course, the reality was not that simple.

There is little doubt that the Roman Catholic Church stood in need of reform of some sort at the beginning of the sixteenth century, and Luther was far from the only person to notice. Protest movements had been a recurrent feature of the previous two centuries of church history – the Lollards and the Hussites were only the most famous.[1] Most – including Luther – hoped precisely to reform the church; they had no ambition of setting up a new movement; they wanted to call the

---

[1] Malcolm Lambert, *Medieval Heresy: Popular Movements from the Gregorian Reform to the Reformation* (Oxford: Blackwell, 3rd edn, 2002) remains an excellent introduction to the stories of many such groups.

old one back to (what they believed to be) its original purity. Some were rather moderate; some extremely radical. They often enough disagreed on what needed changing or reforming. The sixteenth-century movements survived and grew where others had failed at least in part by gaining the support and so protection of the local magistrate.[2]

The splits in the church, and the general uncertainty of the times, seemed to produce a moment when everything could be questioned. Around the edges of the mainstream reform movements were individuals and small groups promoting much more radical ideas. George Williams offered the term 'the radical reformation' to denote this varied and colourful hinterland.[3] Its most famous inhabitants, and the ones Williams focused on most, were those who rejected the link between church and state, and with it the practice of automatically baptizing newborn children (a practice that at least implied that membership in the church was coterminous with membership of the community). These 'anabaptists' often suffered violent persecution, but some communities survived, notably the Mennonites. It included, however, many who doubted or questioned other aspects of the inherited faith and practice, including some who questioned the doctrine of the Trinity.

The Mainline Reformers

All the mainline Reformers were committed to the historic doctrine of the Trinity, believing it to be clearly taught in Scripture. It is so straightforwardly assumed that modern accounts of their theology pass over the doctrine very rapidly, being content to note their acceptance of what was received.[4] That said, particular emphases, often

---

[2] Standard general accounts of the Reformation include Euan Cameron, *The European Reformation* (Oxford: Clarendon, 1991); Carter Lindberg, *The European Reformations* (Oxford: Blackwell, 1996); and *The Reformation in National Context* (ed. Bob Scribner, et al.; Cambridge: CUP, 1994).

[3] George H. Williams, *The Radical Reformation* (Philadelphia: Westminster, 1967).

[4] See, for example, Paul Althaus, *The Theology of Martin Luther* (trans. Robert C. Schultz; Philadelphia: Fortress, 1966), which gives less than two pages to the chapter on the Trinity – pp. 199–200 – compared to, say, twenty-five pages on righteousness, or twenty pages on Christology. François Wendel, similarly, covers the Trinity in Calvin in a quick four-page survey. *Calvin: The Origins and Development of His Religious Thought* (trans. Philip Mairet; London: Collins, 1963), pp. 165–9.

enough connected to their general theological programmes, can be discerned, and Calvin in particular was engaged in some controversial debates over the doctrine, even being accused of Arianism at one point in his career, albeit rather unfairly.[5]

There is no doubt at all that Luther was deeply read in scholastic Trinitarianism;[6] we know that he knew Augustine, Lombard, and Gabriel Biel's commentary on Lombard; he references the fourteenth-century nominalist Pierre d'Ailly; it seems likely that he knew other medieval writers on the doctrine – at least Thomas Aquinas and William of Ockham.[7] He is unquestionably well schooled in the technical debates of the medieval period,[8] even while he can express himself impatient of such theology.[9] Of course, Luther famously had little respect for the dogmatic tradition in other areas; confronted with it at Worms, he delivered his most iconic moment in response, demanding to be convinced 'by the testimonies of the scriptures or by manifest reason'.[10] In the case of the doctrine of the Trinity, he was unconvinced of the ability of manifest reason to say very much (as Thomas Aquinas had been); continued commitment to the doctrine would need to be founded in Scripture.

Luther is not suspicious of the doctrine as some later theologians would be; he does not pick it apart and seek convincing scriptural demonstration for each component; rather, he assumes it is the right interpretation of Scripture and offers it, sometimes as explaining particular features

---

[5] The accusation was made by Pierre Caroli in 1536. For the history of the affair, see Bruce Gordon, *Calvin* (New Haven: Yale UP, 2009), pp. 72–7.

[6] Christine Helmer has published extensively on Luther's doctrine of the Trinity in recent years, and her work will provide the best introduction for the interested student. See her monograph, *The Trinity and Martin Luther: A Study on the Relationship between Genre, Language, and the Trinity in Luther's Works (1523–1546)*, Veröffentlichungen des Institutes für europäische Geschichte/Abteilung abendländische Religionsgeschichte 174 (Mainz: Verlag Philipp von Zabern, 1999); more recent papers have expanded on this in many particulars; amongst them, see especially 'God from Eternity to Eternity: Luther's Trinitarian Understanding', *HTR* 96 (2003): pp. 127–46.

[7] For all this see Simo Knuuttila and Risto Saarinen, 'Luther's Trinitarian Theology and Its Medieval Background', *ST* 53 (1999): pp. 3–12, p. 7.

[8] See, for instance, thesis 14 of the doctoral disputation for Petrus Hegemon (1545), where Luther distinguishes between the idea that the relations cause the *hypostases* and the idea that the *hypostases* cause the relations. *WA* 39.2: p. 340: *Relatio hic non arguit distinctionem rerum, sed res distinctae probant esse relationem.*

[9] See Althaus, *Theology*, p. 200 and references there.

[10] As recorded by Melancthon; Elizabeth Vandiver, et al., *Luther's Lives: Two Contemporary Accounts of Martin Luther* (Manchester: Manchester UP, 2002), p. 31.

of the text (classically on the plural in Gen. 1:26), sometimes as the natural meaning of the Scripture (John 1, for example).[11] Luther's distinctive exegetical procedure centred on a belief that the meaning of the text was 'whatever most exalted Christ'; with this commitment in view, instinctively Trinitarian readings, whether borrowed from the tradition or novel, are not a surprise.

John Calvin[12] similarly simply accepts the received doctrine of the Trinity, assuming and asserting that it is found in Scripture.[13] In his initial summary of Christian doctrine, the 1536 *Institutes*, it is true that he had little to say about the Trinity: he simply assumed the truth of the doctrine.[14] His rapid summary statements are nonetheless enough to demonstrate his commitment to classical orthodoxy: 'Inasmuch as he [the Son] is God, he is one God with the Father, of the same nature and substance or essence, not otherwise than, distinct as to the person which he has as his very own.'[15] The relative silence on the subject, however, allowed Caroli to accuse Calvin (along with his associates, William Farel and – the real target – Pierre Viret) of Arianism. Unsurprisingly, the 1539 edition of the *Institutes* contained a much fuller treatment of the doctrine, which offered many biblical proofs for the deity of the Son and the Spirit, and explored the doctrine with some terminological freedom.[16]

Later, Michael Servetus, who was notorious across Europe as one who denied the deity of Christ, and who had repeatedly sought Calvin's approval for his doctrine (we know of dozens of letters from Servetus to Calvin), chose to present himself in Geneva. Famously, he was executed for his errors. Calvin's role in the proceedings has often been grossly overstated; at the time, he was embroiled in disputes with the secular authorities over who had the right to excommunicate, and they were not about to let him take the lead role in the trial of a

---

[11] Both examples can be found in Mickey L. Mattox, 'From Faith to the Text and Back Again: Martin Luther on the Trinity in the Old Testament', *ProEccl* 15 (2006), pp. 281–303, pp. 286–8.

[12] I am using the electronic edition of the *Calvini Opera* (produced by the Institute for Reformation Research in Apeldoorn, NL).

[13] See, e.g., *Inst.* 1.13.2: 'He reveals himself as the one God in such a manner that he offers himself up to our contemplation in three distinct persons.' John Calvin, *Institutes of the Christian Religion* (trans. Ford Lewis Battles; ed. John T. McNeill; Philadelphia: Westminster, 1960).

[14] An English translation is available: John Calvin, *Institutes of the Christian Religion 1536 Edition* (trans. Ford Lewis Battles; Grand Rapids, MI: Eerdmans, 1975).

[15] *Inst.* 1536, p. 50.

[16] See ch. 4. There is no English translation of which I am aware.

known heretic. Indeed, Calvin's public pronouncements all stress that he had no wish to see Servetus die, desiring (ideally) his recantation, or (realistically) a commutation of sentence.[17] Across Europe, however, death was the prescribed penalty for a heretic,[18] and the city authorities followed normal custom. The affair seemingly made Calvin much more careful in his Trinitarian terminology, striving to express the inherited doctrine with exactness and not to imply anything beyond, and the 1559 edition of the *Institutes* is precise and reticent in its language in comparison with 1539. That said, the first thirteen chapters of the 1559 *Institutes*, dealing with the doctrine of God, are constructed to make four key points: that knowledge of God necessarily involves piety; that knowledge of God is only presently available through the Scriptures; that Scripture condemns idolatry in the strongest possible terms; and that the patristic doctrine of the Trinity is adequate to what Scripture says concerning God.

Calvin believed everything all orthodox Christians had believed since Constantinople:[19] God is simple; Father, Son, and Holy Spirit are three *hypostases* of one ineffable *ousia*; the *hypostases* are differentiated only by relations of origin; everything not related to a relation of origin must be said of all three *hypostases* indivisibly; our language about the divine *ousia* is profoundly limited and analogical. He has one distinctive emphasis, however, in stressing the autotheotic existence of each of the three *hypostases*.[20] For Calvin, the Son is God of himself, not God by gift of the Father – similarly the Spirit. Calvin's argument is essentially that the fullness of deity possessed by Son and

---

[17] Gordon, *Calvin*, pp. 217–32 is a full and balanced history of the dispute.

[18] Bucer, hardly the most aggressive of the Reformers, announced from the pulpit, 'Servetus deserves to be torn into pieces, after having had his entrails ripped out.' So Eric Kayayan, 'The Case of Michael Servetus', *Mid-America Journal of Theology* 8 (1992): pp. 117–46, p. 120.

[19] There are several recent and capable accounts of Calvin's Trinitarian theology in English; perhaps the best (although with no attention to historical development) is Paul Helm, *John Calvin's Ideas* (Oxford: OUP, 2004), pp. 35–57; see also Kurt Anders Richardson, 'Calvin on the Trinity', in *John Calvin and Evangelical Theology: Legacy and Prospect* (ed. Sung Wook Chung; Milton Keynes: Paternoster, 2009), pp. 32–42; and Thomas F. Torrance, 'Calvin's Doctrine of the Trinity', *CTJ* 25 (1990): pp. 165–93.

[20] The point is noted in Helm and Richardson, but by far the best treatment of this theme that I know is a doctoral thesis by Brannon E. Ellis, 'God of Himself: John Calvin, Classical Trinitarianism, and the Self-Existence of the Son of God' (University of Aberdeen, 2010). I understand that a monograph based on the thesis is forthcoming from Oxford University Press; it should be eagerly awaited by all interested in the details of Calvin's Trinitarian doctrine.

Spirit must include aseity, and so that it is improper to speak of the Son's deity as derived from the Father.

Biblical Anti-Trinitarianism

In narrating the history of dogma, we inevitably focus on the new and different, particularly when history shows it to have lasted and become significant. Anti-Trinitarianism in the sixteenth century was not a mass movement, perhaps not even a significant movement, numerically. On any account, Servetus was eccentric and isolated, and his positive doctrine, which was close to a species of what we would now call process theology, positing an account of God changing as the world proceeds, attracted few followers.[21] He is a significant representative, however, of the critical roots of one strand of anti-Trinitarianism that would become important from the sixteenth to the eighteenth century, what we might call biblical anti-Trinitarianism. Servetus was absolutely committed to the authority of Scripture, but regarded the doctrine of the Trinity to be a later distortion of biblical truth, rooted in Greek philosophy rather than in the Scriptures. This argument would become recurrent in rejections of Trinitarian doctrine down the years.

Servetus was not the first to query the received doctrine of the Trinity in the Reformation era;[22] and he was far from being the last.[23] Without question, however, the most famous and influential of the sixteenth-century biblical anti-Trinitarians was Faustus Socinus, the greatest theologian of the anti-Trinitarian Minor Reformed Church of Poland.[24] Although he acknowledged minor historical errors in the

---

[21] On Servetus, see *Michel Servet (1511–1553): Hérésie et pluralisme du XVIe au XXIe siècle* (ed. Valentine Zuber; Paris: Honoré Champion, 2007).

[22] That honour probably goes to Christian Entfelder, whose *Von Gottes und Christi* was published in 1530, a year before Servetus's *On the Errors of the Trinity*.

[23] For a brief survey of some strands, see Williams, *Radical Reformation*, pp. 319–25; for some serious but patchy studies, see *Antitrinitarianism in the Second Half of the 16th Century* (ed. Róbert Dán and Antal Pirnát; Leiden: Brill, 1982).

[24] For the church in general, with much useful material on Socinus, see George H. Williams, *The Polish Brethren* (2 vols; Missoula: Scholars Press, 1980); Earl Morse Wilbur's two-volume *History of Unitarianism* (Boston: Beacon Press, 1945) remains useful in addition. On Socinus himself, David Cory's *Faustus Socinus* (Boston: Beacon Press, 1932) remains the standard work; Alan W. Gomes has recently published several useful articles on aspects of his theology; see especially: 'De Jesu Christo Servatore: Faustus Socinus on the Satisfaction of Christ', *WTJ* 55 (1993):

Bible,[25] he regards it as authoritative in all matters of faith and doctrine; he believes, however, that the doctrine of the Trinity is unscriptural. The Bible teaches that Jesus Christ was a human being, albeit born of a virgin; he was obedient to God and was used by God to teach the true way of life to the world. After his death and resurrection, he ascended into heaven and was received into the divine glory, whence he will return to judge the living and the dead. As a result, it is proper now to worship Christ and to invoke him in prayer (this last point was controversial within the Minor Church, and Socinus had sharp debates over it with another pastor, Francis Dávid).[26] Thus stated, the closest patristic analogue to Socinus's doctrine of the Trinity is clearly dynamic monarchianism, an identification made by Gomes.[27]

Socinus's distinctive doctrines were preserved in the Racovian Catechism of the Polish Brethren, published in 1605.[28] The catechism teaches that God is unipersonal, and must necessarily be, since a person is 'an individual intelligent essence', and therefore if God is one in essence, he must be one in person.[29] Strikingly (and preserving Socinus's own teaching on the point), this is listed not as a dogma necessary to salvation (which the oneness of God is), but as a teaching that is extremely useful, but not necessary.[30] Jesus is called 'God' in the same way that the Psalms speak of many gods: he has been given power and authority by the one true God. Socinus's theme of adoption is played down here, although the catechism retains the possibility of worshipping Jesus.

The Minor Church was outlawed in the Polish Catholic Counter-Reformation in 1656; by then, the works of Socinus, and particularly

pp. 209–21; 'Some Observations on the Theological Method of Faustus Socinus (1539-1604)', *WTJ* 70 (2008): pp. 49–71; 'The Rapture of Christ: The "Pre-Ascension Ascension" of *Jesus in the Theology of Faustus Socinus* (1539–1604)', *HTR* 102 (2009): pp. 75–99.

25 See Gomes, 'Some Observations', pp. 54–5.
26 On which see John C. Gregory, 'Socinus and Christ' and George H. Williams, 'The Christological Issues between Francis Dávid and Faustus Socinus during the Disputation on the Invocation of Christ, 1578–1579', both in Dán and Pirnát, eds, *Antitrinitarianism*, pp. 57–63 and 287–321.
27 Gomes, 'Rapture', pp. 79–80.
28 *Catechesis Racoviensis* . . . (Frankfurt: Johannes Adam Schmidt, 1739) – this is the only edition of the original version I have been able to see. There was a revised edition, *Catechesis Ecclesiarum Polonicarum* . . . (Stauropoli: Eulogethus Philalethes, 1680); an English translation is available, based on the revision: Thomas Rees, *The Racovian Catechism* . . . (London: Longman, et al., 1818).
29 Q. 72: *persona nihil aliud sit, nisi essentia individua intelligens.*
30 Q. 71: . . . *rem vehementa utilia* . . .

the catechism, had been spread across Europe. Biblicist anti-Trinitarianism survived, particularly in England, where the emergence of organized dissent through the Civil War, the 1688 revolution, and the ensuing toleration provided a context of radical and biblicist movements, suspicious of church tradition, where such ideas could thrive.[31] Thomas Edwards's famous *Gangraena*,[32] a catalogue of the various extreme sects that thrived under the Protectorate, identifies several Trinitarian errors he has heard preached:

> 8. That right reason is the rule of Faith, and that we are to beleeve the Scriptures, and the Doctrine of the Trinity, Incarnation, Resurrection, so far as we see them agreeable to reason, and no farther . . .
> 24. That in the unity of the God-head there is not a Trinity of Persons but the Doctrine of the Trinity, beleeved and professed in the Church of God, is a Popish tradition and a Doctrine of *Rome*.
> 25. There are not three distinct Persons in the Divine Essence, but only three Offices; the Father, Son and holy Ghost are not three Persons, but Offices.
> 26. That there is but one Person in the Divine nature.
> 27. That Jesus Christ is not very God, not God essentially, but nominally, not the eternall Son of God by eternall generation, no otherwise may he be called the Son of God but as he was man.[33]

At least some of Edwards's targets were influenced by Socinus, or at least by the Racovian Catechism: his 26th error is a distinctively Socinian position (although not one that could not have been reached independently), and we know of several Socinian sympathizers in Britain at the time.[34] John Biddle, famous as the 'father of English Unitarianism', held to the position that there was only one person in God, defining 'person' in the same way as the catechism,[35] and arguing that the human person Jesus Christ was somehow united to the

---

[31] Philip Dixon, *Nice and Hot Disputes: The Doctrine of the Trinity in the Seventeenth Century* (London: T&T Clark, 2003) offers a helpful introduction to the various anti-Trinitarian movements and figures in England.

[32] Thomas Edwards, *Gangraena, or a Catalogue and Discovery of many of the errours . . .* (London: Ralph Smith, 1646); idem, *The Second Part of Gangraena* (London: Ralph Smith, 1646); idem, *The Third Part of Gangraena* (London: Ralph Smith, 1646).

[33] Edwards, *Gangraena*, pp. 19–21; the numbering is from Edwards's catalogue.

[34] Dixon, *Nice and Hot*, suggests that Paul Best's book, *Mysteries Discovered* (1647), displays 'more than passing acquaintance with the writings of Socinus and his followers', p.44.

[35] He would later (1652) publish an English translation of the *Racovian Catechism*.

one divine person in an adoptionistic way.[36] Biddle spent much of his life in prison for such sentiments, and attracted more rebuttals than followers; that said, his works remained influential after his death, and were known by, amongst others, John Locke.[37]

Biddle's arguments are interesting; some are re-presentations of fourth-century debates (for instance, he asserts 'He that is sent by another, is not God',[38] recalling precisely Augustine's debates over the divine missions); others depend on assertions of points carefully denied by the tradition (so he argues – rightly, according to classical Trinitarianism – that 'He that hath a will distinct in number from that of God is not God',[39] and goes on to assert that the Holy Spirit has a distinct will, which would have been denied by the Fathers. His proof of the point is exegetical, appealing to Romans 8:26–7 in particular as demonstrating a different will in the Spirit than in the Father.) He is at times impatient with traditional Trinitarian vocabulary: 'By Person I understand, as Philosophers do, *suppositum intelligens*, that is an intellectual substance compleat, and not a mood [sic, 'mode'?] or subsistence, which are fantastical & senseless terms, brought in to cozen the simple.'[40] Biddle appears not to see that it is both rather easy and completely pointless to disprove any argument by redefining one of its terms; if 'person' does not mean what Gregory or Augustine or Boethius or John Damascene or Thomas Aquinas took it to mean, then, naturally, their carefully logical usage of it will not be found convincing.

The ongoing debates in the seventeenth century were repeatedly obscured by such terminological problems. Genuine advances in philosophical method – associated with Descartes, Hobbes, and Locke – proposed redefinitions of key Trinitarian vocabulary – 'substance'; 'essence'; 'person' – and so disputants talked past each other, using the same words to mean different things. It is not a surprise that an

---

[36] John Biddle, *A Confession of Faith Touching the Holy Trinity according to the Scripture* (London: s.n., 1648); idem., *XII Arguments Drawn out of Holy Scripture . . .* (London: s.n., 1647).

[37] Locke published nothing concerning the Trinity; given his extensive writing on religious topics, and the extent of the arguments of the 1690s, Dixon's conclusion that 'his silence is not simply strange, it is stunningly eloquent' (*Nice and Hot*, p. 139) seems justified. See, however, Sell's comment that there were 'Trinitarian speech-patterns' in *The Reasonableness of Christianity. Alan P.F. Sell, *John Locke and the Eighteenth Century Divines* (Cardiff: University of Wales Press, 1997), pp. 202–3.

[38] Biddle, *XII Arguments*, p. 6.

[39] Biddle, *XII Arguments*, p. 13.

[40] Biddle, *XII Arguments*, pp. 2–3, marginal note.

appetite grew up amongst those not controversially inclined for a disciplined refusal to go beyond biblical language; at the Salters' Hall Synod of 1719, called in response to the challenge of several recent and powerful anti-Trinitarian texts, notably William Whiston's *Primitive Christianity* (1711) and Samuel Clarke's *Scripture Doctrine of the Trinity* (1712), many ministers, including a majority of the Presbyterians and almost all the General Baptists, declined to sign a proposed statement of faith on the grounds that its language was not found in the Bible. They were not closet anti-Trinitarians; they had merely reached the point of believing that definitions couched in technical language generated argument more often than understanding.[41]

Whiston and Clarke were accused not of Socinianism but of Arianism, reflecting a distinction known to the seventeenth-century controversialists. The 'Arians' were those who believed that the Logos/Son did pre-exist the human person of Jesus, but should not be considered to be divine in the same way as the Father is divine. In fact Whiston's views were more Homoian than Arian, in that he was prepared to accept the eternal, if subordinate, existence of the Son. Whiston's views have to be regarded as eccentric: he became fascinated with an anonymous patristic text, the *Apostolic Constitutions*, which he was convinced was indeed apostolic, and ought to be regarded as the final and crowning book of the New Testament. (In fact the text, although incorporating a complex mixture of earlier sources, can be dated with some confidence to circa 380, and reflects at points a broadly Homoian theology.) He published an edition and translation of this text, coupled with a far-reaching programme for reforming the church's doctrine in accord with its teachings, in his massive *Primitive Christianity Reviv'd*.[42] He would later propose revised liturgies and similar on the same basis.[43]

Samuel Clarke's *Scripture Doctrine of the Trinity* was, by contrast, resolutely biblical.[44] Clarke tells a familiar story of the pristine perfection of

---

[41] That said, the churches represented by the non-subscribing ministers mostly drifted into Unitarianism over the next century, suggesting that technical language and creeds were in fact providing some sort of check on the spread of anti-Trinitarian ideas. On Salters' Hall, and the aftermath, see Michael Watts, *The Dissenters: From the Reformation to the French Revolution* (Oxford: Clarendon, 1978), pp. 371–82.

[42] William Whiston, *Primitive Christianity Reviv'd in Four Parts . . .* (London: s.n., 1712).

[43] His output was voluminous, but see, e.g., William Whiston, *The Liturgy of the Church of England Reduc'd nearer to the Primitive Standard . . .* (London, s.n., 1713).

[44] Samuel Clarke, *The Scripture-Doctrine of the Trinity, in Three Parts . . .* (London: James Knapton, 1712).

the apostolic church, gradually declining, until reaching a nadir in the Middle Ages, from which trough the Reformation is the beginnings of a rise, but one that needs completing. For Clarke, the intrusion of metaphysical arguments into doctrine is the key motor of the decline, and the recovery of pure and simple Bible doctrine is what is needed.[45] He therefore engages in a form of what we would now call 'biblical theology', collecting and exegeting all the relevant New Testament texts in the first part of his book, offering a theological synthesis in the second, and proposing liturgical reforms in the third. He is not averse to speaking of the Son and the Spirit as 'divine persons',[46] insists that the Son is always present with the Father as a distinct person,[47] and accepts that Son and Spirit are worthy of worship. He claims, however, that Scripture nowhere speaks of the mode of generation of the Son (or Spirit), and so we should not speculate; on this basis, he argues that those who teach the *homoousios* are equally worthy of censure with those who teach the created nature of the Son.[48] Like Whiston, his doctrine was closest to a moderate Homoian position; the characterization of it as 'Arian' (which he hotly rejected) was wrong in detail but fair in intent.

Clarke is too early to be considered an Enlightenment figure, but all the characteristic disdain for tradition is there. He had a brilliant mind, and was a fine exegete; in a way, his book reads like an excellent fourth-century contribution, struggling to construct a theology out of Scripture, to work out what must be said and what cannot be said, without any of the help provided by the conceptual clarification of later generations (and, crucially, without any appeal to the Old Testament). He cites patristic texts in his second part, but only to show that others agreed with what he claims to have found in Scripture. On the basis of his own definitions, he asserted that the claim that the Trinity consists of 'three persons of the same individual essence' was necessarily illogical, and so could not be true. Alongside Socinus, Clarke was the greatest of the biblical anti-Trinitarians; he was also amongst the last. After Locke, careful appeals to the limits of understanding of revelation were going to appear at best quaint; a new way of judging the truth of falsity of propositions was on the table, and was going to offer an even more serious challenge to the inherited doctrine of the Trinity.

---

[45] See particularly his 'Introduction', pp. vii–x.
[46] See pp. 241–2.
[47] See pp. 287–8.
[48] See pp. 276–9.

Rational Anti-Trinitarianism

Edward Stillingfleet, bishop of Worcester and an able theologian, published his own *Discourse in Vindication of the Doctrine of the Trinity* in 1697;[49] it stands out from the mass of seventeenth-century works as much for its eirenic tone as for its evident learning and clear argument. Stillingfleet saw the problems with terminology with some clarity, and worked hard to show that the various defenders of the traditional position were all saying the same thing, even if in different words; he also refuted many opponents of the doctrine, amongst whom was John Toland (1670–1722), whose *Christianity Not Mysterious* had appeared the previous year.[50] Toland did not actually mention the Trinity in his book, but the implication that it was one of the doctrines to be discarded because not demonstrably rational was clear enough. Toland's subtitle makes his programme clear: henceforth, reason will be the judge of all doctrine.

Toland is an early representative of a movement commonly known as Deism,[51] which was much feared and written against in the first half of the eighteenth century. The movement was small in numbers of adherents, but powerful, both intellectually, and in the sense that it encapsulated, albeit radically, a prevailing cultural mood. Revelation was, at best, merely the easy presentation for the simple of things that can be known by reason, and are better so known; the true religion is the one that is ancient and universal, written in the hearts of all human beings, and not dependent on historical circumstances or supposed private revelations. Not surprisingly, under such a rubric the doctrine of the Trinity does not fare well; generally it is not even considered worthy of rebuttal, it is so obviously obscure and irrational.

Although Locke (intentionally or not) gave significant impetus to the Deist cause, it pre-dated him. Generally, the origins of English Deism are traced to Lord Herbert of Cherbury, whose *De Veritate* of

---

[49] Edward Stillingfleet, *A Discourse in Vindication of the Doctrine of the Trinity . . .* (London: Henry Mortlock, 1697).

[50] John Toland, *Christianity Not Mysterious, or a Treatise Shewing That There Is Nothing in the Gospel contrary to Reason, nor above It, and That No Christian Doctrine Can Properly Be Call'd a Mystery* (London: s.n., 1696).

[51] Deism is a complex and disputed movement; Jeffrey R. Wigelsworth, *Deism in Enlightenment England: Theology, Politics, and Newtonian Public Science* (Manchester: Manchester UP, 2009) will serve as a good introduction, avoiding the most common distortions. See also B.W. Young, *Religion and Enlightenment in Eighteenth-century England: Theological Debate from Locke to Burke* (Oxford: Clarendon, 1998).

1624 introduced the idea of 'common notions'.[52] Herbert was concerned by his increasing knowledge of the world and its great cultures: it seemed that different and incompatible claims about truth, and about ethics, were everywhere present; how, then, was one to judge what was true and right? His response was to propose five ideas that he believed existed in every religion and culture, because they are generally known and believed by all. His five 'common notions' are: the existence of one supreme deity; the propriety of worshipping said deity (alone); virtue as the essence of religious practice; human sinfulness, and its expiation by sincere repentance; and future rewards and punishments based on merit. From this distance, it is clear that Herbert read some Christian notions into those reports he received of other religious traditions, but the attempt to find that which is held in common was a noble one, and a consistent driver of later Deist – and wider Enlightenment – positions. (A century after Lord Herbert wrote, it is probably fairer to say that the quest was for that which *should be* held in common: people were blinded by custom and tradition, and what was needed was a rational vision that all could be convinced to understand and embrace.)

Perhaps the most famous single work to come out of the Deist movement is Tindal's *Christianity as Old as the Creation*.[53] For Tindal, the criticism of the doctrine of the Trinity is already complete. In 404 pages, he mentions it only twice. The first mention is in passing in a list of technical theological terms ('Divine Person, Essence, Trinity, Messiah, Incarnation, Hypostatical Union, Original Sin, Satisfaction, Justification, Predestination, Grace, Free-will, & all other technical terms') which, he observes, are endlessly redefined and so of endlessly varied meaning. His broader point is that a merely verbal revelation – an inspired text – cannot be an authoritative guide because always subject to interpretation.[54] The second mention is making a similar point: 'Dr S. Clark [*sic*, Samuel Clarke] has reckon'd up more than 1250 texts relating to the doctrine of the Trinity; and how few of them are interpreted alike by the contending parties? . . . had we a Bible translated by *Unitarians*, many texts would be very differently translated . . . and some left out as forg'd [presumably a reference to

---

[52] Edward, Lord Herbert of Cherbury, *De Veritate* (trans. Meyrick Carré; Bristol: University of Bristol, n.d.); the common notions are listed on pp. 289–303.

[53] Matthew Tindal, *Christianity as Old as the Creation: or, the Gospel a Republication of the Religion of Nature* (London: s.n., 1731).

[54] Tindal, *Christianity*, p. 263.

the Johannine comma]'.[55] Tindal is confident that a rational religion which will be capable of commanding the assent of all people can and will be found; it will not need a Bible, and will have no place for such metaphysical speculations as the doctrine of the Trinity.

Into the eighteenth century, French Enlighteners and German neologians assumed the same possibilities and offered the same criticisms of the doctrine. Voltaire, for instance, in his *Dictionnaire Philosophique*,[56] offered a characteristically mocking account of the doctrine under the heading 'Antitrinitaires' (Anti-Trinitarians):

> There are heretics who might not be viewed as Christians. They happen to regard Jesus as saviour and mediator, but they dare to hold that nothing is more unreasonable than what is taught amongst Christians concerning the trinity of persons in one single divine essence, the second of which is begotten by the first, and the third of which proceeds from the two others.
>
> That this unintelligible doctrine is not found anywhere in Scripture. That not one passage can be produced to support it, for which a clearer, more natural meaning, a meaning closer to common sense and basic and unchanging truth, can be found without departing from the spirit of the text . . .
>
> That it is a contradiction to say that there is only one God and that nevertheless there are three persons, each one truly God.
>
> That this distinction, one in essence, and three in persons, is nowhere in Scripture.
>
> That it is obviously false, because it is clear that there are no fewer essences than persons, or persons than essences . . .
>
> That from this it seems that the state of the question between them and the orthodox turns on whether there are three distinctions in God of which we have no idea, and between which there are certain relations of which we have no idea either . . .[57]

---

[55] Tindal, *Christianity*, p. 295.

[56] Voltaire, *Dictionnaire Philosophique* (ed. Raaymond Naves; Paris: Garnier, 1967).

[57] My trans.; the original reads: 'Ce sont des hérétiques qui pourraient ne pas passer pour chrétiens. Cependant ils reconnaissent Jésus comme sauveur et médiateur; mais ils osent soutenir que rien n'est plus contraire à la droite raison que ce qu'on enseigne parmi les chrétiens touchant la trinité des personnes dans une seule essence divine, dont la seconde est engendrée par la première, et la troisième procède des deux autres.

'Que cette doctrine inintelligible ne se trouve dans aucun endroit de l'Écriture.

'Qu'on ne peut produire aucun passage qui l'autorise, et auquel on ne puisse, sans s'écarter en aucune façon de l'esprit du texte, donner un sens plus clair, plus

Voltaire here combines several lines of attack: his essential point is the sheer irrationality of the doctrine: it is assumed in advance to be ridiculous. He buttresses this, however, with an appeal to the biblical anti-Trinitarian position: even if assumed to be true and authoritative, the texts are better explained by another position. He then assumes certain novel definitions of 'person' and 'essence', and points out that the old doctrine makes no sense with these redefinitions. There is actually little that could be classed as rational anti-Trinitarianism in this entry, although this was Voltaire's own position: he believed in the existence of a deity, who could be known by natural reason; he had no time, however, for such absurdities as the doctrine of the Trinity.[58]

Perhaps the crowning statement of this trajectory of thought is Kant's *Religion within the Limits of Reason Alone*,[59] which, however, stands far more in continuity with classical Christianity than most of the Deists. Following through on the transcendental method of his great *Critiques*,[60] in the *Religion*, Kant starts with an idea of radical evil: he believes that it is a truth of universal experience that human beings both know what it would be like to be good, but also know our present failure to live according to those standards. God's perfect ideal for the world is the well-lived human life, which ideal Kant calls the *Logos*; he suggests that it has taken up humanity and become a prototype and example of what a well-lived life would look like for us all. (Kant makes no explicit identification with Jesus in this: he is at least purporting to be arguing for that which is rationally demonstrable in

naturel, plus conforme aux notions communes et aux vérités primitives et immuables . . .

'Qu'il implique contradiction de dire qu'il n'y a qu'un Dieu, et que néanmoins il y a trois *personnes*, chacune desquelles est véritablement Dieu.

'Que cette distinction, un en essence, et trois en personnes, n'a jamais été dans l'Écriture.

'Qu'elle est manifestement fausse, puisqu'il est certain qu'il n'y a pas moins d'*essences* que de *personnes*, et de *personnes* que d'*essences* . . .

'Que l'on peut recueillir de là que l'état de la question entre les orthodoxes et eux, consiste à savoir s'il y a en Dieu trois distinctions dont on n'a aucune idée, et entre lesquelles il y a certaines relations dont on n'a point d'idées non plus' (*Dictionnaire Philosophique*, s.v. 'Antitrinitaires').
[58] See René Pomeau, *La Religion de Voltaire* (Paris: Nizet, 1994).
[59] An excellent translation is found in Immanuel Kant, *Religion and Rational Theology* (trans. and ed. Allen W. Wood and George Di Giovanni; Cambridge: CUP, 1996).
[60] In very brief outline, Kant's transcendental method is the practice of determining the necessary conditions for an experience to be real, for an accepted truth to be true, or for a body of knowledge to be useful.

the sphere of religion, and, as Lessing famously objected, there is a great ditch fixed between logical necessity and historical happenings.) This is, however, merely example, and not necessary example either. Any human being, truly desiring to live well, can do so, whether he or she knows of the example given or not.

As noted above, Kant is perhaps surprisingly orthodox. The belief that sets him apart from earlier Deists most fundamentally is his account of radical evil. He believes, as Tindal and Voltaire did not, that human beings stand in need of salvation. There is no doctrine of the Trinity here at all, however: an inchoate logos-theology in passing, but no more. There is a Christology of a form which becomes remarkably common in the nineteenth and twentieth centuries, however: Jesus as (divinely given) example or pioneer of true humanity (flippantly, one might say that Kant's Christology is summed up in the currently popular slogan 'What would Jesus do?'). The striking thing about this Christological formulation is the extent to which, in Kant's formulation, it marginalizes the historical event of Christ's coming. He is not what is important; the ideal to which he witnessed is. We live best, finally, when we forget the example and live according to the law as he did.

Rational anti-Trinitarianism begins with, and rapidly simply assumes, the claim that the received Trinitarian doctrine is incoherent; it further claims that there is a natural theology that teaches monotheism; and that this natural theology is what is important in matters of belief. The second of these three claims might be debated without prejudice or reference to the doctrine of the Trinity: it is Roman Catholic dogma, after all. The third claim is one that an orthodox Christianity must simply deny: the history of Jesus of Nazareth can never be a truth logically derivable by all people, and must be central. The first point is perhaps the most interesting: as I have tried to show, it turns largely on the acceptance of a redefinition of terms: if 'person' (in particular, but also 'essence', 'substance', etc.) is assumed to mean something radically different from what the Fathers meant by *hypostasis*, then the Trinitarian arguments of the Fathers will appear incoherent. This raises a problem of expression for classical Trinitarianism, but does not constitute a logical demonstration that classical Trinitarianism is false. The programme of rational anti-Trinitarianism must be held to have failed.

Pro-Nicene Theologies in the Early Modern Period

The majority of theological writers from the Reformation down to the end of the eighteenth century were supporters of the received doctrine of the Trinity. Repetitions of received orthodoxy rarely feature highly in histories of theology, of course, unless their authors were innovative in other areas of their thought, but the general orthodoxy of the tradition should not be forgotten. I have not had space to explore many of the conservative responses to the anti-Trinitarians discussed in this chapter, but they were there, and capable (particularly John Owen against English Socinianism, and Daniel Waterland's response to Samuel Clarke); no space at all has been given to the steady stream of carefully orthodox confessions and systems of doctrine proceeding from Roman Catholic, Lutheran, and Reformed writers alike. Richard Muller, after a vast and erudite survey of the Reformed writers from the sixteenth to the eighteenth century, can sum up his findings on the doctrine of the Trinity with the comment: 'In the doctrine of the Trinity, there is a striking continuity . . . mediated through the medieval scholastics, codified at the Fourth Lateran Council and the Council of Florence, respected by the Reformers, and developed as well by the Reformed orthodox . . . assumptions concerning the simplicity of God, the meanings of various attributes, and the patterns of definitions of the Trinity remained constant.'[61]

The same could be said of the Roman and Lutheran traditions.

---

[61] Richard A. Muller, *Post-Reformation Reformed Dogmatics: The Rise and Development of Reformed Orthodoxy, ca. 1530 to ca. 1725, vol. 4: The Triunity of God* (Grand Rapids, MI: Baker, 2003), p. 415.

9.

'A transformation which will go back to its very beginnings': The Doctrine of the Trinity since 1800

Introduction

I used to teach a module, now retired, under the title 'Contemporary issues in Christian doctrine', a title not my own. I would begin the module by explaining to the students how I proposed to interpret 'contemporary', offering the comment that anything that had happened since the French Revolution should not be considered history, but current affairs. I meant this comment seriously, at least when considering the history of Christian doctrine: almost all of the arguments we are now involved in (political and contextual theologies might be the most significant exception) are arguments that began in reaction to Kant and that, whilst they have grown and developed, have not yet been either solved or forgotten. We need to read Hegel and Schleiermacher as earlier voices in our own conversation, not as alien voices from the past. This last chapter, then, is an account of contemporary trends in Trinitarian doctrine.

As such, it will be less determinedly historical than previous chapters. Here I will finally attempt to draw together themes, evaluations, and arguments concerning the nature of the contemporary Trinitarian debate. I began the book with a fairly lengthy account and characterization of the tradition in the twentieth century, which I will not repeat. In returning to the twentieth century at the end of my story, however, I will be attempting to locate the story with which I began against the history I have sketched since. First, however, the nineteenth century beckons, and some towering figures within it.

Rational Trinitarians: Coleridge and Hegel

At the beginning of the nineteenth century, two enormously powerful intellects attempted to offer a recognizably classical account of the doctrine of the Trinity that was developed from rational thought alone. In a sense, the programme was to out-reason the rational anti-Trinitarians of the previous century; certainly, in both cases, there was a desire to overthrow (at least some of) the assumptions of enlightenment, and to find a way beyond Kant. Of the two, Georg Wilhelm Friedrich Hegel's thought became defining for the next two centuries, and remains so; Samuel Taylor Coleridge's ideas remained unpublished until very recently.

Coleridge's reasonings stood in recognizable continuity with a tradition of Christian Platonism that stretched from the Fathers through John Scotus Eriugena, Nicholas of Cusa, and – Coleridge's immediate inspirations – the Cambridge Platonists of the seventeenth century: Ralph Cudworth; Henry More; Benjamin Whichcote; and others. The tradition was generally mystical in piety, seeing ascent to God as the primary human good, and believed (perhaps because of this: the real connection of the human soul to God postulated in this mysticism suggests an availability of the divine without revelation) in the possibility of a rational theology – and often the reality of an ancient unrevealed theology, the *prisca theologia* – in which the truth of the doctrine of the Trinity was available to all who thought carefully about the nature of the divine.

Coleridge begins with the belief,[1] which he holds to be rationally demonstrable, that the primordial reality is will: 'The Will, the absolute Will, is that which is essentially causative of reality, essentially and absolutely . . .'[2] He accepts, also, the position that divine perfection implies the lack of potentiality in God: *actus purus sine ulla potentia*. Therefore, primordial will does not remain merely potent, but wills to be. Its existence first is as the Supreme Mind, which again cannot remain merely potent, and so eternally contemplates itself,

---

[1] I have written more expansively on Coleridge's Trinitarian development in my chapter 'Coleridge', in *The Blackwell Companion to Nineteenth Century Theology* (ed. David Fergusson; Oxford: Blackwell: 2010), pp. 76–96; my exposition here will follow that argument closely, and assume some of the points I was able to argue in the longer piece.

[2] Kathleen Coburn, ed., *The Collected Works of Samuel Taylor Coleridge*, Bollingen Series 75 (jointly published by Routledge & Kegan Paul [London] and Princeton University Press [Princeton, NJ], vol. 15, p. 220.

producing ('begetting') the Supreme Idea, the Logos. The eternal self-realization of primordial will, however, must remain united, and so there is a third existence, the unity which Mind and Idea, or Father and Son, share: the Holy Spirit. The eternal act of self-realization of primordial will, therefore, just is the Trinity, and one may – and Plato did – think oneself to this position without ever having heard the name of Jesus Christ. The primordial will, Coleridge claims, 'abideth in the Father, the Word and the Spirit, totally and absolutely in each, one and the same in all.'[3] A worked-through doctrine of the Trinity – not just a vague triad, but an account of three hypostatic existences of the same essence – is presented as derived solely from reasoning about the nature of primordial will.

It is not, of course, difficult to unpick the smuggled assumptions in Coleridge's argument (why does will manifest first as supreme mind?); the argument that the doctrine of the Trinity is derivable through natural theology is a striking one, however, and one Coleridge upheld in print more than once.[4] He unfortunately never completed or published his fully worked-out account of how speculative reasoning may prove Trinitarian doctrine[5] and so we cannot tell how influential it might have been. I suppose that it would have been found eccentric: there are few, if any, examples of anyone not already convinced of the truths of Christianity following a path of reasoning such as Coleridge sketches out, and that alone makes his proposal implausible.

Hegel did publish, very extensively, and became one of the most influential thinkers of the modern period. At the heart of his system was a concept and a method. The concept was *Geist* – the German can carry senses of 'mind', 'spirit', or even 'ghost' in English, but the general English translation is 'spirit'. For Hegel, this replaces more traditional concepts of 'substance' or 'being' – or indeed God – as being more dynamic and energetic. *Geist* does not simply subsist; it acts. Hegel's fundamental method was the dialectic: almost everything in history, politics, metaphysics, and religion unfolds through a process of an initial thesis giving birth to its own antithesis, and the two finding union in a synthesis. In his *Lectures on the Philosophy of Religion*,[6]

---

[3] *Collected Works* 15, p. 222.
[4] See, e.g., *Collected Works* 9, p. 177.
[5] *Collected Works* 15 was the first publication of the fragments, in 2002.
[6] G.W.F. Hegel, *Lectures on the Philosophy of Religion* (3 vols; ed. and trans. Peter C. Hodgson, et al.; Berkeley: UC Press, 1984–7). The best analysis of the text in English is Hodgson's own: Peter C. Hodgson, *Hegel and Christian Theology: A Reading of the Lectures on the Philosophy of Religion* (Oxford: OUP, 2005).

Hegel describes the self-manifestation of *Geist*/absolute spirit through a dialectic process: absolute spirit first creates that which is not absolute spirit, both finite spirit and matter; then absolute spirit embraces that which is not itself, overcoming the distinction in a greater unity.[7] Hegel identifies this threefold pattern with the economic action of the persons of the Trinity. The Father creates that which is not-God; the Son becomes that which is not-God and embraces total otherness from the Father – death – to bring about reconciliation, the Spirit-filled eschaton where all things are gathered up in God.

Hegel does have a concept of an eternal Trinity behind the economic: in the eternal life of God is a pattern of identity begetting otherness, and togetherness proceeding from the two together. That said, Hegel's God inevitably creates the world: the logical pattern of God's own life needs enacting in reality, 'which is not merely a play of love with itself but an engaged and serious love for others.'[8] God is possessed of his own immanent perfection, but needs to be oriented toward the future in which he will have overcome the God-world distinction and become the unity of the Holy Spirit.

Clearly, Hegel's ideas are profoundly speculative; he himself, with fine Christian humility, saw them as the final synthesis of the thesis of Enlightenment rationalism and its antithesis in Romantic irrationalism, and so as the last word in the history of philosophy which had now revealed the truth of the world. History judged somewhat differently, of course, but Hegel's ideas have been profoundly influential. Whilst his school disintegrated into competing wings, each emphasizing one area of his thought and downplaying another, in Germany in the middle of the nineteenth century (and even the later flowering of British idealism died away early in the twentieth century), certain ideas of Hegel's have become standard assumptions of much modern theology. His demand for a more dynamic account of God's essential being, whilst arguably a simple misunderstanding of the dynamism of the *actus purus* tradition of Thomas Aquinas, has become a rallying cry for such different traditions and schools as the process theology of Hartshorne and the work of Karl Barth.[9] Equally, his account of God's

---

[7] See Hegel, *Lectures*, 3:273–4.
[8] Hodgson, *Hegel*, p. 130.
[9] See Colin E. Gunton, *Becoming and Being: The Doctrine of God in Charles Hartshorne and Karl Barth* (London: SCM, 2nd edn, 2001) for a revealing account which begins from the assumption that the 'classical doctrine of God' (p. 1) has been sufficiently critiqued that it is untenable, and looks to Barth and Hartshorne as alternative options for what will replace it.

life as being lived out through the life of the world is repeatedly assumed in modern theology.

Perhaps Hegel's most influential move, considered in the light of twentieth-century Trinitarianism, however, is more subtle, but more far-reaching, than the above. In rejecting the inherited doctrine, the anti-Trinitarianism of the previous centuries had also rejected the theme, fundamental to Athanasius and Basil, that there is a basic metaphysical gulf between Creator and creation. The adoptionist ideas of Socinus could perhaps maintain this, although it does not seem to have been a major theme for him; Clarke's *Scripture Doctrine* reverts to an idea of metaphysical gradations, and the location of the Son and Spirit between the Father and creation, ontologically speaking. Hegel has a basic gulf, but he locates it in the Father-Son relation, not in the God-world relation, and proposes that it will be overcome in the eschatological synthesis which is spirit-filled life. (Coleridge, in locating 'alterity' in the Father-Son relation, and the possibility of all that is distinct from God in the life of the Son, had done something similar.)

Recent Trinitarian theology has again and again followed Hegel in this: the basic distinction in reality is the Father-Son distinction, not the God-world distinction. It is important not to read the classical doctrine into this move: it is emphatically not an attempt to place the Son on the created side of a Creator-creation distinction. As with Hegel, it is an account of how the life of the world becomes a part of the life of God; the fundamental ontological distinction that used to be implied in the doctrine of *creatio ex nihilo* has essentially been rejected as unhelpful, because the eschatological expectation is the overcoming of all such distinctions, the embracing of all things in the life of the divine. Creation is not fundamentally, then, the bringing into being of that which is not God, but the distention of God's own life in unstable ways, which require a history of redemption for a new, enlarged, stability to emerge. The basis of this distention is located in the fundamental account of otherness, the begetting of the Son by the Father.

Useless Orthodoxy? Schleiermacher and Hodge

Hegel's more explicitly theological thought was developed in direct conversation with F.D.E. Schleiermacher,[10] his colleague in Berlin. There

---

[10] Helpful recent studies on Schleiermacher in English include Terrence N. Tice, *Schleiermacher* (Nashville: Abingdon, 2006) and the various papers in Jacqueline

is a familiar story told of Schleiermacher, that, horrified by the Romantic rejection of religion, he proposed (in the *Speeches on Religion*) a startlingly new apologetic based on an appeal to human religious experience (presumed to be universal and fairly uniform); this was then codified into a theological system in *The Christian Faith*, a system which begins by establishing the validity of theology from discussions of universal religious experience. Certainly, the *Speeches* offer a brilliant Christian apologetic based on religion as 'the sensibility and taste for the infinite'[11] and Schleiermacher's own profoundly Christocentric and experiential piety; recent scholarship has been less ready to assume that the organization of *The Christian Faith* reflects Schleiemacher's views on the proper intellectual basis of theology, however, instead seeing the opening sections as serving to locate the present theological task historically.[12]

In contrast to Hegel, Schleiermacher is self-consciously conservative in his outlines of doctrine, repeatedly referencing Scripture and the confessional statements of the Reformed churches; he is prepared to accept the need to overthrow traditional arguments and terminology as no longer meaningful in his particular historical context, but, in *The Christian Faith*[13] in particular, displays throughout a concern to be responsible to the theological tradition. The tradition, however, is an inheritance to which we must be responsible in doing theology at our own moment of history, not a body of timeless knowledge which we must master (or be mastered by) and then pass on unchanged.

This acute sense of the historical development of thought is of particular importance in the context of Schleiermacher's account of the Trinity in *The Christian Faith*.[14] Schleiermacher witnesses to the essential stability of church doctrine from the medieval period to the eighteenth century with which I ended the last chapter, and regards it as an enormous,

---

Mariña, *The Cambridge Companion to Friedrich Schleiermacher* (Cambridge: CUP, 2005); in the latter, see especially Francis Schüssler Fiorenza, 'Schleiermacher's Understanding of God as Triune', pp. 171–88.

[11] The standard English translation is Friedrich Schleiermacher, *On Religion: Speeches to Its Cultured Despisers* (ed. and trans. Richard Crouter; Cambridge: CUP, 2000); this quotation is on p. 23.

[12] The best introduction to this tradition of reading in English is now Christine Helmer, 'Schleiermacher', in *Blackwell Companion to Nineteenth-Century Theology* (ed. Fergusson), pp. 31–57. See especially the phrasing of the question on p. 32, contrasting §§1–31 read as 'a philosophical foundation' with it read as 'a preliminary contextualization', and the developed account on pp. 48–50.

[13] F.D.E. Schleiermacher, *The Christian Faith* (trans. J.S. Stewart and H.R. Mackintosh; Edinburgh: T&T Clark, 1928).

[14] Schleiermacher, *The Christian Faith*, §§170–72.

almost intractable, problem. For Schleiermacher, there is a periodic need for reconstructions of doctrines to reassert their continuing relevance in successive stages of history; the peculiar value of the Reformation, on his account, was its wholesale and successful restatement of so many Christian doctrines; the Trinity, however, was left untouched. His analysis of the situation in which this leaves the doctrine is uncompromising: 'so there must still be in store for it a transformation which will go back to its very beginnings' (§172). Schleiermacher is concerned that the early conciliar statements of the doctrine contained many attempts to avoid heathen polytheism, and yet to maintain the necessary confession of plurality in the Godhead; such strictures are no longer needed, since polytheism is no longer a live teaching (in Europe . . .). Schleiermacher does not think himself capable of providing the necessary reconstruction, however: he ends his great work with a claim that he has attempted to restate and clarify the more immediate doctrines, those that give us direct language to name our religious experiences, and that this is the necessary preliminary to a restatement of the Trinity; he does not, however, propose to offer such a restatement himself (§172.3).

This comment on the historical location of the doctrine introduces the three most criticized features of Schleiermacher's Trinitarian doctrine: its placement, as the last word in the book (and a brief word at that); the claim that, in contrast to all other doctrines treated, it 'is not an immediate utterance concerning the Christian self-consciousness, but only a combination of several such utterances' (§170); and its relative poverty, with a minimal, perhaps unacceptable, account of the doctrine presented and several apparent indications that Schleiermacher despairs of the possibility of giving anything better. The placement at the end is often taken to be deliberately marginalizing, the reduction of the doctrine to a mere appendix.[15] Schleiermacher in fact explains his placement: in the contemporary need for doctrinal reformulation, the doctrine of the Trinity stands as a means of drawing together the developed statements of several other doctrines, and insisting that they in fact belong together (most basically, it is the claim that the two claims that we meet the divine in Christ, and that the Spirit indwells the church, do not stand in opposition to each other); given this, even if in logical presentation it might belong as the first word of theology, as the doctrine on which all others depend, in the task of restatement it must be the last doctrine to be considered.

---

[15] For a representative sample of such charges, see Fiorenza, 'Schleiermacher's Understanding', pp. 172–3.

This already explains something of the placement of the doctrine, but Schleiermacher's general treatment of the doctrine of God should also be considered. *The Christian Faith* contains no separate section on the doctrine of God; instead, it argues from aspects of Christian experience towards accounts of what must be true of the divine for that experience to be authentic. So a consideration of our inescapable awareness of sin leads to the deductions that God is holy, just, and merciful; again, a consideration of our awareness of our own finitude leads to a doctrine of creation and the propositions that God is eternal, omnipresent, omnipotent, and omniscient. Schleiermacher proceeds by a series of abstractions from narrations of the Christian life to his doctrine of God, and the highest abstraction is the doctrine of the Trinity, which is fundamentally an assertion that all these other experiences find their union in one divine life.[16] As such, Schleiermacher describes the doctrine as 'the coping-stone of Christian doctrine' (§170.1) – the crowning glory which gives shape and completeness to the whole.

Turning to the alleged poverty of Schleiermacher's doctrine, three complaints need to be distinguished: the first is that he does not, in fact, say very much; the second that even what he does say is wrong; and the third that he seems to suggest that an adequate account can never be given. On the first, and as already noted, Schleiermacher is quite open about the fact that he is not offering a developed doctrine, and that this needs to be done; the criticism is fair, then, but hardly interesting, in that it is merely highlighting a defect that the author himself has cheerfully admitted to in the text. The second and third criticisms are potentially more interesting, and at first sight seem supported. Schleiermacher asserts and argues that simultaneously fully asserting the unity and the triunity of God is impossible: we either emphasize one at the expense of the other, or 'remain hesitating between the two' (§171.3), not expressing either adequately. This certainly appears to be a denial of the received doctrine, and a claim that it is impossible to ever find an adequate statement.

However, this comment needs to be read in the light of Schleiermacher's general historical treatment. As already noted, he believes that the context of apologetic against pagan polytheism led to an unhappy fascination with, put crudely, the numerical aspects of the doctrine. As long as we think the doctrine is a logical problem to do with combining ones and threes, we will never express it adequately.

---

[16] Fiorenza, 'Schleiermacher's Understanding', is very good on this.

Rather, we are searching for a doctrine which allows us to gather up the redemptive experience of Christ, the communal work of the Spirit, and all the divine perfections he has identified, and point to the essential unity of them all, without losing their real particularity, in the divine essence. This is not, as far as I can see, a denial of anything central, nor is it a despairing assertion that we cannot find an adequate doctrine of the Trinity; it may be a call for us to find different modes of expression from those our predecessors used, but that, right or wrong, is hardly an embracing of heresy.

Schleiermacher simply accepts the critique of classical Trinitarian terminology: persons and nature are no longer meaningful or useful terms (see especially §97.2, on Christology, on this); he goes further, and asserts the unintelligibility at our moment in history of the classical formulae. The doctrine of the Trinity stands in need of re-narration. This, however, is not such a pressing task as the doctrine itself is useless in terms of Christian practice: it is logically essential, in crowning and defining the grand edifice of doctrine, but it has no direct connection with Christian piety, experience, or action. This same concern over the practical uselessness of the doctrine can be found in a much more conservative theologian, Charles Hodge from old Princeton.

Hodge's exposition of the Trinity[17] begins with what I take to be a deliberate and direct response to Schleiermacher, although the German is never named. The doctrine of the Trinity is the heart of revealed truth, and it is of the essence of revealed truth to be useful. Assertion of the practical uselessness of the doctrine must be wrong, even if coupled with a claim of its logical centrality in a system. 'Truth is in order to holiness. God does not make known his being and attributes to teach men science, but to bring them to saving knowledge of Himself.'[18] How, then, is it useful? Hodge soon offers an answer:

> It [the doctrine of the Trinity] is the unconscious or unformed faith, even of those of God's people who are unable to understand the term by which it is expressed. They all believe in God, the Creator and Preserver . . . They . . . believe in a divine Redeemer and a divine Sanctifier. They have, as it were, the factors of the doctrine of the Trinity in their own religious convictions (p. 443).

---

[17] Charles Hodge, *Systematic Theology*, vol. 1 (Peabody, MA: Hendrickson, 2003), pp. 442–82.

[18] Hodge, *ST* p. 442.

It is immediately striking how direct a response to Schleiermacher this is: Hodge couches his account of the usefulness of the doctrine in an analysis of the inchoate religious consciousness of ordinary believers. However, as Schleiermacher would have been quick to point out, this is not the received doctrine of the Trinity. Rather, it is modalism, an account of the three *hypostases* as playing different economic roles. Hodge knows this well enough: '[t]he terms Father, Son, and Spirit do not express different relations of God to his creatures. They are not analogous to the terms Creator, Preserver, and Benefactor.'[19] Or, presumably, to the terms Creator, Redeemer, and Sanctifier. Hodge knows, and defends as biblical, the doctrine that the external acts of the Trinity are undivided.[20]

How are we to understand this apparent contradiction? It might be that Hodge is intending only to indicate that the rudimentary and unarticulated spiritual experience of the ordinary Christian is essentially triadic, and is not expecting us to derive any doctrinal consequences from it. If so, however, his opening and strident assertions of the usefulness of Trinitarian doctrine are left without any content, unless we are prepared to accept an inchoate modalism. Hodge wants to give content to the usefulness of the received doctrine, but cannot.

For the rest, Hodge attempts to offer a careful restatement of what was received, together with demonstrations or (more commonly) assertions that it is all biblical, and a glance at the history. Along the way, he accepts a redefinition of the word 'person' seemingly unwittingly. His operative definition is 'a person is an intelligent subject who can say I, who can be addressed as Thou, and who can act and can be the object of action' (p. 444). This definition does not force him to deviate very much from the received doctrine (he holds to the singularity of the divine intellect and will, for instance), but is an indication of a turn towards an interest in the personal that was a significant movement in nineteenth-century theology and an important influence on twentieth-century Trinitarianism.

Dorner and the Turn to the Person

P.T. Forsyth, writing at the beginning of the twentieth century, but summing up a nineteenth-century move, announced that the highest

---

[19] Hodge, *ST* p. 444; see also the discussion of Sabellianism on p. 459.

[20] More accurately, he asserts that 'the persons of the Trinity concur in all external acts' (*ST* p. 445), which, it will be observed, is not quite the same as the received doctrine. I take it that this deviation is a result of his redefinition of 'person' noted below.

goal of modern theology was the completion of the project begun at the Reformation, of the 'moralizing' of dogma, the replacing of the metaphysics of substance that had underlain traditional constructions with a 'metaphysics' based on morals.[21] Behind this lay a conviction that the understanding of God, and so ultimate reality, is moral and personal, rather than metaphysical. He learned this conviction from Isaak Dorner,[22] who had in the mid-nineteenth century argued for a basic shift in theology from regarding God as absolute substance to seeing God as absolute personality.[23] As Malysz sums up Dorner's central concern, 'the doctrine conceives of God as the utterly simple substance, and only as an afterthought does it half-heartedly attempt to reconcile the attribute of simplicity with the claim that God is also subjective and personal.'[24] On Dorner's telling, the definition of God as a simple, immutable, substance needs to be replaced with God as utterly and irreducibly personal.

Dorner developed these views in conscious dependence on Schleiermacher. In his *Divine Immutability*,[25] he offers a lengthy account of the historical development of the doctrine from Augustine to Schleiermacher. Traditional concepts of divine perfection stem from a demythologizing of pagan, anthropomorphic accounts of deity; God is the supreme good, not capricious, not jealous, not changing, a settled ethical perfection. This is unstable, however, because it appears to deny the possibility of God's action in the world. It is prone to collapse in one of two directions: Deism, maintaining the immutable perfection of the divine, but separating God from the world; or pantheism, identifying God with all the change and flux in the world.

---

[21] P.T. Forsyth, *The Person and Place of Jesus Christ* (London: Independent Press, 5th edn, 1946; original edn, 1909), pp. 213–24.

[22] See Leslie McCurdy, *Attributes and Atonement: The Holy Love of God in the Theology of P.T. Forsyth* (Carlisle: Paternoster Press, 1999), pp. 5–7, for evidence of Dorner's influence on Forsyth. McCurdy focuses simply on the definition of God as 'Holy Love' here, and so does not explicitly recognize either the centrality of a turn from metaphysical to moral conceptions of deity (a point which is made elsewhere in his book), or the dependence of this central Forsythian move on Dorner (a point which is absent).

[23] See I.A. Dorner, *A System of Christian Doctrine*, vol. 1 (trans. Alfred Cave; Edinburgh: T&T Clark, 1880), p. 412ff. For an excellent examination of this theme in Dorner, see Jonathan Norgate, *Isaak A. Dorner: The Triune God and the Gospel of Salvation* (London: T&T Clark, 2009), pp. 10–52.

[24] Piotr J. Malysz, 'Hegel's Conception of God and Its Application by Isaak Dorner to the Problem of Divine Immutability', *ProEccl* 15 (2006), pp. 448–71, p. 466.

[25] I.A. Dorner, *Divine Immutability: A Critical Reconsideration* (trans. R.R. Williams and Claude Welch; Minneapolis: Fortress, 1994).

Schleiermacher cuts through all this with his method of theology as the analysis of the necessary underlying reality to the Christian experience of sinfulness and redemption. This reconception of the work of theology allows for a revisiting of the problem of immutability, one which Schleiermacher did not, however, fully carry through.[26]

Schleiermacher held to the older idea of the perfection of God: 'simple self-sameness and self-identical, without opposition. In this simplicity, no real distinction between attributes, no distinction between knowledge and will . . . nothing potential in God that does not become eternally actual . . .'[27] Dorner believes this makes historical reality an illusion: in God's eternity everything has been willed with one immutable will, known with one immediate perception. This is at odds, however, with Schleiermacher's focus on the lived experience of crisis and resolution in Christian experience. Therefore a new doctrine of immutability, one which allows for the reality of history, is needed.

Dorner returns to the Euthyphro dilemma, the *locus classicus* for appeals to divine simplicity. Is what God wills good because there is an external standard of goodness by which to judge him? Clearly not. Is it good merely because God wills it? No, because this would make divine goodness a creation of the divine will, not something basic. So the good must be somehow identical with God's life, neither external nor arbitrary. Thus far, the argument is the standard one for simplicity. Dorner's original move, however, is to further insist that goodness must be willed and chosen, not merely innate: it must be ethical, not merely metaphysical. So, claims Dorner, 'God is to be conceived *first* as the ethically necessary being or as the holy, *second* as the ethically free, through both of these, God actualizes himself eternally as self-conscious, holy and free love.'[28] This, of course, is a Trinitarian formula: Father and Son together in the Spirit. The argument could be seen as a Hegelian dialectic: the personality of the divine life is the synthesis of necessary goodness and freely chosen goodness. The personal God, then, can only exist in multiple – specifically three – modes

---

[26] This is a summary of the whole of Part 2 of *Divine Immutability*. For some helpful analyses, see Robert R. Williams, 'I.A. Dorner: The Ethical Immutability of God', *JAAR* 54 (1986): pp. 721–38; Robert Sherman, 'Isaak August Dorner on Divine Immutability: A Missing Link between Schleiermacher and Barth', *JR* 77 (1997): pp. 380–401. For an account of a different genealogy, see Robert F. Brown, 'Schelling and Dorner on Divine Immutability', *JAAR* 52 (1985): pp. 237–49.

[27] Dorner, *Divine Immutability*, p. 124.

[28] Dorner, *Divine Immutability*, p. 171.

of being;[29] but God must be personal, so the doctrine of the Trinity is central to the maintenance of an adequate theology.

Dorner thus witnesses to a new interest in the category of person-hood, but knows enough history not to casually assume that in the divine this 'personal' category must be applied to the 'persons'. (I have already commented on Barth's appropriation of Dorner's views in this respect.)[30] He thus represents some sort of mediating position between the classical doctrine and the late twentieth-century accounts of three fully personal *hypostases* united by their shared relationships. Whence, though, this interest in the category of the personal? It is, after all, in danger of seeming crudely anthropomorphic: we take an aspect of our own experience – a nexus of self-awareness, possession of volition, and ratiocination – and assert that it is necessary for God to be like this. *Pace* Dorner, what is wrong with a deity who is neces-sarily good in a metaphysical sense? (Dorner's argument against Schleiermacher is, after all, susceptible to some very well-rehearsed defences of the compatibility of divine providence and human free-dom on the basis of the relationship of eternity to time; Dorner was too good a theologian not to have known this.)

I have suggested elsewhere that the influence of the Romantic movement was key. The Romantic rebellion against the mechanistic philosophies of the Enlightenment is one we still live with; in the face of suggestions that the only necessary metaphor to understand the world was 'machine', the Romantic movement reasserted self-con-sciousness, beauty, emotion, and the spiritual experience of humanity as the highest good. Personhood, then, understood as being funda-mentally about self-determination, and so about volition, and so expressed primarily in spontaneous emotional reaction, became the highest good, the essence and height of what it is to be human. Given this, there has been and is still an enormous cultural pressure to assert that this currently popular cultural construction of the good be applied to God also (and if some believe that Romanticism died away, consider the equivalent demands of personalism or existentialism – and in a more extreme and juvenile form, of pop culture, supremely in the 1960s, but also ever since).

In Dorner and Barth – and in others since – there is a refusal to allow this novel and modern sense of 'person' (consider that in the seven-teenth and eighteenth centuries Locke and Voltaire – hardly diehard

---

[29] Williams, 'I.A. Dorner', pp. 73–5 is an excellent summary of this argument in Dorner.

[30] See above, p. 5–8.

defenders of classical theology – were still assuming that 'person' meant 'individual intelligent substance') to infect the technical term 'person'. For Dorner and Barth, God is personal in this sense of the word, but not tri-personal in this sense of the word. I confess to having hesitations even to such a concession: on the one hand, if normal rules of theological discourse are to apply, it is at best an analogy, and a stretched one at that: to take only one of many possible examples, it seems to me that the discursive nature of my intellect is intrinsic to my being personal in this sense: the interior conversation of teasing out and testing ideas that is my inevitable experience is quintessentially personal, defining my self-awareness in decisive ways. It is a standard piece of doctrine, however, to insist that God's knowledge, being perfect, is not discursive but complete and immediate: God in one instant act of apprehension perceives all things, and all relations between them, perfectly. Already, it seems to me, the contemporary definition of 'personhood' is being stretched to, or beyond, breaking point by this single example. Far better, if the term must be used, to borrow coinages such as 'suprapersonal'. More pertinently, it is not clear to me why we should allow a set of ideas, often enough hazy or inchoate, and derived from a Romantic reaction to Enlightenment philosophy, to become decisive for our theological constructions.

The practice of speaking of three 'persons' in this sense in the divine life, of asserting a 'social doctrine of the Trinity', a 'divine community' or an 'ontology of persons in relationship' can only ever be, as far as I can see, a simple departure from (what I have attempted to show is) the unified witness of the entire theological tradition. Why, then, has it become so popular? In part at least, I think, because of a fundamental sense of dislocation. Dorner suggests that Schleiermacher pointed out a fundamental weakness in the inherited doctrine of God which then needed correcting; Forsyth and Barth followed him in this belief, although in neither case showing any explicit awareness that it came from Schleiermacher. More generally, the harvest of nineteenth-century theology includes a broad sense that the discipline stood in need of fundamental reformulation, as Schleiermacher had said it did. If we try to analyze this logically, it tends to reduce to a series of claims about the broad narrative of the theological tradition – such as the claim that it became profoundly infected by Greek metaphysics in the patristic period – which were based on nineteenth-century historical work; we all now know that the historical work was inadequate in many ways, but the sense that the tradition we have received is somehow warped or broken remains strong. For an example of this, I turn to my final nineteenth-century witnesses, Ritschl and von Harnack.

Ritschl, von Harnack, and the History of Religion

Hegel and Schleiermacher in different ways had brought the idea of historical development to the fore in theology; the task of describing a rational history of religion was one to which a number of great German theologians gave themselves in the nineteenth century.[31] We might start the story with F.C. Baur's elaborate and extravagant – yet brilliant – account of Catholic Christianity as the triumphant outcome of a Hegelian synthesis between Pauline and Petrine parties somewhere in the mid-second century; whilst profoundly fanciful at times, relying on many highly speculative reconstructions, and, as is now obvious, fatally flawed in needing to date the New Testament documents so late, Baur offered a brilliantly plausible conflict motif to explain the peculiar shape of the New Testament, which not only seemed to explain many otherwise intractable features of the text, but also resonated with the intellectual fashions of the age. Amongst Baur's students was David Friedrich Strauss, whose great work, the *Life of Jesus*, inaugurated what has become famous as 'the quest for the historical Jesus'.[32] In the closing decades of the nineteenth century, when the 'quest' had gained maturity but before Schweitzer's brilliant demolition of its presuppositions and assumed results, it seemed that good scholarship had proved that the religion taught by Jesus was simple and ethical; miracles – particularly the resurrection – and a fascination with eschatology (including themes of sin and redemption) and metaphysics, were later accretions to the simple original gospel.

Whence the accretions? By some Paul was blamed, in a survival of some of Baur's ideas, at least. Paul, it was argued, took the teaching of Jesus and turned it into a mystery cult that would be acceptable as a religious option for the Greek world. Every suggestion concerning

---

[31] On Baur, see for introduction Stephen Neill and Tom Wright, *The Interpretation of the New Testament, 1861–1986* (Oxford: OUP, 19882), pp. 20–30 and for critical engagement P.C. Hodgson *Ferdinand Christian Baur on the Writing of Church History* (Oxford: OUP, 1968). His own summary of his work on early Christianity can be found in *Paulus der Apostel*; an old English translation was recently reissued: F.C. Baur, *Paul the Apostle of Jesus Christ* (Peabody, MA: Hendrickson, 2003).

[32] Presumably a misappropriation of Schweitzer's title, *The Quest of the Historical Jesus*.

Christological pre-existence, atonement, miracle, and a coming eschaton, was a Pauline addition to the original purity of the gospel of Jesus. In dogmatics, this focus on the ethical finds its clearest exponent in Albrecht Ritschl, Dorner's successor in the chair at Göttingen. Ritschl believed passionately that theology must have a firm historical foundation, and that the study of the history of ideas was the route to purifying them. In a similar manner to Kant, he saw Jesus as the instantiation of God's will for the world, which, in Ritschl's understanding, is the inauguration and growth of a truly ethical community, the Kingdom of God.

Ritschl's work gave rise to the 'History of Religions school', which re-narrated the distortion of the ethical gospel of Jesus as the result of a transposition of those ideas into a cultic context.[33] For Bousset and others, the pressure of the cultic act of reflection on the teachings of Jesus led to the focus shifting from the Kingdom to the King, from what Jesus sought to promote to Jesus himself. The greatest account of this reconstruction of the history, however, came from Adolf von Harnack.[34] Christianity loses its primarily ethical character, and gains instead doctrine, as a result of reaction to Gnosticism, just as it gains a canon as a result of reaction to Marcion. The doctrine of the deity of Christ, and with it the doctrine of the Trinity, are held up as the classic examples of this process, perversions of primitive Christianity to make it acceptable and defensible in the context of a new, Hellenistic, cultural setting.

Baur's reconstruction has been simply and comprehensively destroyed by good historical evidence; probably no serious scholar would accept the later arguments either; however, their prevalence for a century seems to have left a curious legacy, in which there is a presumption that in some unspecified and shadowy way, there was a Hellenistic distortion of Christian theology early on, and there is a remaining theological task of reconstructing doctrine in a way that is free of this distortion. The doctrine of God, in particular, was shifted away from biblical presentations to an embracing of some Greek metaphysical ideas – notably simplicity, impassibility, eternity, and the like – which are alien to the Bible and have led to a distorted

---

[33] On the school, see in summary Mark D. Chapman, 'The History of Religion School', in *Blackwell Companion* (ed. Fergusson), pp. 434–54.

[34] The best study might still be Agnes von Zahn-Harnack, *Adolf von Harnack* (Berlin: H. Bott, 1936); for some more recent critical comments, however, see Martin Rumscheidt, ed., *Adolf von Harnack: Liberal Theology at Its Height* (London: Collins, 1989).

doctrine. For a particularly blunt statement of this theme, consider Colin Gunton: 'the impersonal attributes come from Greece, the Greek philosophical tradition; the personal ones come from the Bible and don't appear to be consistent with them.'[35]

Of course, this might be right. The development of the doctrine of the Trinity took place in the context of an intellectual culture that was shaped by Greek philosophy, and it could be argued that this became determinative. However, the argument needs to be made; as far as I am aware it has not really been seriously essayed since von Harnack, even if it has been regularly assumed. After all, as I have tried to show, the debate down to Augustine was almost entirely exegetical, the search for a set of concepts that would allow every text of Scripture (including the Old Testament texts) to be true in what it affirmed; as concepts were borrowed, refined, sometimes redefined, in this process, it is more easy to believe that the concepts were forced to fit the shape of Scripture than vice versa, and this was certainly the belief of those involved; an argument to the contrary at least needs credible evidence.

The Dawn of the Twentieth Century: Had the Doctrine Been Lost?

The standard narrative of the Trinitarian revival with which I began asserts that the doctrine was lost by the beginning of the twentieth century; we are now in a position to assess whether this is true.

Certainly, the doctrine had been 'lost' in the sense that a doctrine that had been assumed without much challenge from the close of the fourth century to the dawn of the eighteenth was now subject to repeated and hard challenges over its coherence, over the use of its technical vocabulary, and over its adequacy to its stated purpose, to represent adequately the biblical revelation of God. It is noticeable, however, that in the nineteenth century there seems still to be creative and significant Trinitarian theology being done – by Hegel, Schleiermacher, and Dorner in Germany and by Coleridge, Hodge, and Forsyth in the English-speaking world. That said, almost all of this work

---

[35] Colin E. Gunton, *The Barth Lectures* (ed. P.H. Brazier; London: T&T Clark, 2007), p. 94. This is, to be fair, a posthumously published transcript of a lecture, and so perhaps a blunter statement than Gunton would have offered in public by choice; however, the same point, albeit in more nuanced language, is made in (e.g.) *Act and Being* (London: SCM, 2003), pp. 39–54.

has become speculative (Hodge would be the exception): the doctrine of the Trinity becomes an account of God's self-becoming (Hegel), or a necessary deduction of who God must be on the basis of prior philosophical commitments (Coleridge; Dorner), or a necessary supposition to make a theological scheme work (Schleiermacher); Trinitarian theology is happening in the nineteenth century, but, outside of confessional contexts, it seems to have forgotten the name of Jesus.

In this sense, the twentieth-century Trinitarian revival can be seen to have begun in the right places: Barth, insisting that revelation, divine identity, and the narrative of redemption demand a doctrine of the Trinity; Rahner, insisting that accounts of the immanent Trinity must be somehow responsible to the economy of salvation. There was, without question, a need for theology to find a better way of speaking of God whilst remaining faithful to the biblical witness. The work of the various theologians I described in the opening chapter of this book – Zizioulas; Pannenberg; Moltmann; Jenson; Boff; Volf; Plantinga; Leftow; and Rea – and of a whole host of others who could have been covered, including, as a very minor contribution, some of my own earlier work – can be seen as an attempt to respond to this admittedly pressing challenge. We could have returned to careful readings of the Fathers and the classical tradition, but we chose to see the doctrine taught by the Fathers as the problem, not a potential solution. Why so? I suppose that we were too convinced of the rightness of some of the nineteenth-century criticisms and positions: we wanted to involve God in history, and believed a story, however vague, of Hellenistic infestation.

As a result, we developed the positions I described in the first chapter. There I suggested some common themes: a focus on the gospel narratives, largely to the exclusion of other biblical data, particularly of the Old Testament; an unshakeable belief in the full personality, in the modern sense, of the three divine persons; a commitment to univocal language applying to the divine; and a willingness to entangle God's life with the history of the world. As a result we believed Schleiermacher's prophecy that 'there must still be in store for it [the doctrine of the Trinity] a transformation which will go back to its very beginnings.'

This might usefully be compared to the summary of patristic Trinitarianism I offered earlier:

1. The divine nature is simple, incomposite, and ineffable. It is also unrepeatable, and so, in crude and inexact terms 'one'.

2. Language referring to the divine nature is always inexact and trophic; nonetheless, if formulated with much care and more prayer, it might adequately, if not fully, refer.
3. There are three divine *hypostases* that are instantiations of the divine nature: Father, Son, and Holy Spirit.
4. The three divine *hypostases* exist really, eternally, and necessarily, and there is nothing divine that exists beyond or outside their existence.
5. The three divine *hypostases* are distinguished by eternal relations of origin – begetting and proceeding – and not otherwise.
6. All that is spoken of God, with the single and very limited exception of that language which refers to the relations of origin of the three *hypostases*, is spoken of the one life the three share, and so is indivisibly spoken of all three.
7. The relationships of origin express/establish relational distinctions between the three existent *hypostases*; no other distinctions are permissible.

In our accounts of a Trinitarian revival, we wanted little or nothing to do with such strictures. As a result, we set out on our own to offer a different, and we believed better, doctrine. We returned to the Scriptures, but we chose (with Tertullian's Praxeas, Noetus of Smyrna, and Samuel Clarke) to focus exclusively on the New Testament texts, instead of listening to the whole of Scripture with Tertullian, Hippolytus, and Daniel Waterland. We thought about God's relationship with the creation in the economy, but we chose (with the Valentinians, Arius, and Hegel) to believe that the Son must be the mode of mediation of the Father's presence to creation, instead of following Irenaeus and Athanasius in proposing God's ability to mediate his own presence. We tried to understand the divine unity, but we chose (with Eunomius and Socinus) to believe that we could reason adequately about the divine essence, instead of following Basil, Gregory of Nyssa, Augustine, Thomas Aquinas, and John Calvin in asserting divine unknowability. We addressed divine simplicity, and chose (with Socinus and John Biddle) to discard it, rather than following Basil and the rest in affirming it as the heart of Trinitarian doctrine. We thought about Father, Son, and Holy Spirit, but chose (with Sabellius, Arius, and Eunomius) to affirm true personality of each, rather than following Augustine and John of Damascus in believing in one divine personality.

We called what we were doing a 'Trinitarian revival'; future historians might want to ask us why.

Bibliography of Works Cited

Ancient Texts

Anselm

Schmitt, F.S. *Anselmi Cantuariensis Archiepiscopi Opera Omnia* (6 vols; Edinburgh: Thomas Nelson and Sons, 1940–61).

Alexander of Alexandria

'Letter to Alexander of Thessalonica'. Trans. in Rusch, William G. *The Trinitarian Controversy* (Philadelphia: Fortress Press, 1980).

Athanasius

Decr. Opitz, *Werke* 2.1; best Eng. trans. is *NPNF*.
Syn. Opitz, *Werke* 2.1; best Eng. trans. is *NPNF*.
C. Ar. Metzler/Savvidis, *Werke* 1.1; best Eng. trans. is *NPNF*.

Athenagoras

Legatio. Markovich, ed. Patristische Texte und Studien 31 (W. de Gruyter, 1990). Eng trans.: Schoedel, W.R. *Athenagoras: Legatio and De Resurrectione* (Oxford: Clarendon Press, 1972).

Augustine of Hippo

Serm. PL 38.
Trin. CCSL 50–50A; Augustine, *The Trinity* (trans. Hill; New York: New City Press, 1991).

Civ. CCSL 47–8; *The City of God* (trans. Dyson; Cambridge: Cambridge University Press, 1998).

Basil of Caesarea

De Spir. SC 17; *St Basil the Great on the Holy Spirit* (trans. Jackson; Crestwood: St Vladimir's Seminary Press, 1980).
C.E. SC 299 and 305.

Boethius

OS. The Theological Tractates. Loeb Classical Library (trans. H.F. Stewart and E.K. Rand; London: Heinemann, 1962).

Cyril of Alexandria

Comm. Is. PG 70.

Eunomius

Vaggione, R.P. *Eunomius: The Extant Works.* Oxford Early Christian Texts (Oxford: Clarendon Press, 1987) (editions and translations).

Eusebius of Caesarea

Com. Isa. Ziegler, Joseph, ed. *Eusebius Werke: Neunter Band: Der Jesajakommentar*, Der Griechischen Christlichen Schriftsteller (Berlin: Akademie-Verlag, 1975).
Hist. eccl. Eusebius: Ecclesiastical History Loeb Classical Library (trans. K. Lake; Harvard University Press, 1989).

Gregory of Nazianzus

Or. SC 250; St Gregory of Nazianzus. Pages 25–148 in *On God and Christ* (trans. F. Williams and L. Wickham; Crestwood: St Vladimir's Seminary Press, 2002).
Ep. Gallay, P., ed. and trans. *Saint Grégoire de Nazianze: Lettres* (2 vols; Paris: Belles Lettres, 1964–7).
De vita sua, White, C., ed. and trans. *Gregory of Nazianzus: Autobiographical Poems* (Cambridge: Cambridge University Press, 1996).

Gregory of Nyssa

Jaeger, W., ed. *Contra Eunomium Libri*. Gregorii Nysseni Opera 1 and 2 (Leiden: Brill, 1960).

Ad ablab. Mueller, F., ed. *Gregorii Nysseni Opera Dogmatica Minora.* Gregorii Nysseni Opera 3.1 (Leiden: Brill, 1958); trans. Cyril C. Richardson. Pages 256–67 in *Christology of the Later Fathers* (ed. E.R. Hardy; London: SCM Press, 1954).

Hilary of Poitiers

De syn. PL 10:479–546; the most recent Eng. trans. is in *NPNF* 9.

De Trin. SC 462; trans. Stephen McKenna FC 25.

Hippolytus

Refutatio. Marcovich, M., ed. *Patristiche Texte und Studien* 25 (Berlin: de Gruyter, 1986).

Noet. Butterworth, R., ed. and trans. *Hippolytus of Rome: Contra Noetum* (London: Sheed & Ward, 1999).

Irenaeus

Haer. SC 263–4; the most recent Eng. trans. is *ANF*.

Epid. SC 406; trans. J. Behr, St Vladimir's Seminary Press, 1997.

John of Damascus

De fid. orth. Kotter, B., ed. *Die Schriften des Johannes von Damaskos* (5 vols; Berlin: de Gruyter, 1969–88). Pages 7–239 in vol. 2. The most recent Eng. trans. is *NPNF*.

Justin Martyr

Dial. Bobichon, P., ed. *Dialogue avec Tryphon* (Friborg: Academic Press, 2003); the most recent Eng. trans. is *ANF*.

Lactantius

Inst. Heck E. et A. Wlosok, eds. *Divinarum institutionum libri septum* (Monachii et Lisiae: Saur, 2005–); Lactantius, *Divine Institutes* (trans. A. Bowen and P. Garnsey; Liverpool: Liverpool UP, 2003).

Marcellus of Ancyra

Vinzent, Markus, hrsg. *Markell von Ankyra: Die Fragmente der Brief an Julius von Rom.* Supp. *VC* 39 (Leiden: Brill, 1997).

Novatian

De Trin. CCSL vol. 4; trans. FC 67.

Origen of Alexandria

Princ. SC 252, 253, 268, 269 and 312; *Origen: On First Principles* (trans. H. Butterworth; Gloucester: P. Smith, 1973).
Hom. in Acta. PG 51.
Hom. in Rom. PG 60.
Dial. Scherer, J., ed. *Entretien d'Origène avec Héraclide et les évêques . . .* (Cairo: IFAO, 1949); trans. J.R. Daly, *Origen: Treatise on Passover . . .* (New York: Paulist Press, 1992).
Comm. Jo. SC 120 bis, 157, 222, 290 and 385; trans. FC 80 and 89.
Cels. SC 132, 136, 147, 150 and 227; trans. H. Chadwick (Cambridge: Cambridge University Press, 1953).

Peter Lombard

Sent. Sententiae . . . (2 vols; Spicilegium Bonaventurianum 4–5, 1971–81).

Philostorgius

Hist. eccl. PG 65.

St Photius the Great

Mystagogy (text and trans.; New York: Studion, 1983).

Plato

Tim. Burnet, ed. *Opera*, vol. 4; many Eng. trans. are available.

Pseudo-Cyril

De SS. Trin. PG 77.

Richard of St Victor

De Trin. SC 68.

Socrates of Constantinople

Hist. eccl. SC 505; trans. *NPNF.*

Tertullian

Prax. Evans, E., ed. and trans. *Tertullian's Treatise against Praxeas* (London: Society for the Promotion of Christian Knowledge, 1948).

Theophilus of Antioch

Autol. Grant, R.M. *Theophilus of Antioch: Ad Autolycum* (Oxford: Clarendon Press, 1970).

Thomas Aquinas

Opera Omnia. Leonine edn (1882–).
Contra errores Graecorum. Tomus 40A.
ST. Toma 4–12.

Modern Works

Aageson, James W. *Written Also for Our Sake: Paul and the Art of Biblical Interpretation* (Louisville, KY: Westminster John Knox Press, 1993).
Allert, Craig D. *Revelation, Truth, Canon and Interpretation: Studies in Justin Martyr's Dialogue with Trypho.* Supplements to *Vigiliae christianae* 64 (Leiden: Brill, 2002).
Althaus, Paul. *The Theology of Martin Luther* (trans. Robert C. Schultz; Philadelphia: Fortress Press, 1966).
Anatolios, Khaled. *Athanasius: The Coherence of His Thought* (London: Routledge, 2nd edn, 2005).
Anon. *Catechesis Ecclesiarum Polonicarum* . . . (Stauropoli: Eulogethus Philalethes, 1680).
Anon. *Catechesis Racoviensis* . . . (Frankfurt: Johannes Adam Schmidt, 1739).
Arnim, J. von, ed. *Stoicorum Verterum Fragmenta* (4 vols; Lipsiae [*sic*, Leipzig]: Teubner, 1903–24).

Astruc-Morize, Gilberte et Le Boulluec Alain. 'Le sens caché des Écritures selon Jean Chrysostome et Origène'. Studia pastristica 25 (1993): pp. 1–26.

Ayres, Lewis. 'Athanasius' Initial Defence of the Term ὁμοούσιος: Rereading the De decretis'. *Journal of Early Christian Studies* 12 (2004): pp. 337–53.

— *Augustine and the Trinity* (Cambridge: Cambridge University Press, 2011).

— *Nicaea and Its Legacy: An Approach to Fourth-Century Trinitarian Theology* (Oxford: Oxford University Press, 2004).

— '"Remember That You Are Catholic" (*Serm.* 52.2): Augustine on the Unity of the Triune God'. *Journal of Early Christian Studies* 8 (2000): pp. 39–82.

— and G. Jones, eds. *Christian Origins: Theology, Rhetoric, and Community* (London: Routledge, 1998).

Bark, William. 'Boethius' Fourth Tractate, the so-called De Fide Catholica'. *Harvard Theological Review* 39 (1946): pp. 55–69.

Barnes, M. and D.H. Williams, eds. *Arianism after Arius* (Edinburgh: T&T Clark, 1993).

Barnes, M.R. 'Exegesis and Polemic in Augustine's De Trinitate I'. *Augustinian Studies* 30 (1999): pp. 43–59.

— '"One Nature, One Power": Consensus Doctrine in Pro-Nicene Polemic'. Studia patristica 29 (1997): pp. 205–23.

— *'The Power of God': Dunamis Theology in Gregory of Nyssa's Trinitarian Theology* (Washington, DC: Catholic University of America Press, 2000).

Barnes, Michel R. 'The Arians of Book V, and the Genre of De trinitate'. *Journal of Theological Studies*, NS 44 (1993): pp. 185–95.

Barnes, T.D. *Athanasius and Constantius: Theology and Politics in the Constantinian Empire* (Cambridge, MA: Harvard University Press, 1993).

— *Constantine and Eusebius* (Cambridge, MA: Harvard University Press, 1981).

Barnes, Timothy. 'The Collapse of the Homoeans in the East'. Studia patristica 29 (1997): pp. 3–16.

Barnes, Timothy David. *Tertullian: A Historical and Literary Study* (Oxford: Clarendon Press, 1971).

Barth, Karl. *Church Dogmatics* (14 vols; Edinburgh: T&T Clark, 1956–75).

Barthes, Roland. 'La mort de l'auteur'. En Barthes, *Oeuvres Complètes, Tome 2: 1966–1973* (ed. Éric Marty; Éditions de Seuil, 1994).

— *Image-Music-Text* (trans. and ed. Stephen Heath; London: Flamingo Paperbacks, 1984).

Barton, John, ed. *The Cambridge Companion to Biblical Interpretation* (Cambridge: Cambridge University Press, 1998).

Bauckham, Richard. *Jesus and the God of Israel: God Crucified and Other Studies on the New Testament's Christology of Divine Identity* (Grand Rapids, MI: Eerdmans, 2008).

— *Moltmann: Messianic Theology in the Making* (Basingstoke: Marshall Pickering, 1987).

— *2 Peter and Jude*, Word Biblical Commentary (Waco: Word, 1983).

— *The Theology of Jürgen Moltmann* (Edinburgh: T&T Clark, 1995).

Baur, F.C. *Paul the Apostle of Jesus Christ* (Peabody, MA: Hendrickson, 2003).

Beasley-Murray, George R. *John*. Word Biblical Commentary (Waco: Word, 1987).

Beckwith, Carl. 'Photinian Opponents in Hilary of Poitiers' Commentarium in Matthaeum'. *Journal of Ecclesiastical History* 58 (2007): pp. 611–27.

Behr, John. *Formation of Christian Theology, vol. 1: The Way to Nicaea* (Crestwood, NY: St Vladimir's Seminary Press, 2001).

— *The Nicene Faith (Formation of Christian Theology*, vol. 2), (2 vols; Crestwood, NY: St Vladimir's Seminary Press, 2004).

Biddle, John. *A Confession of Faith Touching the Holy Trinity according to the Scripture* (London: s.n., 1648).

— *XII Arguments Drawn out of Holy Scripture . . .* (London: s.n., 1647).

Blaising, Craig A. and Carmen S. Hardin, eds. *Psalms 1 – 50*. Ancient Christian Commentary on Holy Scripture Old Testament 7 (Downers Grove, IL: Inter-Varsity Press, 2008).

Boff, Leonardo. *Trinity and Society (Liberation and Theology, vol. 2)* (Tunbridge Wells: Burns & Oates, 1998).

Bonner, Gerald. *St Augustine of Hippo: Life and Controversies* (Norwich: The Canterbury Press, 1986).

Bousset, W. *Die Religion des Judentums im späthellenistischen Zeitalter* (ed. H. Gressmann; Tübingen: JCB Mohr, 3rd edn, 1926).

Brakke, David. *Athanasius and the Politics of Asceticism* (Oxford: Clarendon Press, 1995).

Braun, René. *Deus Christianorum: Recherches sur le vocabulaire doctrinal de Tertullian* (Paris: Études Augustiniennes, 2nd edn, 1977).

Brennecke, Hanns C. *Studien zur Geschichte der Homöer: Der Osten bis zum Ende der homöischen Reichskirche* (Tübingen: JCB Mohr, 1988).

Brent, Allen. *Hippolytus and the Roman Church in the Third Century: Communities in Tension before the Emergence of a Monarch-Bishop. Supplements to Vigiliae christianae* 31 (Brill: Leiden, 1995).

Brown, Colin, ed. *New International Dictionary of New Testament Theology* (Exeter: Paternoster Press, 1975–86).

Brown, Robert F. 'Schelling and Dorner on Divine Immutability'. *Journal of the American Academy of Religion* 52 (1985): pp. 237–49.

Brueggemann, Walter. *Theology of the Old Testament: Testimony, Dispute, Advocacy* (Minneapolis: Fortress Press, 1997).

Burrus, Virginia. 'Rhetorical Stereotypes in the Portrait of Paul of Samosata'. *Vigiliae christianae* 43 (1989): pp. 215–25.

Busch, Eberhard. *Karl Barth: His Life from Letters and Autobiographical Texts* (London: SCM Press, 1976).

Calvin, John. *Institutes of the Christian Religion* (trans. Ford Lewis Battles; ed. John T. McNeill; Philadelphia: Westminster, 1960).

— *Institutes of the Christian Religion 1536 Edition* (trans. Ford Lewis Battles; Grand Rapids, MI: Eerdmans, 1975).

— *Iohannes Calvini opera quae supersunt omnia* (ed. Wilhelm Baum, et al.; Brunswick: A. Schwetschke & Son, 1863–1900).

Cameron, Euan. *The European Reformation* (Oxford: Clarendon Press, 1991).

Campenhausen, H. von. *The Formation of the Christian Bible* (trans. J.A. Baker; Minneapolis: Fortress Press, 1972).

Chadwick, Henry. *Boethius: The Consolations of Music, Logic, Theology, and Philosophy* (Oxford: Oxford University Press, 1981).

Childs, B.S. *The Struggle to Understand Isaiah as Christian Scripture* (Grand Rapids, MI: Eerdmans, 2004).

Chung, Sung Wook, ed. *John Calvin and Evangelical Theology: Legacy and Prospect* (Milton Keynes: Paternoster, 2009).

Clarke, Samuel. *The Scripture-Doctrine of the Trinity, in Three Parts . . .* (London: James Knapton, 1712).

Coakley, Sarah, ed. *Re-thinking Gregory of Nyssa* (Oxford: Blackwell, 2003).

Coleridge, Samuel Taylor. *The Collected Works of Samuel Taylor Coleridge.* Bollingen Series 75 (ed. Kathleen Coburn; jointly published by Routledge & Kegan Paul [London] and Princeton University Press [Princeton, NJ]).

Collins, Paul. *Trinitarian Theology West and East: Karl Barth, the Cappadocian Fathers, and John Zizioulas* (Oxford: Oxford University Press, 2001).

Congar, Yves. *I Believe in the Holy Spirit*, vol. 3 (New York: Seabury Press, 1983).

Conticello, Vassa L. 'Pseudo-Cyril's "De SS. Trinitate": A Compilation of Joseph the Philosopher'. *Orientalia christiana periodica* 61 (1995): pp. 117–29.

Cory, David. *Faustus Socinus* (Boston: Beacon Press, 1932).

Cross, Richard. 'Quid tres? On What Precisely Augustine Professes Not to Understand in De Trinitate V and VII'. *Harvard Theological Review* 100 (2007): pp. 215–32.

Crouzel, Henri. *Théologie de l'image de Dieu chez Origène* (Paris: F. Aubier, 1956).

— and A. Quacquarelli, eds. *Origeniana Secunda* (Rome: Editiona dell'Ateneo, 1980).

Cunningham, David S. *These Three Are One: The Practice of Trinitarian Theology* (Oxford: Blackwell, 1998).

Curd, Patricia and Daniel W. Graham, eds. *The Oxford Handbook of Presocratic Philosophy* (Oxford: Oxford University Press, 2008).

Dán, Róbert and Antal Pirnát, eds. *Antitrinitarianism in the Second Half of the 16th Century* (Leiden: Brill, 1982).

Daniélou, Jean. 'Eunome l'Arien et l'exégèse platonicienne du Cratyle'. *Revue D'Études Grecques* 69 (1956): pp. 412–32.

Davies, Brian and Brian Leftow, eds. *The Cambridge Companion to Anselm* (Cambridge: Cambridge University Press, 2004).

Dawson, D. *Allegorical Readers and Cultural Revision in Ancient Alexandria* (Berkeley: University of California Press, 1992).

DelCogliano, Mark. *Basil of Caesarea's anti-Eunomian Theology of Names* (Leiden: Brill, 2010).

Dixon, Philip. *Nice and Hot Disputes: The Doctrine of the Trinity in the Seventeenth Century* (London: T&T Clark, 2003).

Doignon, Jean. *Hilaire de Poitiers: Disciple et témoin de la vérité* (Paris: Études Augustiniennes, 2005).

Dorner, I.A. *Divine Immutability: A Critical Reconsideration* (trans. R.R. Williams and Claude Welch; Minneapolis: Fortress Press, 1994).

— *A System of Christian Doctrine*, vol. 1 (trans. Alfred Cave; Edinburgh: T&T Clark, 1880).

Driscoll, J., ed. *Imaginer la théologie catholique: Permanence et transformations de la foi en attendant Jésus-Christ* (Rome: Centro Studi S. Anselmo, 2000).

Drobner, H.R. and Christoph Klock, eds. *Studien zu Gregor von Nyssa und der Christlichen Spätantike* (Leiden: Brill, 1990).

Dunn, G.D. 'The Diversity and Unity of God in Novatian's De Trinitate'. *Ephemerides theologicae lovanienses* 78 (2002): pp. 385–409.

Dünzl, Franz. *A Brief History of the Doctrine of the Trinity in the Early Church* (trans. John Bowden; London: T&T Clark, 2007).

Edward, Lord Herbert of Cherbury. *De Veritate* (London, 1633; ET: Meyrick H. Carré; Bristol: University of Bristol Press, 1937).

Edwards, M.J. 'Did Origen Apply the Word homoousios to the Son?' *Journal of Theological Studies* NS 49.2 (1998): pp. 658–70.

Edwards, Thomas. *Gangraena, or a Catalogue and Discovery of Many of the Errours . . .* (London: Ralph Smith, 1646).

— *The Second Part of Gangraena* (London: Ralph Smith, 1646).

— *The Third Part of Gangraena* (London: Ralph Smith, 1646).

Eichrodt, Walther. *Theology of the Old Testament*, vol. 1 (London: SCM Press, 1961).

Ellis, Brannon E. 'God of Himself: John Calvin, Classical Trinitarianism, and the Self-Existence of the Son of God' (PhD Thesis, University of Aberdeen, 2010).

Emery, Gilles. 'Le Traité de saint Thomas sur la Trinité dans la Somme contre les Gentils'. *Revue Thomistique* 96 (1996): pp. 5–40.

— *The Trinitarian Theology of St Thomas Aquinas* (trans. Francesca Murphy; Oxford: Oxford University Press, 2007).

— *Trinity in Aquinas* (Ypsilanti, MI: Sapienta Press, 2003).

Fedwick, Paul J., ed. *Basil of Caesarea: Christian, Humanist, Ascetic: A Sixteen-hundredth Anniversary Symposium* (2 vols; Toronto: Pontifical Institute of Mediaeval Studies, 1981).

Feenstra, Ronald J. and Cornelius Plantinga, eds. *Trinity, Incarnation, and Atonement: Philosophical and Theological Essays* (Notre Dame: University of Notre Dame Press, 1989).

Fergusson, David, ed. *The Blackwell Companion to Nineteenth Century Theology* (Oxford: Blackwell, 2010).

Flint, Thomas H. and Michael C. Rea, eds. *The Oxford Handbook to Philosophical Theology* (Oxford: Oxford University Press, 2009).

Flogaus, Reinhard. 'Palamas and Barlaam Revisited: A Reassessment of East and West in the Hesychiast Controversy of 14th Century Byzantium'. *St Vladimir's Theological Quarterly* 42 (1998): pp. 1–32.

Forsyth, P.T. *The Person and Place of Jesus Christ* (London: Independent Press, 5th edn, 1946).

Fraigneau-Julien, B. 'Un traité anonyme de la Sainte Trinité attribué à s. Cyrille d'Alexandrie'. *Recherches de Science Religieuse* 49 (1961): pp. 188–211, 386–405.

Goldingay, John. *Old Testament Theology, vol. 2: Israel's Faith* (Milton Keynes: Paternoster, 2006).

Gomes, Alan W. 'De Jesu Christo Servatore: Faustus Socinus on the Satisfaction of Christ'. *Westminster Theological Journal* 55 (1993): pp. 209–21.

— 'The Rapture of Christ: The "Pre-Ascension Ascension" of Jesus in the Theology of Faustus Socinus (1539–1604)'. *Harvard Theological Review* 102 (2009): pp. 75–99.

— 'Some Observations on the Theological Method of Faustus Socinus (1539-1604)'. *Westminster Theological Journal* 70 (2008): pp. 49–71.

Gordon, Bruce. *Calvin* (New Haven: Yale University Press, 2009).

Grant, R.M. 'The Book of Wisdom at Alexandria: Reflections on the History of the Canon and Theology'. *Texte und Untersuchungen* 92 [= Studia patristica 7] (1966).

Grant, Robert M. *Irenaeus of Lyons* (London: Routledge, 1997).

Grenz, Stanley. *Rediscovering the Triune God: The Trinity in Contemporary Theology* (Minneapolis: Fortress Press, 2004).

Gunton, Colin E. *Act and Being* (London: SCM Press, 2003).

— *The Barth Lectures* (ed. P.H. Brazier; London: T&T Clark, 2007).

— *Becoming and Being: The Doctrine of God in Charles Hartshorne and Karl Barth* (London: SCM Press, 2nd edn, 2001).

— *The Triune Creator: A Historical and Systematic Study* (Edinburgh: Edinburgh University Press, 1998).

— and Christoph Schwöbel, eds. *Persons Divine and Human* (Edinburgh: T&T Clark, 1991).

Gwynn, David M. *The Eusebians: The Polemic of Athanasius of Alexandria and the Construction of the 'Arian Controversy'* (Oxford: Oxford University Press, 2007).

Hanson, R.P.C. *Allegory and Event* (Minneapolis: John Knox Press, 1959).

— *Origen's Doctrine of Tradition* (London: SPCK, 1954).

— *The Search for the Christian Doctrine of God* (Edinburgh: T&T Clark, 1988).

Harnack, Adolf von. *Der kirchengeschichtliche Ertrag der exegetischen Arbeiten des Origenes, Erster Teil: Hexateuch und Richterbuch.* Texte und Untersuchungen 42.3 (1918).

Hector, Kevin W. 'God's Triunity and Self-Determination: A Conversation with Karl Barth, Bruce McCormack and Paul Molnar'. *International Journal of Systematic Theology* 7/3 (2005): pp. 246–61.

Hegel, G.W.F. *Lectures on the Philosophy of Religion* (3 vols; ed. and trans. Peter C. Hodgson, et al.; Berkeley: University of California Press, 1984–7).

Heine, R.E. 'The Christology of Callistus'. *Journal of Theological Studies* NS 49 (1998): pp. 56–91.

Helm, Paul. *John Calvin's Ideas* (Oxford: Oxford University Press, 2004).

Helmer, Christine. 'God from Eternity to Eternity: Luther's Trinitarian Understanding'. *Harvard Theological Review* 96 (2003): pp. 127–46.

— *The Trinity and Martin Luther: A Study on the Relationship between Genre, Language, and the Trinity in Luther's Works (1523–1546).* Veröffentlichungen des Institutes für europäische Geschichte/ Abteilung abendländische Religionsgeschichte 174 (Mainz: Verlag Philipp von Zabern, 1999).

Hennessy, Kristin. 'An Answer to de Régnon's Accusers: Why We Should Not Speak of "His" Paradigm'. *Harvard Theological Review* 100 (2007): pp. 179–97.

Heppe, Heinrich. *Reformed Dogmatics* (ed. Ernest Bizer; trans. G.T. Thomson; Grand Rapids, MI: Baker, 1978).

Hodge, Charles. *Systematic Theology* (3 vols; Peabody, MA: Hendrickson, 2003).

Hodgson, Leonard. *The Doctrine of the Trinity: Croall Lectures, 1942–3* (London: Nisbet, 1943).

Hodgson, P.C. *Ferdinand Christian Baur on the Writing of Church History* (Oxford: Oxford University Press, 1968).

Hodgson, Peter C. *Hegel and Christian Theology: A Reading of the Lectures on the Philosophy of Religion* (Oxford: Oxford University Press, 2005).

Holmes, Stephen R. *Listening to the Past: On the Place of Tradition in Theology* (Carlisle: Paternoster Press, 2002).

Houssiau, Albert. *La Christologie de Saint Irénée* (Louvain: Publications Universitaires de Louvain, 1955).

Hunsinger, George. 'Election and the Trinity: Twenty-Five Theses on the Theology of Karl Barth'. *Modern Theology* 24/2 (2008): pp. 172–98.

Hurtado, Larry. *Lord Jesus Christ: Devotion to Jesus in Early Christianity* (Grand Rapids, MI: Eerdmans, 2003).

— *One God, One Lord: Early Christian Devotion and Ancient Jewish Monotheism* (London: T&T Clark, 2nd edn, 1998).

Hussey, M. Edmund. 'The Palamite Trinitarian Models'. *St Vladimir's Theological Quarterly* 16 (1972): pp. 83–9.

Inwagen, Peter van and Dean Zimmerman, eds. *Persons: Human and Divine* (Oxford: Oxford University Press, 2007).

Janowski, Bernd and Peter Stuhlmacher, eds. *The Suffering Servant: Isaiah 53 in Jewish and Christian Sources* (trans. Daniel P. Bailey; Grand Rapids, MI: Eerdmans, 2004).

Jensen, Anne. 'Prisca – Maximilla – Montanus: Who Was the Founder of "Montanism"?' Studia patristica 26 (1993): pp. 147–50.

Jenson, Robert W. *Systematic Theology, vol. 1: The Triune God* (Oxford: Oxford University Press, 1997).

— *The Triune Identity: God according to the Gospel* (Philadelphia: Fortress Press, 1982).

Jüngel, E. *God's Being Is in Becoming: The Trinitarian Being of God in the Theology of Karl Barth* (trans. J. Webster; Edinburgh: T&T Clark, 2004).

Kannengiesser, Charles. *Athanase d'Alexandrie évêque et écrivain: Une lecture des traités contre les Ariens* (Paris: Beauchesne, 1983).

— *Hilaire et son Temps* (Paris: Études Augustiniennes, 1969).

Kant, Immanuel. *Religion and Rational Theology* (trans. and ed. Allen W. Wood and George Di Giovanni; Cambridge: Cambridge University Press, 1996).

Karfíková, L., S. Douglass and J. Zachhuber, eds. *Gregory of Nyssa: Contra Eunomium II: An English Version with Supporting Studies* (Leiden: Brill, 2007).

Kayayan, Eric. 'The Case of Michael Servetus'. *Mid-America Journal of Theology* 8 (1992): pp. 117–46.

Kecskeméti, Judit. 'Exégèse Chrysostomienne et Exégèse Engagée'. Studia patristica 22 (1989): pp. 136–47.

Kelly, J.N.D. *Early Christian Creeds* (Harlow: Longman, 3rd edn, 1972).

Kerr, Fergus. *After Aquinas: Versions of Thomism* (Oxford: Blackwell, 2002).

Kilby, Karen. 'Aquinas, the Trinity and the Limits of Understanding'. *International Journal of Systematic Theology* 7 (2005): pp. 414–27.

— *Karl Rahner: Theology and Philosophy* (London: Routledge, 2004).

King, Karen L. *What Is Gnosticism?* (Cambridge, MA: Belknap Press, 2003).

Kittel G., ed. *Theologisches Wörterbuch zum Neuen Testament* (Stuttgart: Kolhammer, 1933–79).

Knight, Douglas H., ed. *The Theology of John Zizioulas: Personhood and the Church* (Aldershot: Ashgate, 2007).

Knuuttila, Simo and Risto Saarinen. 'Luther's Trinitarian Theology and Its Medieval Background', *Studia theologica* 53 (1999): pp. 3–12.

Kretzman, Norman and Eleanor Stump, eds. *The Cambridge Companion to Thomas Aquinas* (Cambridge: Cambridge University Press, 1993).

Lambert, Malcolm. *Medieval Heresy: Popular Movements from the Gregorian Reform to the Reformation* (Oxford: Blackwell, 3rd edn, 2002).

Levering, Matthew. *Scripture and Metaphysics: Aquinas and the Renewal of Trinitarian Theology* (Oxford: Blackwell, 2004).

Lindberg, Carter. *The European Reformations* (Oxford: Blackwell, 1996).

Logan, Alistair H.B. 'Marcellus of Ancyra and the Councils of 325: Antioch, Ancyra, and Nicaea'. *Journal of Theological Studies* NS 43 (1992): pp. 428-46.

Longenecker, Richard N. *Biblical Exegesis in the Apostolic Period* (Grand Rapids, MI: Eerdmans, 1975).

Louth, Andrew. *St John Damascene: Tradition and Originality in Byzantine Theology* (Oxford: Oxford University Press, 2002).

Luther, Martin. D. *Martin Luthers Werke. Kritische Gesamtausgabe* (= WA) (Weimar: Böhlaus Nachfolger, 1883–).

Luttikhuizen, Gerard P. *Gnostic Revisions of Genesis Stories and Early Jesus Traditions*. Nag Hammadi and Manichaean Studies 58 (Leiden: Brill, 2006).

Lyons, J.A. *The Cosmic Christ in Origen and Teilhard de Chardin: A Comparative Study* (Oxford: Oxford University Press, 1982).

McCall, Thomas H. *Which Trinity? Whose Monotheism? Philosophical and Systematic Theologians on the Metaphysics of Trinitarian Theology* (Grand Rapids, MI: Eerdmans, 2010).

McCormack, Bruce. 'Election and the Trinity: Theses in Response to George Hunsinger'. *Scottish Journal of Theology* 63/2 (2010): pp. 203–24.

McCruden, Kevin. 'Monarchy and Economy in Tertullian's Adversus Praxean'. *Scottish Journal of Theology* 55 (2002): pp. 325–37.

McCurdy, Leslie. *Attributes and Atonement: The Holy Love of God in the Theology of P.T. Forsyth* (Carlisle: Paternoster Press, 1999).

MacDonald, Nathan. *Deuteronomy and the Meaning of 'Monotheism'* (Tübingen: Mohr Siebeck, 2001).

McGowan, Andrew. 'Tertullian and the "Heretical" Origins of the "Orthodox" Trinity'. *Journal of Early Christian Studies* 14 (2006): pp. 437–57.

McGuckin, John. 'Perceiving Light from Light in Light: The Trinitarian Theology of St Gregory the Theologian'. *Greek Orthodox Theological Review* 39 (1994): pp. 7–32.

Malysz, Piotr J. 'Hegel's Conception of God and Its Application by Isaak Dorner to the Problem of Divine Immutability'. *Pro Ecclesia* 15 (2006): pp. 448–71.

Marenbon, John. *Boethius* (Oxford: Oxford University Press, 1993).

— ed. *The Cambridge Companion to Boethius* (Cambridge: Cambridge University Press, 2009).

Mariña, Jacqueline. *The Cambridge Companion to Friedrich Schleiermacher* (Cambridge: Cambridge University Press, 2005).

Marshall, Bruce D. *Trinity and Truth* (Cambridge: Cambridge University Press, 2000).

Mattox, Mickey L. 'From Faith to the Text and Back Again: Martin Luther on the Trinity in the Old Testament'. *Pro Ecclesia* 15 (2006): pp. 281–303.

Metzger, Bruce. *The Canon of the New Testament* (Oxford: Clarendon Press, 1987).

Metzger, Paul, ed. *Trinitarian Soundings in Systematic Theology* (London: T&T Clark, 2005).

Molnar, Paul. *Divine Freedom and the Doctrine of the Immanent Trinity: In Dialogue with Karl Barth and Comtemporary Theology* (London: T&T Clark, 2002).

— 'The Trinity, Election and God's Ontological Freedom: A Response to Kevin W. Hector'. *International Journal of Systematic Theology* 8/3 (2006): pp. 294–306.

Moltmann, Jürgen. *The Crucified God: The Cross of Christ as the Foundation and Criticism of Christian Theology* (trans. R.A. Wilson and John Bowden; London: SCM Press, 2001).

— *Experiences of God* (trans. Margaret Kohl; London: SCM Press, 1980).

— 'Political Theology'. *Theology Today* 28 (1971): pp. 6–23.

— *Theology of Hope: On the Ground and Implications of a Christian Eschatology* (trans. J.W. Leitch; London: SCM Press, 1967).

— *The Trinity and the Kingdom of God* (trans. M. Kohl; London: SCM Press, 1981).

Moutsoulas, E. 'Le problème de la date des "Trois Discours" contre les Ariens d'Athanase d'Alexandrie'. *Studia patristica* 16 (1985).

Mowry LaCugna, Catherine. *God for Us: The Trinity and Christian Life* (New York: HarperCollins, 1991).

Mühlenberg, Ekkehard. *Die Unendlichkeit Gottes bei Gregor von Nyssa: Gregors Kritik am Gottesbegriff der klassischen Metaphysik* (Göttingen: Vandenhöck & Ruprecht, 1966).

Muller, Richard A. *Post-Reformation Reformed Dogmatics: The Rise and Development of Reformed Orthodoxy, ca. 1530 to ca. 1725, vol. IV: The Triunity of God* (Grand Rapids, MI: Baker, 2003).

Musurillo, Herbert, trans. *The Acts of the Christian Martyrs* (Oxford: Clarendon Press, 1972).

Neill, Stephen and Tom Wright. *The Interpretation of the New Testament, 1861–1986* (Oxford: Oxford University Press, 2nd edn, 1988).

Norgate, Jonathan. *Isaak A. Dorner: The Triune God and the Gospel of Salvation* (London: T&T Clark, 2009).

Norris, F.W. 'Paul of Samosata: Procurator Ducenarius'. *Journal of Theological Studies* NS 35 (1984): pp. 50–70.

Osborn, Eric. *Irenaeus of Lyons* (Cambridge: Cambridge University Press, 2001).

Otto, Randall. 'Moltmann and the Anti-Monotheist Movement'. *International Journal of Systematic Theology* 3/3 (2001): pp. 293–308.

Otto, Rudolph. *The Idea of the Holy* (Harmondsworth: Penguin, 1959).

Paddison, Angus and Andrew T. Lincoln, eds. *Christology and Scripture: Interdisciplinary Perspectives* (London: T&T Clark, 2007).

Pannenberg, Wolfhart. 'God's Presence in History'. *Christian Century* 98 (1981): pp. 260–63.

— ed. *Revelation as History* (trans. David Granskou; London: Sheed & Ward, 1979).

— *Systematic Theology*, vol. 1 (trans. Geoffrey W. Bromiley; Edinburgh: T&T Clark, 1991).

Papadakis, Aristeides. *Crisis in Byzantium: The Filioque Controversy in the Patriarchate of Gregory II of Cyprus (1283–1289)* (Crestwood, NY: St Vladimir's Seminary Press, 1997).

Papanikolaou, A. 'Is John Zizioulas an Existentialist in Disguise? A Response to Lucian Turcescu'. *Modern Theology* 20 (2004): pp. 601–7.

Parvis, Sara. *Marcellus of Ancyra and the Lost Years of the Arian Controversy 325–345* (Oxford: Oxford University Press, 2006).

Patterson, L.G. *Methodius of Olympus: Divine Sovereignty, Human Freedom, and Life in Christ* (Washington, DC: Catholic University of America Press, 1997).

Pearson, Birger A. *Ancient Gnosticism: Traditions and Literature* (Minneapolis: Fortress Press, 2007).

Pelikan, Jaroslav. 'Montanism and Its Trinitarian Significance'. *Church History* 25 (1956): pp. 99–109.

Peters, F.E. *Greek Philosophical Terms: A Historical Lexicon* (New York: New York University Press, 1967).

Peterson, Erik. *Der Monotheismus als politisches Problem: Ein Beitrag zur Geschichte der politischen Theologie im Imperium Romanum* (Leipzig: Jakob Hegner, 1935).

Piché, David. *La Condemnation parisienne de 1277* (Paris: Vrin, 1999).

Pomeau, René. *La Religion de Voltaire* (Paris: Nizet, 1994).

Prestige, G.L. *God in Patristic Thought* (London: SPCK, 2nd edn, 1952).

— *St Basil the Great and Apollinaris of Laodicea* (London: SPCK, 1956).

Rahner, Karl. *Theological Investigations*, vol. 4 (London: Darton, Longman and Todd, 1966).

— *The Trinity* (trans. Jospeh Donceel; Tunbridge Wells: Burns & Oates, 1970).

Ramelli, I.L.E. 'Origen's Anti-Subordinationism and Its Heritage in the Nicene and Cappadocian Line'. *Vigiliae christianae* 65 (2011): pp. 21–49.

Rauser, Randal. 'Rahner's Rule: An Emperor without Clothes?' *International Journal of Systematic Theology* 7 (2005).

Rees, Thomas. *The Racovian Catechism . . .* (London: Longman, et al., 1818).

Régnon, Theodore de. *Études de théologie positive sur la Sainte Trinité* (4 vols; Paris: Victor Retaux, 1892-8).

Robertson, Jon M. *Christ as Mediator: A Study of the Theologies of Eusebius of Caesarea, Marcellus of Ancyra, and Athanasius of Alexandria* (Oxford: Oxford University Press, 2007).

Rougé, J. et R. Turcan. *Les Martyrs de Lyon* (177) (Paris: CNRS, 1978).

Roy, Olivier du. *L'Intelligence de la Foi en la Trinité selon Saint Augustin: Genèse de sa Théologie Trinitaire jusqu'en 391* (Paris: Études Augustin-iennes, 1966).

Rumscheidt, Martin, ed. *Adolf von Harnack: Liberal Theology at Its Height* (London: Collins, 1989).

Runia, David T. *Philo in Early Christian Literature* (Minneapolis: Fortress Press, 1993).

Sanders, James A. *Canon and Community: A Guide to Canonical Criticism* (Philadelphia: Fortress Press, 1984).

Schleiermacher, F.D.E. *The Christian Faith* (trans. J.S. Stewart and H.R. Mackintosh; Edinburgh: T&T Clark, 1928).

Schleiermacher, Friedrich. *On Religion: Speeches to Its Cultured Despisers* (ed. and trans. Richard Crouter; Cambridge: Cambridge University Press, 2000).

Schroeder, H.J. *Disciplinary Decrees of the General Councils: Text, Translation and Commentary* (St Louis: B. Herder, 1937).

Schwöbel, Christoph, ed. *Trinitarian Theology Today* (Edinburgh: T&T Clark, 1995).

Scribner, Bob, et al., eds. *The Reformation in National Context* (Cambridge: Cambridge University Press, 1994).

Sell, Alan P.F. *John Locke and the Eighteenth Century Divines* (Cardiff: University of Wales Press, 1997).

Sherman, Robert. 'Isaak August Dorner on Divine Immutability: A Missing Link between Schleiermacher and Barth'. *Journal of Religion* 77 (1997): pp. 380–401.

Shortwell, W.A. *The Biblical Exegesis of Justin Martyr* (London: SPCK, 1965).

Siecienski, A.E. *The Filioque: The History of a Doctrinal Controversy* (Oxford: Oxford University Press, 2010).

Simone, R.J. *The Treatise of Novatian the Presbyter on the Trinity: A Study of the Text and the Doctrine* (Rome: Institutum Patristicum Augustinianum, 1970).

Simonetti, Manlio. *Biblical Interpretation in the Early Church* (trans. J. Hughes; Edinburgh: T&T Clark, 1994).

— *La Crisi Ariana nel IV Secolo* (Rome: Augustinianum, 1975).

— *Testi Gnostici in Lingua Greca e Latina* (Vincenza: Fondazione Lorenzo Valla, 1993).

Smith, Carl B. *No Longer Jews: The Search for Gnostic Origins* (Peabody: Hendrickson, 2004).

Smulders, P. *Hilary of Poitiers' Preface to His Opus Historicum* (Leiden: Brill, 1995).

Sopko, Andrew J. '"Palamism before Palamas" and the Theology of Gregory of Cyprus'. *St Vladimir's Theological Quarterly* 23 (1979): pp. 139–47.

Stanley, Christopher D. *Arguing with Scripture: The Rhetoric of Quotations in the Letters of Paul* (London: T&T Clark International, 2004).

Stead, Christopher. *Divine Substance* (Oxford: Oxford University Press, 1977).

Stillingfleet, Edward. *A Discourse in Vindication of the Doctrine of the Trinity . . .* (London: Henry Mortlock, 1697).

Stramara, Daniel F. 'Gregory of Nyssa's Terminology for Trinitarian Perichoresis'. *Vigiliae christianae* 52 (1998): pp. 257–63.

Tetz, Martin. 'Markellianer und Athanasios von Alexandrien: Die markellianische Expositio fidel ad Athanasium des Diakons Eugenios von Ankyra'. *Zeitschrift für die Neutestamentliche Wissenschaft* 64 (1973): pp. 75–121.

Tice, Terrence N. *Schleiermacher* (Nashville: Abingdon, 2006).

Tindal, Matthew. *Christianity as Old as the Creation: or, the Gospel a Republication of the Religion of Nature* (London: s.n., 1731).

Toland, John. *Christianity Not Mysterious, or a Treatise Shewing That There Is Nothing in the Gospel contrary to Reason, nor above It, and That No Christian Doctrine Can Properly Be Call'd a Mystery* (London: s.n., 1696).

Torjesen, Karen Jo. *Hermeneutical Procedure and Theological Method in Origen's Exegesis*. Patristiche Texte und Studien 28 (Berlin: de Gruyter, 1986).

Torrance, Alan. *Persons in Communion: An Essay on Trinitarian Description and Human Participation* (Edinburgh: T&T Clark, 1996).

Torrance, Thomas F. 'Calvin's Doctrine of the Trinity'. *Calvin Theological Journal* 25 (1990): pp. 165–93.

Torrell, Jean-Pierre. *Saint Thomas Aquinas, vol. 2: Spiritual Master* (Washington, DC: Catholic University of America Press, 2003).

Trier, Daniel J. and David Lauber, eds. *Trinitarian Theology for the Church: Scripture, Community, Worship* (Nottingham: Apollos, 2009).

Tuggy, Dale. 'The Unfinished Business of Trinitarian Theorizing'. *Religious Studies* 39 (2003): pp. 165–83.

Turcescu, L. '"Person" vs "Individual", and Other Modern Misreadings of Gregory of Nyssa'. *Modern Theology* 18 (2002): pp. 527–39.

Vaggione, R.P. *Eunomius: The Extant Works. Oxford Early Christian Texts* (Oxford: Clarendon Press, 1987).

Vandiver, Elizabeth, et al. *Luther's Lives: Two Contemporary Accounts of Martin Luther* (Manchester: Manchester University Press, 2002).

Vanhoozer, Kevin J., ed. *Dictionary of Theological Intepretation of the Bible* (Grand Rapids, MI: Baker, 2005).

Veroeven, Theodorus. *Studiën over Tertullianus' Adversus Praxean* (Amsterdam: Noord-Hollandsche Uitgevers Maatschappij, 1949).

Vinzent, Markus, hrsg. *Markell von Ankyra: Die Fragmente der Brief an Julius von Rom. Supplements to Vigiliae christianae* 39 (Leiden: Brill, 1997).

Volf, Miroslav. *After Our Likeness: The Church as the Image of the Trinity* (Grand Rapids, MI: Eerdmans, 1998).

— '"The Trinity is Our Social Program": The Doctrine of the Trinity and the Shape of Social Engagement'. *Modern Theology* 14 (1998): pp. 403–23.

Voltaire. *Dictionnaire Philosophique* (ed. Raaymond Naves; Paris: Garnier, 1967).

Watson, Francis. *Text, Church, and World: Biblical Interpretation in Theological Perspective* (Edinburgh: T&T Clark, 1994).

Watts, Michael. *The Dissenters: From the Reformation to the French Revolution* (Oxford: Clarendon Press, 1978).

Webster, John, ed. *The Cambridge Companion to Karl Barth* (Cambridge: Cambridge University Press, 2000).

— *Karl Barth* (London: Continuum, 2nd edn, 2004).

Weedman, Mark. 'Hilary and the Homoiousians: Using New Categories to Map the Trinitarian Controversy'. *Church History* 76 (2007): pp. 491–510.

— *The Trinitarian Theology of Hilary of Poitiers*. Supplements to *Vigiliae christianae* 89 (Leiden: Brill, 2007).

Weinandy, Thomas, et al., eds. *Aquinas on Doctrine: A Critical Introduction* (London: T&T Clark, 2004).

Wendel, François. *Calvin: The Origins and Development of His Religious Thought* (trans. Philip Mairet; London: Collins, 1963).

Whiston, William. *The Liturgy of the Church of England Reduc'd nearer to the Primitive Standard* . . . (London, s.n., 1713).

— *Primitive Christianity Reviv'd in Four Parts* . . . (London: s.n., 1712).

Wickham, L.R. 'The Syntagmation of Aetius the Anomean'. *Journal of Theological Studies* NS 19 (1968): pp. 532–69.

Widdicombe, Peter. *The Fatherhood of God from Origen to Athanasius* (Oxford: Clarendon Press, 1994).

Wigelsworth, Jeffrey R. *Deism in Enlightenment England: Theology, Politics, and Newtonian Public Science* (Manchester: Manchester University Press, 2009).

Wilbur, Earl Morse. *History of Unitarianism* (2 vols; Boston: Beacon Press, 1945).

Wilkins, Jeremy D. '"The Image of This Highest Love": The Trinitarian Analogy in Gregory Palamas's Capita 150'. *St Vladimir's Theological Quarterly* 47 (2003): pp. 383–412.

Williams, D.H. *Ambrose of Milan and the End of the Arian-Nicene Conflicts* (Oxford: Clarendon Press, 1995).

— 'Monarchianism and Photinus of Sirmium as the Persistent Heretical Face of the Fourth Century'. *Harvard Theological Review* 99 (2006): pp. 187–206.

Williams, George H. *The Polish Brethren* (2 vols; Missoula: Scholars Press, 1980).

— *The Radical Reformation* (Philadelphia: Westminster Press, 1967).

Williams, Michael A. *Rethinking 'Gnosticism': An Argument for Dismantling a Dubious Category* (Princeton: PUP, 1996).

Williams, Robert R. 'I.A. Dorner: The Ethical Immutability of God'. *Journal of the American Academy of Religion* 54 (1986): pp. 721–38.

Williams, Rowan. *Arius: Heresy and Tradition* (London: SCM Press, 2nd edn, 2001).

— ed. *The Making of Orthodoxy: Essays in Honour of Henry Chadwick* (Cambridge: Cambridge University Press, 1989).

Wingren, Gustav. *Man and the Incarnation: A Study in the Biblical Theology of Irenaeus* (trans. R. Mackenzie; Edinburgh: Oliver & Boyd, 1959).

Young, B.W. *Religion and Enlightenment in Eighteenth-Century England: Theological Debate from Locke to Burke* (Oxford: Clarendon Press, 1998).

Young, Frances. *Biblical Exegesis and the Formation of Christian Culture* (Cambridge: Cambridge University Press, 1997).

Zahn-Harnack, Agnes von. *Adolf von Harnack* (Berlin: H. Bott, 1936).

Zizioulas, John D. *Being as Communion: Studies in Personhood and the Church* (London: Darton, Longman and Todd, 1985).

— *Communion and Otherness* (ed. Paul McPartlan; London: T&T Clark, 2006).

Zuber, Valentine, ed. *Michel Servet (1511–1553): Hérésie et pluralisme du XVIe au XXIe siècle* (Paris: Honoré Champion, 2007).

Index of Biblical Texts Cited

Index of Technical Terms/Phrases in Latin/Greek

General Index of Authors and Subjects

W.E. Sangster

A Critical Analysis of the doctrines of Sanctification and Perfection in the Thought of W.E. Sangster

Andrew J. Cheatle

STUDIES IN EVANGELICAL HISTORY AND THOUGHT

W.E. Sangster (1900–1960), once termed 'the prince of preachers' and 'a preacher without peer in the world' is the subject of this book. Perhaps no other twentieth century British Methodist has written or spoken as much about the characteristic doctrines of Methodism as Sangster. This book is unique in that it addresses the chief theological concern of W.E Sangster – holiness of life. It outlines and examines the influences that helped shape his thought, the direction in which that thought went over against that of Wesley, and his central theological and pastoral theme of the human condition.

'This book sets something of a benchmark against which others will inevitably be set,' – **Rev Prof Kenneth G.C. Newport, Pro Vice-Chancellor, Liverpool Hope University**

Andrew Cheatle lectures at Liverpool Hope University.

978-1-84227-216-9

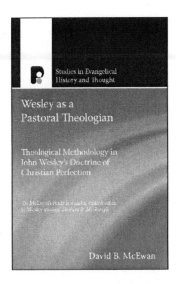

Wesley as a Pastoral Theologian

Pastoral Theology in the Context of the Doctrine of Perfection

David B. McEwan

STUDIES IN EVANGELICAL HISTORY AND THOUGHT

Wesley as a Pastoral Theologian examines Wesley's life from his time in Oxford to the point at which he becomes the leader of the Methodist Movement and beyond and demonstrates that he was a theologian concerned more with the living relationship between humanity and God than with an academic comprehension of propositional truths about God.

'I warmly commend Dr McEwan's study as a major contribution to Wesley studies, for its biblical and theological emphases but particularly for the significant contribution it makes to the current interest in John Wesley's pastoral and practical theology – **Herbert B. McGonigle, Senior Lecturer in Historical Theology and Wesley Studies, Nazarene theological College, Manchester, UK.**

David B. McEwan is Academic Dean and Lecturer in Theology at Nazarene Theological College, Brisbane, Australia

978-1-84227-621-1

Tradition and the Baptist Academy

Roger A. Ward and Philip E. Thompson

STUDIES IN BAPTIST HISTORY AND THOUGHT

This volume is the fruit of a meeting of the Young Scholars in the Baptist Academy that explore some ways Baptist Christians live in the transmission of tradition and Gospel practice from our places in the Academy. The essays in this volume explore the essence of Christianity and religious practices that are 'handed down'"through generations, and the characteristic Baptist resistance to such traditions and how this can be overcome or modified.

> 'These Baptists, therefore, have given a gift to the whole church just to the extent that their critical engagement with what it means to be Baptist should inform all ecclesial traditions as we struggle to discover our catholicity. There is not a weak essay in this volume. I hope it will be read not only by Baptists but by others as we have much to learn here' – **Stanley Hauerwas, Gilbert T. Rowe Professor of Theological Ethics at the Divinity School of Duke University, USA.**

Roger Ward is Professor and Chair of Philosophy and Director of the Center for Christian Discernment and Academic Leadership at Georgetown College, Kentucky, USA. **Philip Thompson** is Professor of Systematic Theology and Christian Heritage, Sioux Falls Seminary, South Dakota, USA.

978-1-84227-327-2

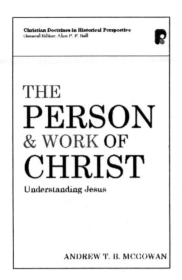

The Person and Work of Christ

Understanding Jesus

Andrew T. B. McGowan

CHRISTIAN DOCTRINES IN HISTORICAL PERSPECTIVES

This book is a fresh and exciting exercise in historical theology. McGowan examines the gradual development, over the centuries, of the church's understanding of the person and work of Jesus Christ, assessed in the light of what the Scriptures have to say on the subject. The book highlights the developing understanding, together with the mistakes and heresies that forced the church into defining the truth about Christ more clearly. The great debates of the first five centuries and of the period of Reformation are examined with unique insight and sensitivity, and the debate is brought right up to the present day with application for the contemporary church.

978-1-84227-749-2